THE ONCE & FUTURE QUEEN

Guinevere in Arthurian Legend

NICOLE EVELINA

The Once and Future Queen

Nicole Evelina

© 2017 Nicole Evelina

All rights reserved. This book or any portion thereof may not be reproduced or used in any manner whatsoever without the express written permission of the author, Nicole Evelina, or the publisher, Lawson Gartner Publishing, except for the use of brief quotations in a book review.

Lawson Gartner Publishing
PO Box 2021
Maryland Heights, MO, 63043
www.lawsongartnerpublishing.com

Printed in the United States of America
First Printing, 2017
ISBN 978-0-9967632-2-6
Library of Congress Control Number: 2017915670
Editor: Kelly Gamble, Joy Editing
Cover Design: Jenny Quinlan, Historical Editorial
Layout: Nada Qamber, Najla Qamber Designs

Cover Image: *Lancelot and Guinevere* by Herbert James Draper, 1890s. Image is public domain.

Publisher's Cataloging-In-Publication Data
(Prepared by The Donohue Group, Inc.)

Names: Evelina, Nicole.
Title: The Once and Future Queen : Guinevere in Arthurian legend / by Nicole Evelina.
Description: Maryland Heights, MO : Lawson Gartner Publishing, [2017] | Includes bibliographical references and index.
Identifiers: ISBN 9780996763226
Subjects: LCSH: Guenevere, Queen (Legendary character)--In literature. | Arthurian romances--History and criticism. | Women in literature.
Classification: LCC PN686.G8 E94 2017 | DDC 809.9337--dc23

For Persia Woolley.
Thanks for blazing the trail.
May you rest in peace.

Table Of Contents

INTRODUCTION 1
    Emphasis and Scope 4
    A Note on Names 11

CHAPTER ONE: An Overview of the Character 13
    Literary Identity vs. Historical Fact 13
    How Many Guineveres Were There? 16
    Guinevere's Lineage and Family 18
    Guinevere's Children and Lovers 19
    End of Life 22
    A Changing Woman 25

CHAPTER TWO: Beginnings: Guinevere in Celtic Literature 30
    Guinevere in Poetry and Literature 30
    Triad 56 35
    Triad 80 37
    Triad 53 37
    Triad 54 38

CHAPTER THREE: The Middle Ages Part One: Gildas and Geoffrey of Monmouth 41
    Women in the Middle Ages 41
    Life of Gildas 46
    Geoffrey of Monmouth 48

CHAPTER FOUR: The Middle Ages Part Two: Wace and Layamon 55
    Eleanor as Inspiration 55
    Roman de Brut 57
    Layamon 60

CHAPTER FIVE: The Middle Ages Part Three: Chrétien De Troyes and
Marie De France   64
    Lancelot or The Knight of the Cart   64
    Guinevere and Lancelot as Models of Courtly Love   68
    Chrétien's Motivations   73
    Marie de France   76

CHAPTER SIX: The Middle Ages Part Four: The Vulgate Cycle   82
    Importance of the Vulgate Cycle   82
    The True and False Guineveres   83
    Guinevere in The Vulgate Cycle   86

CHAPTER SEVEN: The Middle Ages Part Five: Alliterative Morte
Arthure and Thomas Malory   90
    Alliterative Morte Arthure   90
    Thomas Malory   94
    The Poisoned Apple   95
    Le Morte d'Arthur   98
    Guinevere as Symbol   103

CHAPTER EIGHT: The Renaissance to the Nineteenth Century   107

CHAPTER NINE: Tennyson, Idylls of the King   110
    About the Idylls   110
    Guinevere as a Character   112
    Guinevere as a Reflection of Victorian Society   119

CHAPTER TEN: William Morris, The Defence of Guenevere   125
    Defense or Deception?   125

CHAPTER ELEVEN: Guinevere in the Early Twentieth Century and T.
H. White   132
    Arthuriana for a New Age   132
    T. H. White—The Once and Future King   137

CHAPTER TWELVE: Guinevere, Victim of the Patriarchy (1960's—Early 1980's) — 145

CHAPTER THIRTEEN: Marion Zimmer Bradley—The Mists of Avalon — 151
- Women in the Fore — 151
- Guinevere: Christian in a Pagan World — 153
- Feminist or Feminot? — 159

CHAPTER FOURTEEN: Parke Godwin and Gillian Bradshaw — 161
- A New Type of Guinevere — 161
- Gillian Bradshaw — 166

CHAPTER FIFTEEN: Sharan Newman — 172
- Guinevere as Superwoman — 172
- Sharan Newman — 177

CHAPTER SIXTEEN: Persia Woolley — 185
- "Through the Eyes of a Real Woman" — 185

CHAPTER SEVENTEEN: Nancy Mckenzie and Rosalind Miles — 191
- Guinevere and Elaine — 191
- Rosalind Miles — 194
- Every Woman a Goddess — 198
- Strong, not Feminist — 200

CHAPTER EIGHTEEN: Guinevere Post-2000 and Lavinia Collins — 205
- The Arthurian Market Slows — 205
- Lavinia Collins — 207
- The Sexual Side of Guinevere — 210
- A Mixed Reaction — 213

CHAPTER NINETEEN: Nicole Evelina — 216
- Guinevere and Me: Personal Reflections — 216

Breaking with Tradition by Inventing Guinevere's Early Years   220
Pagan vs. Christian   222
The Dark Side of History   226
A Woman in a Man's World   227
Rejecting the Convent   228

CONCLUSION   231
SOURCES   235
INDEX   249
BEFORE YOU GO   262
ACKNOWLEDGEMENTS   263
ABOUT THE AUTHOR   265

Timeline Of Arthurian Fiction Mentioned In This Book

c. 800s – Welsh Triads – (from oral sources; approximate dates first written down, author unknown)

c. 1100-1225 – *The Mabinogion* (from oral sources; approximate dates first written down, author unknown)

c. 1130-1150 – *The Life of Gildas* by Caradoc of Llancarven

c. 1136 – *The History of the Kings of Britain* by Geoffrey of Monmouth

c. 1155 – *Roman de Brut* by Wace

c. 1170 – *Erec and Enid* by Chrétien de Troyes

c. 1170-1215 – *Lanval* by Marie de France *The Romance of Yder* (author unknown)

c. 1176 – *Cliges* by Chrétien de Troyes

c. 1177-1181 – *Lancelot, or The Knight of the Cart* by Chrétien de Troyes
Yvain, the Knight by Chrétien de Troyes

c. 1190-1215 – *Brut* by Layamon

c. 1195 – *Lanzelet* by Ulrich von Zatzikhoven

c. 1200-1250 – The Lancelot-Grail Cycle or Vulgate Cycle (authors unknown)

c. 1200-1210 – *Perlesvaus* (author unknown)

1220 – *Diu Crone* by Heinrich von dem Türlin

1268 – *Claris et Laris* (author unknown)

c. 1400 – *Alliterative Morte Arthure* (author unknown)

1485 – *Morte d'Arthur* by Thomas Malory

1587 – *The Misfortunes of Arthur* by Thomas Hughes

1590-1596 – *The Faerie Queen* by Edmund Spenser

1801 – *The Fairy of the Lake* by John Thelwall

1858 – *Defence of Guenevere* by William Morris

1869 – *Idylls of the King* by Alfred Lord Tennyson

1956 – *The Great Campaigns* by Henry Treece

1958 – *The Once and Future King* by T. H. White

1956 – *The Green Man* by Henry Treece

1963 – *Sword at Sunset* by Rosemary Sutcliff

1978 – *Lancelot: A Novel* by Peter Vansittart

1980 – *Firelord* by Park Godwin

1981 – *Guinevere* by Sharan Newman

1982 – *In Winter's Shadow* by Gillian Bradshaw

1983 – *The Mists of Avalon* by Marion Zimmer Bradley
The Chessboard Queen by Sharan Newman

1984 – *Beloved Exile* by Parke Godwin

1985 – *Guinevere Evermore* by Sharan Newman

1987 – *Child of the Northern Spring* by Persia Woolley

1990 – *Queen of the Summer Stars* by Persia Woolley

1991 - *Guinevere: The Legend in Autumn* by Persia Woolley

1994 – *The Child Queen* by Nancy McKenzie

1995 – *The High Queen* by Nancy McKenzie

1998 – *Guenevere: Queen of the Summer Country* by Rosalind Miles

2000 – *The Knight of the Sacred Lake* by Rosalind Miles

2001 – *The Child of the Holy Grail* by Rosalind Miles

2002 – *Queen of Camelot* by Nancy McKenzie (combined re-issue of *The Child Queen* and *The High Queen*)

2014 – *Warrior Queen* by Lavinia Collins
A Champion's Duty by Lavinia Collins
Day of Destiny by Lavinia Collins
Guinevere: A Medieval Romance by Lavinia Collins (boxed set)

2016 – *Daughter of Destiny* by Nicole Evelina
Camelot's Queen by Nicole Evelina

2018 – *Mistress of Legend* by Nicole Evelina
Guinevere's Tale by Nicole Evelina (boxed set)

INTRODUCTION

The name "Guinevere" conjures up evocative images from the pages of literature and the celluloid frames of film. From the long-haired queen weeping in contrition at Arthur's feet while a heartbroken Lancelot looks on, to the ermine-clad Vanessa Redgrave singing a prayer to St. Genevieve while opining the simple joys of maidenhood, she does nothing by halves. Whether a reader first encounters her in the works of Thomas Malory or in a modern movie or TV adaptation, one thing is clear: Queen Guinevere is a woman to be reckoned with. She will not easily be lost within the pages of history, even if her better-known husband threatens to eclipse her and her reputation is lost in favor of tawdry remembrances of her sin.

History has proven Guinevere will not go down without a fight. Over the last thousand years, she has become a symbol of each society for which she is written, taking on its mores, personifying its deepest fears, and providing a warning: take heed lest you too become a victim of sin. In more recent years, as women have come to demand an equal place in society, she has become a symbol of feminism, the queen who owns her sexuality and isn't willing to apologize for taking what she wants from life. To some, she is still a man-eater (as T. H. White famously dubbed her), but to others, she is the model of liberated womanhood they so desperately seek.

While the main subject of this book is the evolution of the character of Guinevere, it will also, by necessity, touch upon the roles of women, feminism, and the subject of religion; each is tightly interwoven with how Guinevere is portrayed by her authors. Religion, up until the last century or so, was a vital part of society and the everyday life of most people in Europe and the Americas. As such, it unconsciously affected the way they read Guinevere's actions and the consequences she deserved. So when the Catholic Church became involved in crafting the Arthurian legend in the twelfth century, Guinevere took on the role of scapegoat for Arthur's downfall, becoming both a victim of her own lust and the willing perpetrator of evil—the Eve for the world of Camelot. It is only when religion becomes less important to an increasingly secular society that Guinevere begins to be redeemed.

Likewise, the role of women in society was a given until women started to enter the workplace during World War I and later, in the 1970s, began to demand equal treatment outside the home. So it is not surprising that Guinevere started out as a peripheral character who was there to do her husband's bidding and, at best, entertain his knights. Throughout the Middle Ages and even into the beginning of the twentieth century, women were treated as second class citizens whose role was to serve their husbands and bear children. While Guinevere excelled at the former, being barren, she failed to fulfill one of the key duties assigned to her as a woman and a queen: to bear a child. As such, she is fundamentally tainted, virtually predisposed to evil and weakness, as though she bore an extra original sin that doomed her to an unsavory fate.

As women began to fight for their rights in the 1970s and 1980s, Guinevere slowly emerged from the shadows, becoming a woman with a full backstory, a childhood, opinions and agendas of her own, and a life after King Arthur's death. With this success as a backdrop, authors of the twenty-first century felt freer to experiment with well-known aspects of the Arthurian story in order to gild their Guinevere with the sex appeal and strength needed to attract an increasingly literature-deficient and mentally-distracted generation.

This is due in no small part to the fact that from the mid-1980s onward, the authors of Guinevere's story began, for the first time in history, to be predominately female. Women writing the female experience brought a whole new perspective to the character, a well-roundedness that male authors could not hope to achieve. As Sara Cooley notes in her thesis, "it is because these male authors, more often than not, *did* write women, and wrote them *terribly*, in ways that are not only frustrating, but also damaging, that we must revisit the canon through a feminist perspective."[1] Elsewhere, she continues, "While we will never know firsthand what it is like to be a queen, or a high priestess, or a knight errant, we will know it better than any man who has ever failed to write

---

1   Cooley, Sara Diane, "Re-vision from the Mists: The Development of a Literary Genre of Feminist Arthuriana as an Allegorical Response to Second Wave Feminist Politics" (Senior Capstone Projects, Paper 520, Vassar College, 2015), 11.

us as such"[2] or, as any man wrote us as such through male eyes.

Emphasis and Scope

Stephanie Comer very eloquently captures the essence of the idea behind this book: "Guinevere has existed in literature for nearly a millennium, evolving to suit societal values and mores. She has metamorphosed from Arthur's noble queen to Lancelot's jealous lover, from a motherly sovereign to a vindictive adulteress as each author struggled to apply his own literary and societal conventions to a character that is both inherited and created."[3] Building upon this idea, this book chronicles the evolution the character of Guinevere has undergone in the last one thousand years of her existence, showing how she changed with the view of women at the time she was written or rewritten to serve as either a warning or a role model for those hearing her story. As Comer notes, "any beginning fiction writer is told the old adage of 'write what you know…' [Each Arthurian writer] retold a basic story in terms that they and their readers would understand and relate to. The knights might have been stuck in the quasi-medieval age in which they had been conceived, but Guinevere had the ability to be formed and reformed according to societal standards. She is a barometer, reflecting attitudes and ideas on how society views love,

---

[2] Ibid., 12.
[3] Comer, Stephanie, "Behold Thy Doom is Mine: The Evolution of Guinevere in the Works of Chrétien de Troyes, Sir Thomas Malory, and Alfred, Lord Tennyson" Master's, Eastern Michigan University, 2008), iv.

marriage, the battle of the sexes, and, most importantly, women."[4]

As it would be impractical to cover in a single book every version of the Arthurian legend in a single designation of time, much less within one thousand years, this volume is limited to the most popular and influential works, those that are most accessible to the average reader with a post-secondary education. This study is also limited to works written for adult audiences, although there has been a resurgence of interest in the Arthurian legend, especially of that focusing on Guinevere, for children and young adult readers in recent years.

While this book focuses on British, French, and American Arthurian portrayals of Guinevere, it is worth noting that the Germans and Spanish also had their own strong Arthurian traditions. "Medieval Arthurian works [appear] in at least 29 languages ranging from Aragonese and Breton to Tagalog, Welsh and Yiddish."[5] In fact, Guinevere is consistently much more positively portrayed in the German tradition than any other. The reason for not including these in the book is simply a matter of controlling the scope. Readers will most likely be familiar with the British, French, and American traditions, so this book focuses on those.

The goal is to bring the evolution of Guinevere out of the halls of academia where she has been intensely studied for at least half a century and into the consciousness of everyday readers. There are not many books that attempt to do so. While Andrea

---

4 Comer, "Behold Thy Doom," 75.
5 Gordon-Wise, Barbara, *The Reclamation of a Queen: Guinevere in Modern Fantasy* (New York: Greenwood Press, 1991).

Hopkins' *The Book of Guinevere* provides a broad overview of the evolution of certain aspects of the character's personality, it does not cover works more recent than Tennyson, nor does it provide a possible explanation for the character's change. Therefore, in addition to covering the classic ground of medieval through Victorian Arthuriana, this book will provide a study of the major novels written about Guinevere in the last part of the twentieth and early twenty-first centuries and link her growth to cultural and societal influences.

Moreover, there is little information on Guinevere outside of scholarly works written for academics, which the lay reader is not likely to seek out. Thus, this book fills a void by presenting a summation of Guinevere's treatment since the legend's inception for a lay audience.

Chapter One will give a broad overview of the character of Guinevere in order to orient or refresh the reader who is not overly familiar with her tradition. Included is a discussion regarding what is known about her from history and literature, the tradition of multiple women named Guinevere in myth, and a summary of what we know of her family, children, lovers, and the end of her life.

In Chapter Two, we examine the earliest extant references to Guinevere to ponder her origins in Welsh poetry and myth, as well as the enigmatic Welsh triads. Though these mentions are brief and Guinevere's role minor, they provide the fodder on which a thousand years of tradition is built and the basis of many of Guinevere's less desirable qualities.

Chapter Three covers the beginning of the Middle Ages, with *The Life of Gildas* and Geoffrey of Monmouth as the early determiners of her character. This section begins with a discussion of how women were treated during this period and how prevailing thoughts and attitudes might have influenced Guinevere. There follows a discussion of how Guinevere's kidnapping by Melwas, which Gildas introduced, could be connected to the story of the rape of the Flower Bride in Celtic myth. Next, we see how Geoffrey of Monmouth establishes the passive Guinevere, beginning a centuries-long tradition of her being regarded as little more than a royal beauty whose lust was Camelot's undoing.

Chapter Four takes us deeper into the Middle Ages where Wace and Layamon rewrite Geoffrey to give us more of the story we recognize today. We'll uncover the origins of Guinevere's personality, including her much-touted feelings of guilt over her affair, and see how Layamon's changes take her from a conflicted woman to a villainous whore, a reputation she will struggle to overcome.

Chapter Five focuses on the monumental contributions of the French to Arthurian legend, especially Chrétien de Troyes' many unique introductions to the story and Marie de France's odd representation of a truly evil Guinevere. This chapter also features a discussion of courtly love and how it may have influenced how Chrétien approached the legend and its characters.

Chapter Six delves into the role of the Cistercian monks in changing the course of the legend in the Vulgate Cycle, including through the stories of the True and False Guineveres and by adding a distinctly religious element to Guinevere's sin, forever linking her to Biblical figures such as Eve and Mary Magdalene.

Chapter Seven marks the high point of the Middle Ages and the part of the legend that is the most well-known today. But before turning to what is familiar, we explore the lesser-known *Alliterative Morte Arthure* (1400), which depicts a very negative Guinevere. We then turn to Thomas Malory with his "Poisoned Apple" and the famous *Morte d'Arthur* (1485). By examining the contradictions inherent in Malory's Guinevere, we see the polarities of the character in sharp relief and experience her becoming the guardian of morality, a role she'll continue to hold for the next four centuries.

Chapter Eight provides a brief overview of the disinterest in the Arthurian legend from the Renaissance to the nineteenth century. It also briefly explores how changing morals and the shift of religious sentiment from Catholic to Protestant resulted in a dearth of Arthurian material for approximately two hundred years.

In Chapter Nine, we visit the Victorian era and the resurgence of interest in the Arthurian legend. Here we'll look at how Victorian morality influenced Tennyson's famous *Idylls of the King* (1869) and how Guinevere reflected this society's simultaneous abhorrence of and fascination with the figure of the fallen woman.

Chapter Ten looks at William Morris' controversial poem "In Defence of Guenevere," which, despite its title, may not be any defense at all. Or conversely, it may be a cry for independence from a woman written for a highly constrained Victorian audience—we'll examine both viewpoints.

Chapter Eleven moves us into the twentieth century with a discussion of society's unrelenting fascination with the Arthurian legend, which is reflected in the sheer number of Arthurian novels and short stories published during this century. Following is a discussion of T. H. White's famous *The Once and Future King* (1958) and how he appears to have transferred his issues with women onto the female characters he wrote, including poor Guinevere, who took on many of his mother's negative qualities.

Chapter Twelve begins with a look at how the changes in women's rights, including the rise of feminism and women's studies programs in colleges, affected the way Arthurian legend was viewed from the period of 1960-1980. Next is a discussion of two rather un-feminist portrayals of Guinevere in Rosemary Sutcliffe and Mary Stewart's famous Arthurian books.

In Chapter Thirteen, we look at one of the most famous modern Arthurian novels, Marion Zimmer Bradley's *The Mists of Avalon* (1983). Core to this chapter is a discussion of why, for all of the novel's feministic triumphs with Morgaine and other female characters, Guinevere is still a weak woman, very much at the mercy of the men in her world. To answer this question, we must examine the motivations Bradley gives Guinevere and statements she is trying to make about the patriarchy.

Chapter Fourteen brings us to two authors who bridge the gap between the patriarchal versions of Guinevere to date and the ultra-feministic ones to come. This chapter examines how in the early-to-mid-1980s, Parke Godwin gave us the first Guinevere who showed agency, intelligence, and a willingness to be Arthur's equal. We also explore the Guinevere of Gillian Bradshaw's *In Winter's Shadow* (1982), another highly active and independent woman, but in ways markedly different from the one Godwin created.

Chapter Fifteen opens with an examination of how the second wave of feminism—and its attendant stressors on women to be simultaneously perfect wives, perfect mothers, and perfect career women—pushed women into the (sometimes mistaken) belief that they could do it all. This is followed by an analysis of Sharan Newman's Guinevere trilogy, which shaped the future of the legend by being the first to explore Guinevere's early life.

Chapter Sixteen is devoted to the writings of Persia Woolley, who takes Guinevere back to her pagan Celtic roots and purposefully shows her as Arthur's equal. As the chapter will show, the changes she makes to the legend appear to correspond with events and concerns of the late 1980s and early 1990s.

Similarly, Chapter Seventeen looks at two additional female writers focused on Guinevere with two very different takes on the famous queen. A discussion of Nancy McKenzie's works shows us a bratty, immature queen who is cowed by her cousin, Elaine, while Rosalind Miles' Guinevere is decisive and bold—just don't call her a feminist construction.

Chapter Eighteen begins with an analysis of why fictional portrayals of Guinevere seemed to drop off the radar of traditional publishing after the year 2000 and how independent authors took up Guinevere's cause in their novels. What follows is an analysis of the Guineverian writings of one such indie author:

Lavinia Collins. Utilizing reader reviews left on Amazon and Goodreads, we see a Guinevere who is very much written for the new millennium, a strong woman who is not afraid to own her sexuality or take what she wants.

Finally, Chapter Nineteen is where I explain my own Guinevere novels in the context of their time and society. They are too new to know what their cultural impact will be through the eyes of critics, so included is an explanation of why my Guinevere is written as she is and what I hoped to achieve by telling my specific version of her story.

A Note on Names

Guinevere's name has changed with the location of the author and the time period in which her story is written. *The Arthurian Material in the Chronicles* lists twenty-one variations of her name.[6] Some of these include: Gwehywfar (Welsh), Guanhumara/Guenhumara (Geoffrey of Monmouth in Latin),[7] Wenneuereia (Gerad of Wales), Gwynnever (Middle English), Guinevere (French), Guenever (T. H. White), Ginevra/Givevara/Ginover (German), Wehaver/Wenhaver (Layamon), Winlogee

---

6 Fletcher, Robert Huntington, "The Arthurian Material in the Chronicles Especially Those of Great Britain and France," in *Studies and Notes in Philology and Literature*, Vol. X (Boston: Ginn and Company, 1906), 298.

7 Bromwich, Rachel, "Celtic Elements in Arthurian Romance: A General Survey," in *The Legend of Arthur in the Middle Ages: Studies presented to A.H. Diverres by Colleagues, Pupils, and Friends*, ed. P. B. Grout et al. (Cambridge: D.S. Brewer; Torowa N.J., U.S.A.: Biblio Distribution Services, 1983), 42. Bromwich notes that Geoffrey must have "derived [this name] from a written source in Old Welsh."

(Breton),[8] Gaynore/Waynor (*The Alliterative Morte Arthure*), and Gwinfreda (a Saxon in John Gloag's 1976 novel *Artorius Rex*).

The meaning of Guinevere's name is variously translated as "the white phantom or fairy,"[9] "the white or fair enchantress,"[10] "the white fay or ghost," or the "white shoulders." Her name's etymology derives from "white, fair, or holy" and "magical being,"[11] which is both interesting and unexpected because in most traditional Arthurian legend, it is Morgan who is associated with magic and the Otherworld rather than Guinevere.

For ease of reading, in this book the name of Arthur's queen will be spelled Guinevere unless another spelling is used in a direct quote, as this spelling is the one most commonly known by modern readers. Likewise, I will use these spellings for the other main Arthurian characters: Arthur, Lancelot, Morgan, and Merlin.

---

8   Matthews, John and Caitlin, *The Complete King Arthur: Many Faces, One Hero* (Rochester, Vermont: Inner Traditions, 2017), 175. The name comes from an image in the Modena Cathedral in Italy.
9   Ibid., 175.
10 Bromwich, Rachel, "Celtic Elements in Arthurian Romance," 42.
11 "Guinevere," Wikipedia, accessed January 23, 2017, https://en.wikipedia.org/wiki/Guinevere

CHAPTER ONE

An Overview Of The Character

Literary Identity vs. Historical Fact

Before we delve deep into history, it will be helpful to have a refresher of what the Arthurian tradition tells us about Guinevere. In relation to other characters such as Arthur, Lancelot, and Merlin, we know precious little about Guinevere. Nevertheless, there are some constants. Nearly all versions of the story agree on these facts:

- She was the wife of Arthur and the queen of Camelot.
- At some point, she takes a lover in an adulterous affair. Sometimes he is Mordred or Bedivere, but most commonly after the twelfth century, he is Lancelot.
- One or more times during the story, she is kidnapped by Malegant/Mordred/Melwas/Kay, depending on the tradition. Sometimes she suffers rape and/or abuse at his hands. Most of the time her rescuer is Lancelot, but in a few versions, it is Arthur. This element is believed to have its basis in "a Celtic narrative in which a fairy leaves her otherworldly mate to become the wife of a mortal only to

be reclaimed later by her original partner."[12]
- For her crimes, which vary from adultery and treason to witchcraft, she is sentenced to burn at the stake.
- Lancelot rescues her. Oftentimes, Arthur follows the couple, leaving Mordred free to take over Camelot. The ensuing power struggle leads to the battle of Camlann, where both men are killed.

Like the rest of the Arthurian legend, scholars believe most of this is the fantasy of literature, rather than historical fact. Historically, we know that someone did gather the British tribes in a coordinated defense against and defeat of the invading Saxons sometime between 490 and 530 CE that resulted in a period of peace. This information comes to us from two ancient historians, a monk named Gildas who wrote *De Excidio Britanniae (The Ruin of Britain)* in the mid-500s and Nennius, who gives us the basic story: "The twelfth [battle of King Arthur] was a most severe contest, when Arthur penetrated to the Hill of Badon. In this engagement nine hundred and forty fell by his hand alone, no one but the Lord affording him assistance."[13] However, this is as much as we can say with any certainty.

If Arthur lived, chances are good he had a wife, but her name and biographical details would have been different. As John and Caitlin Matthews write:

---

[12] Walters, Lori. "Introduction." *Lancelot and Guinevere: A Casebook*, ed. Lori Walters (New York: Routledge, January 4, 2002), xv.
[13] Nennius, Bill Gunn and Mark the Hermit, ed. *The Historia Brittonum* (London: John and Arthur Arch, 1819), 35.

Despite efforts on the part of some scholars to identify Guinevere with an actual historical woman, there is no conclusive evidence to support this.... The version in the *Historia* [*The History of the Kings of Britain* by Geoffrey of Monmouth] is plausible, since it is likely that Arthur would have known Guinevere as a child, growing up in the court of Cador and might even have fallen for her then—making his choice (other than her renowned beauty and her Roman blood) a reasonable one...[but] as ever with these accounts, we are almost certainly seeing a mixture of real and legendary material, so that there may indeed have been a real person named Guinevere, who might indeed have been married to Arthur, even though we have no firm evidence of this.[14]

As Arthurian scholar Tyler Tichelaar points out in his book *King Arthur's Children*, the old Welsh stories are likely closest to the truth. "If a historical Guinevere ever lived, she probably was mother to Arthur's children, did not commit adultery, and died before Camlann, meaning she was innocent of all the charges brought against her."[15]

---

14 Matthews, John and Caitlin, *The Complete King Arthur* (Rochester: Inner Traditions, 2017), 217-218.
15 Tichelaar, Tyler, *King Arthur's Children* (Ann Arbor, Michigan: Modern History Press, 2010), 64.

How Many Guineveres Were There?

Asking this question of any other character might seem odd, but it is a valid question when speaking of Guinevere because the answer varies. We will delve into this more in depth later, but for now, it is enough to note that there may only have been one or as many as three.

Welsh tradition is the source of the three Guineveres. "There is a long tradition of Arthur having married three women named Guinevere," write John and Caitlin Matthews in *King Arthur: Many Faces, One Hero*.[16] It is well-documented that the Welsh—and the Celtic people before them—loved memorializing things in threes, so the three Guineveres may well be a holdover from this tradition. In the Welsh Triads, we find "Three Great Queens of Arthur's Court: Gwehywfar daughter of Cywyrd Gwent, and Gwehywfar daughter of Gwyther ap Greidawl, and Gwehywfar daughter of Gogfran the Giant."[17] For many years, this was explained away as tradition, but now modern feminist scholars such as Caitlin Matthews argue the three Guineveres represent the triune goddess who is Maiden, Mother, and Crone, while scholars Barbara Gordon-Wise and Shulamith Shahar point out that Guinevere fulfills a very different triplicate role, that of The Virgin Mary/Eve/Mary Magdalene. As Arthur's queen, she is expected to be a paragon of virtue like The Virgin Mary. However, through her affair with Lancelot, she becomes

---

16   117.
17   Bromwich, Rachel, *Trioedd Ynys Prydein* (Cardiff: University of Wales Press, 2014), Triad 56.

the fallen Eve. But later through her repentance, she is like Mary Magdalene.[18]

The concept of two Guineveres comes to us from Triad 53 of the Welsh Triads, where Gwenhwyfawr strikes Gwenhwyfach. This brief mention was greatly expanded by the Cistercian monks who penned the Vulgate Cycle of Arthurian legend. In these tales, the two Guineveres are twins conceived on the same night by the same father but by different mothers. The True Guinevere was protected by Lancelot, while The False takes Guinevere's place for a while, before eventually betraying King Arthur. It is interesting to note that while tradition identifies them as The True and The False, they are never actually called that in the text. One is known as Gwenhwy-fawr, or "Gwenhwy the Great," while the other is Gwenhwy-fach, or "Gwenhwy the less."[19]

One Guinevere is the tradition that most people are familiar with. Even here, there is a scholarly debate about what she may represent. Arthurian and Celtic scholar John Matthews argues that Guinevere and Morgan are two sides to one coin, the positive and negative aspects of sovereignty, as well as the light and dark aspects of the Goddess.[20] This is a relatively modern argument that has entered the Arthurian sphere in the wake of the feminist movement of the 1970s-1990s that connects the female members of Camelot's court to an ancient goddess who

---

18 Gordon-Wise, *The Reclamation of a Queen*, 63.
19 Bethlehem, Ulrike, "Guinevere, a Medieval Puzzle: Images of Arthur's Queen in the Medieval Literature of England and France" (Doctoral Universität, Bochum, 2001), 34.
20 Matthews, John, *King Arthur: Dark Age Warrior and Mythic Hero* (New York: Rosen Publishing, 2008), 77.

may have been worshiped in Celtic Britain or may be a product of the New Age movement.

Guinevere's Lineage and Family

It is telling that no matter the tradition, Guinevere is identified by the man she is most closely related to, usually her father. There is never a mention of her mother, as power and property were handed down through the male line and women were considered property with no personal identity during the Middle Ages. Plus, medieval tales were written by men primarily for consumption by other men (as well as some women at the court), and few would have cared about her female relatives in a male-dominated society.

In one of the earliest works mentioning Guinevere, Geoffrey of Monmouth's *History of the Kings of Britain* (1136), all we know is that she is of Roman lineage. By 1485, when *Le Morte d'Arthur* was published, Guinevere is commonly identified as the daughter of King Leodgrance of Cameliard, while Welsh tradition calls her father Gogrvan or Ocvran and the 1220 German poem *Diu Crone* identifies her father as King Garlin of Gore. In the 1801 play *The Fairy of the Lake* (1801), John Thelwall makes her the daughter of Vortigern. Regardless of Guinevere's father's identity, the authors make it clear that Guinevere is of noble descent and a worthy wife for the high king.

Some traditions mention siblings of Guinevere. As noted above, the most well-known is that of her sister/twin in Welsh legend. This sister struck Guinevere, leading to the battle of

Camlann. Both Welsh tradition and French romance give Guinevere an identical half-sister who takes her place for a while. In the German *Diu Crone*, she has a brother called Gotegrin, while in the 1980s retellings *Firelord* (1980) and *Beloved Exile* (1984), both by Parke Godwin, she has a brother named Peredur. In a twist not seen elsewhere in the Arthurian legend, in some versions of Wace's *Roman de Brut* (1155), Guinevere is Mordred's sister.[21] This is unusual because elsewhere in Arthurian legend, Mordred is only connected to Arthur, being his nephew or son.

Guinevere's Children and Lovers

Thanks to the pervasive influence of medieval works much as *Le Morte d'Arthur*, modern readers tend to think of Guinevere as barren, but in a few instances, she has children. In some parts of Welsh poetic tradition, Guinevere is Arthur's second wife, and in the *Historia Brittonum* he has a son named Amr or Anir but Guinevere is not mentioned, so this child may be from another marriage or it may be that the author didn't think it was important to mention the mother's identity.

Welsh tradition, as well the French *Lanzelet* and *Perlesvaus*, name Guinevere's son Llacheu or Loholt. The poem *Morte Arthure* (not to be confused with Malory's work of a similar name) says Guinevere and Mordred were the parents of two unnamed sons after she married Mordred during his revolt. Finally, the 1898

---

21 Korrel, Peter, *An Arthurian Triangle: A Study of the Development and Characterization of Arthur, Guinevere and Mordred* (Leiden: E.J. Brill, 1984.), 191.

work *The Birth of Galahad* by Richard Hovey makes Guinevere the mother of Galahad with Lancelot.

Guinevere as an unfaithful wife seems to be an ancient tradition. In his 1891 book *Studies in Arthurian Legend*, John Rhys says that in some parts of Wales, to call a girl Gwenhwyvar is "as much as to suggest she is no better than she should be,"[22] that is to call her sexual morals into question. He goes on to note that "in the literature of the Welsh, her guilt is rather assumed than proved; but it is quite possible that popular tales dwelling on her levity have been lost."[23]

Lancelot is, of course, Guinevere's most famous lover. Their affair was most likely created at the urging of Marie of France, Countess of Champagne, who was the patron of Chrétien de Troyes in the twelfth century. Scholars believe Chrétien was not entirely comfortable with the addition to the story, but he had no choice but to include it because the countess desired it to be included. Her motivations are even less clear. It may be that because she promoted the idea of courtly love in her court, Marie de France wished to make the pair an example of its ideal fulfillment.

The next most popular lover for Guinevere is Kay, who is in many traditions Arthur's foster brother and/or right-hand man, much like Lancelot is in later versions. Guinevere's affair with him is implied in the Welsh stories. If he was as close to Arthur as the stories seem to indicate, his betrayal would have

---
22 Rhys, John, *Studies in Arthurian Legend* (Oxford, Clarendon Press, 1891), 49.
23 Ibid., 50.

been a great blow to the king, perhaps even more so than that dealt by Lancelot.

Other traditions give Guinevere a variety of lovers, with names both familiar and obscure. In *Lanzelet* (1195), it is Gawain. In Chrétien de Troyes' story *Erec* (1170) a knight called Guiamor leaves Morgan for Guinevere. Marie de France's lay (a type of poem) *Lanval* (1170-1215) has Guinevere make a sexual offer to a knight named Lanval, but he refuses her. The French also implicate knights named Claris (in *Claris et Laris* written in 1268) and Yder (in *The Romance of Yder*, written at the end of the twelfth or beginning of the thirteenth century). Many modern authors, including Rosemary Sutcliff and Mary Stewart, make Bedivere the guilty party, thus implicating another of Arthur's closest friends.

Why is there such a long and varied tradition of Guinevere's unfaithfulness? In some of the earliest Arthurian stories, King Arthur is a tyrant to whom it would not be easy being married. But one of the strongest arguments, one we will see played out later as we explore the evolution of the legend, is that the authors needed a reason for the downfall of Camelot. They purposefully painted King Arthur as an ideal king and needed a plausible reason for their perfect hero to be defeated and betrayed by Mordred. Guinevere was a convenient scapegoat.

In addition, when medieval monks got hold of the story in the twelfth century, they used it to caution their readers against the dangers of the female temptress. As we will see, under their pens, Guinevere became conflated with Eve, another sinful woman whose weakness led to the downfall of a utopian paradise. By so closely aligning the two women, they imparted to their readers the need to be wary of the sins of the flesh, lest they, too, be brought low.

End of Life

Thanks to the popularity of the musical *Camelot*, many people in the twenty-first century are most familiar with the idea of Guinevere ending her days in a convent. This part of the story began early in the tradition as a reflection of how disposable women were in the Middle Ages. During that time, women who were widowed, outcast, or no longer necessary to society were often sent to or voluntarily sought refuge in convents. For some, this was due to religious fervor or a desire for repentance, but for many it was a matter of survival, as convents were the only place that would take them in. As Barbara Gordon-Wise says,

> While Arthur dies or is carried off to Avalon, the queen apparently lives on in piety and obscurity. On the one hand, her enclosure in a nunnery may be interpreted as the final suppression of a troublesome queen; representing the patriarchal order of medieval Christendom, the nunnery provides a secure imprisonment for a faithless queen and the story of the queen's retirement serves as a cautionary tale which warns of the dangers of the world and of the flesh. On the other hand, historically, the convent or nunnery also provided one of the few spheres

where a medieval woman might enjoy relative freedom from patriarchal control.[24]

Indeed, a convent was one of the only places a medieval woman could gain an education and hold a position of power. Nuns often learned to read, write, and perform basic calculations in order to run the business side of a busy convent and read their prayer books. Some also worked in scriptoriums, which created beautiful works of illuminated art that were in high demand with the nobility. While technically beholden to the bishop, many abbesses held as much, if not more power than their male counterparts, running large estates that produced wine, wheat, produce, and other goods that made them an important part of the surrounding kingdom. They were also centers of great wealth, so the abbess could be thought of as akin to a noblewoman given the large budget and number of workers she oversaw.

In the Arthurian tradition, Guinevere can be seen benefiting from this cultural construct in Gillian Bradshaw's final Arthurian novel, *In Winter's Shadow* (1982). After the fall of Camelot, Guinevere flees to the convent. But instead of leading a life of humble repentance, she uses the skills she learned as queen to lead the nuns and oversee the transfer of the literate culture she and Arthur built to the Irish monastery of Iona. Guinevere is so revered in this position that even she recognizes that it has redeemed her of her sins in the eyes of her people.

While this is the ending we know the best, it is by no

---

24   Gordon-Wise, *The Reclamation of a Queen*, 61.

means the only one. Andrea Hopkins points out, "As the medieval authors had a very broad spectrum of appreciation for Arthur's queen, so they also devised a number of very different endings for her. Guinevere's fate ranges from the very gruesome to a more demure ending where she repents of her sins dedicating the rest of her days to prayers and good deeds."[25]

In a few stories, Guinevere dies before the fall of Camelot. In *Perlesvaus* (1200-1210), she dies of grief over the death of her son Loholt in Arthur's lifetime. In the MS *Lancelot*, she dies before Arthur goes to war with Mordred. There is also a French tradition of Guinevere dying before the battle of Camlann, although this one plays out very differently. "In the French prose *Genievere*, Mordred is shut in a prison cell with the decaying body of Guinevere and is forced to resort to cannibalism before dying miserably of starvation."[26]

Hector Boece, a Scottish historian who wrote *Scotorum Historiae* (1552), originated the idea that Guinevere went north after her disastrous affair, but before King Arthur died. He tells us she ended her life a prisoner of the Picts and that Arthur ordered her to be dragged to death by wild horses or dogs in revenge for her affair. Whether or not this is true, there is a local legend that Guinevere fled to the town of Meigle in Scotland where she may be buried.

Boece is not alone in laying Guinevere's death at Arthur's feet. Layamon's *Brut* (1190-1215) hints that Arthur murdered Guinevere, then put a curse on her head. We will examine this

---

25 Hopkins, Andrea, *The Book of Guinevere* (Salford, England, Saraband, 2004), 24.
26 Ibid.

ending more closely in the chapter on Layamon's influential work.

In contrast, many modern retellings let Guinevere live, giving her respite in her old age. She most often retreats to the countryside, where finally retired from a life of politics, she provides the services of a healer, herbalist, and teacher. In the 1980s and 1990s' trilogies of Sharan Newman, Rosalind Miles, and Persia Woolley, Guinevere ends her life as a resourceful, independent dowager queen, widely respected for her wisdom and accomplishments.[27]

But what about the famous grave of Arthur and Guinevere at Glastonbury? Despite being a tourist attraction to this day, carbon dating and other scientific study has proven it a hoax. Not long before its "discovery" in 1190, the abbey suffered a tremendously damaging fire. It is believed by most scholars that the monks invented the famous grave to attract tourists to their abbey because more tourists meant more funds they could use to rebuild. Regardless of the truth, the site's ongoing mystique attracts tens of thousands of visitors each year and reminds us of the human desire to grasp something physical related to our heroes, even if they have their source in legend, rather than in fact.

A Changing Woman

As we will see, Guinevere underwent changes as the society for which she was written evolved and changed, both in their attitudes

---

[27] Noble, James, "Guinevere, the Superwoman of Contemporary Arthurian Fiction, *Florilegium*, vol. 23.2 (2006): 197-210, 199, https://journals.lib.unb.ca/index.php/flor/article/viewFile/12554/20003.

toward women and their "proper" place in society. As Barbara Gordon-Wise asserts, "the treatment of Arthur's queen in every historical time period has been influenced by basic sociological and ideological pressures.... The study of the development of Guinevere over the course of almost a thousand years of literature suggests far-ranging implications concerning Western attitudes toward women, for Guinevere has developed into a secular Eve with Camelot a parallel to the lost Garden of Eden in Genesis."[28]

She is, then, a representative figure for the fears, hopes, lusts, and dreams of society. Guinevere is an archetype like the figures of old, only instead of being a fixed representation, she is ever morphing to meet the needs of her reader. "The enduring legacy of the Arthurian lady is the mirror she holds up to the psyche of creator and reader: the idealized women of Arthurian literature reflect the social mentalities and sexual preoccupations of their class."[29]

Guinevere begins her Arthurian journey as very much a peripheral character with no real identity or agency outside of her interactions with Arthur. Arthurian scholar Maureen Fries writes that in many of her early incarnations and even into the Middle Ages, "Guinevere exists, like heroines of Arthurian and other romance, to get into trouble that the hero must get her out of. The incentive to heroic action, she is at the same time its reward. Functionally, Guinevere is unable to act on her own. She

---

28 Gordon-Wise, *The Reclamation of a Queen*, 2, 6.
29 Lacy, Norris J., *The New Arthurian Encyclopedia: New Edition* (New York: Taylor and Francis, 2013), 524.

is carried off and imprisoned; fought for and defended; freed and returned home; and fought for again: all at the will of and/or agreement between the males in the tale."[30]

This is a theme we see over and over again, as Guinevere, like the real-life women of the time, is treated like a means to an end, rather than a person with her own intrinsic value. Katherine Bonner writes, "The medieval authors, Geoffrey, Wace and Layamon, merely present Guinevere as a flat character, a tool in their narrative. She is not a woman in her own right...In the works of Malory and Chrétien, Guinevere is given more dialogue and is mentioned much more frequently...still [they] predominately portray her as merely a part of the action, not its center. Moreover they virtually ignore her emotions and motivations."[31]

Over time, the situation improves, but only by degrees, often taking one step forward—as in Morris' "The Defence of Guenevere"—only to take two back—as she is next portrayed as a harpy by T. H. White or a self-centered shrew by Marion Zimmer Bradley. Bonner adds, "The authors of the late 1800's [sic] and early 1900's [sic], Tennyson, Morris and White...still present her as a one-sided character.... Neither [Tennyson or Morris] presents her as a self-sufficient character with story all her own, nor does White.... While Guinevere may be the 'villain' of Bradley's novel, Bradley nevertheless give Guinevere much more

---

30 Fries, Maureen, "Female Heroes, Heroines, and Counter Heroes," in *Popular Arthurian Traditions*, ed. Sally K. Slocum (Bowling Green: B.G.S.U.P.P., 1992), 9.
31 Bonner, Katherine Alice, "Guinevere as Heroine: Her Development, Dynamics and Demise in the Works of the Middle Ages Through the Present" (M.A., Georgia College & State University, 2000), 10-12.

status and attention than the authors of previous years.... [She] keeps Guinevere in the forefront of her narrative."[32]

In novels such as Bradley's *The Mists of Avalon*, Guinevere is not so much valued for herself, but for the light she sheds on other female characters, being a foil for them or a reflection of the proper place of all female characters. As Gordon-Wise notes, through the mid-1980s, Guinevere's role "serves as a vehicle for assigning women their proper subordinate position within a hierarchy of gender-determined relations. The representation of Arthur's queen has been traditionally conditioned by a masculine interpretation of woman."[33]

It is only from the mid-1980s onward that Guinevere comes into her own. Perhaps this is only fitting because it is when the second wave of feminism (at least in the United States) was starting to give women their due. Women were fighting for equality, for an end to sexual harassment in the workplace, and to show they could be mothers and wives as well as working women. It is during this time that authors like Sharon Newman, Rosalind Miles, Persia Woolley, and Nancy Mackenzie bring Guinevere out of Arthur's shadow and into the spotlight. For the first time, female authors have seized control of the narrative of this very powerful woman and made her their own. No longer do we have to see Guinevere through the filter of the male gaze; she is allowed to speak for herself, to show us what being a woman means, rather than simply to reflect others' perceptions.

---

32   Ibid., 12.
33   Gordon-Wise, *The Reclamation of a Queen*, 2.

Finally, in the late twentieth and early twenty-first centuries, a millennium and a half after her name was first uttered, Guinevere has her due, with modern authors building entire books, series, and worlds around this strong female figure. She is a woman of all trades: a queen, wife, lover, and often a mother, who rules over both the political and domestic spheres alongside her husband. Andrea Hopkins points out that "if a real test of character lies in how a person handles catastrophe, then Guinevere triumphs. It is in the face of imminent disaster that the queen's innate nobility emerges, whether she be bravely confronting an enemy endangering the lives of her knights or resolutely facing the consequences when her love affair is exposed."[34] She has become the embodiment of the modern woman's dream, able to handle anything, to overthrow the patriarchy and finally usher in the elusive era of equality women have been actively campaigning for since they first whispered the notion of suffrage nearly two hundred years before.

---

34 Hopkins, Andrea, *The Book of Guinevere*, 80.

CHAPTER TWO

BEGINNINGS: GUINEVERE IN CELTIC LITERATURE

"Gwehywfar, daughter of Ogfran the Giant—bad when little, worse when big."[35] *— Welsh popular rhyme*

Guinevere in Poetry and Literature

The origins of Guinevere in Celtic literature are shrouded in the mists of time. The extant sources were all written down after the year 1100, but likely existed orally long before then. Today, we call the people who told these tales Welsh—as the Celtic tribes of Britain were driven into what is modern-day Wales by the invading Saxons, Vikings, and Normans—but when these tales were popular, they were likely from a variety of tribes. Barring a major archeological find, where these stories began, how, and why are questions unlikely ever to be answered.

As the quote that opens this chapter illustrates, Guinevere's name can be seen in common rhyme as well as in high literature. Another example is an eleventh or twelfth century Welsh poem called "Ymddiddan Melwasa Gwenhwyfar" ("The Dialogue

---

35 Matthews, *Dark Age Warrior*, 37.

of Melwas and Gwenhwyfar"). In this story, an imprisoned Guinevere mocks Melwas, calling him short and making fun of his youth (and one can surmise, naiveté) while her rescuer, Cai, waits for his turn to fight him. Here Guinevere is no victim; she is calm, intelligent, and even provokes violence between Cai and Melwas,[36] a very different interpretation than we will see in later years, suggesting she may well have started out as a heroine in her own right.

However, it is literature that gives us the closest thing we have to "proof" of Guinevere's existence before the year 1100. The earliest mention we have is in two stories within *The Mabinogion*, a collection of Welsh tales first written down between 1100-1225. Guinevere's name is mentioned three times in "Culhwch and Olwen," believed to be the earliest known reference to her.[37] In this story, as Estelle Vallas explains, Arthur treats her as a possession, naming her last in the list of exceptions to the boon he offers to the hero Kulwch. "He begins with the biggest item he owns and enumerates smaller objects until he finishes off with his dagger, and finally, his wife. Guinevere's purpose is to add beauty to his surroundings, which reinforces his magnificence and pride."[38]

While this may sound like a massive dose of male chauvinism (and it is), it is also at least partially accurate and

---

36 Matthews, John and Caitlin, *The Complete King Arthur*, 176.
37 Ibid., 174.
38 Vallas, Estelle, "Feminist Icon or Ruthless Warrior? Guinevere in Bernard Cornwell's The Warlord Chronicles," in *Theorising the Popular*, ed. Michael Brennen (Newcastle upon Tyne, UK: Cambridge Scholars Publishing, 2017), 138.

likely reflects attitudes of the time. As Jean Markale points out, in the Celtic world, "the laws protecting [women] were made by men living in an androcratically structured society,"[39] so they reflect male concerns and prejudices. Celtic women may have had many rights and served alongside their men as warriors, but they were still bought and paid for with a bride price or *coibche*, which is much like a dowry, only a portion of it was set aside for the woman.[40]

These women were better off than their counterparts in other ancient cultures, but the Celtic world was not a matriarchal utopia, nor did its women have equal rights. Celtic studies scholar Sharon Paice MacLeod writes, "Officially women did not generally have an enormous amount of independent legal capacity."[41] They could not act as a witness, could not enter into contracts without their husband or father's consent, and had limited rights of property ownership and inheritance.[42] "Strangely, a queen had no official or special legal rights independent of her husband," [43] MacLeod notes. Peter Ellis agrees. "No serious commentator can argue that Celtic women lived in a socially liberated paradise. On the other hand, the society they lived in was a truly remarkable one and women enjoyed considerable freedoms compared to

---

39 Markale, Jean, *Women of the Celts* (Rochester, VT: Inner Traditions International, 1986, 1972), 247.
40 Ellis, Peter, *Celtic Women: Women in Celtic Society and Literature* (Grand Rapids: William B. Eerdmans Publishing Company, 1995), 122.
41 Macleod, Sharon Paice, *Celtic Myth and Religion: A Study of Traditional Belief* (Jefferson:North Carolina, McFarland & Co., Inc., 2012),188.
42 Ibid.
43 Ibid., 189.

their Greek and Roman sisters, not to mention the women of the restrictive, militaristic Anglo-Saxon culture."[44]

In addition to "Culhwch and Olwen," Guinevere also appears in *The Mabinogion* stories of "Rhonabwy's Dream," "Peredur, Owein and Lunet," and "Gereint and Enid." Here we see the germ forming of the Arthurian legend that later audiences will come to know well. Arthur is said to have three sons, Gwydre, Llacheu, and Amhar, but none of them are connected to Guinevere, so either that fact wasn't mentioned or Arthur had another wife. While Arthur was away, another powerful warlord named Medraut pillaged Arthur's lands and took his throne. He took Gwehywfar from the throne and raped her. Later, he returned and kidnapped her. In these stories, she has a champion who has two affairs and then happily marries a faithful wife. At no time is there a hint of any affair involving Guinevere. In fact, she is known to have a peaceful relationship with her husband.[45]

"Culhwch and Olwen" is likely the source of the two love triangles we will see in later Arthurian legend, between Guinevere/Lancelot/Arthur and Isolde/Tristan/Mark. In this story, a woman named Creiddylad is desired by both Gwyn ap Nudd and Gwythyr ap Greidawl. They appeal to King Arthur for help in ending their feud. He rules that they will "fight over her every May day til doomsday,"[46] designating her the Flower Bride of spring, who is fought over by summer and winter—a

---

44 Ellis, Peter, *Celtic Women*,. 141.
45 Walters, "Introduction," xv.
46 Matthews, John and Caitlin, *The Complete King Arthur*, 176-177.

popular theme in Celtic legend.⁴⁷ When this myth is applied to the Arthurian legend, "the implication here is that Arthur, the older husband of a younger wife, is a winter rival for the hand of the lovely Flower Bride of Spring, while Melwas, whose realm is the Summer Country, represents the summer rival."⁴⁸ Later, this idea is passed on in the story of Tristan and Isolde, when Arthur rules that Tristan can have Isolde while the leaves are on the trees. At first, this may seem like Mark will get custody of her for the winter season, much like Hades does with Persephone, but Isolde sees the greater wisdom. Because the holly, ivy, and yew (and the pine) never lose their leaves, Arthur is really saying she can stay with Tristan always.

Our other ancient source is the Welsh Triads, a group of related stories dating from 1235 though likely first written down in the ninth century,⁴⁹ that preserve early folklore, mythology, and oral history. They are called triads because everything is listed in groups of three, which was likely a mnemonic device to help the early bards remember copious amounts of information. Three was also a sacred number to the Celts.

Guinevere appears in four of the triads: 53, 54, 56, and 80. Since their numbers don't indicate the order in which they should be read, we will examine them in order of richness of information, least to most.

---

47   Ibid., 177.
48   Ibid.
49   Fries, Maureen, "The Poem in the Tradition of Arthurian Literature" in *The Alliterative Morte Arthure: A Reassessment of the Poem*, ed. Karl Heinz Goller (Cambridge: D.S. Brewer), 31.

Triad 56

"*Three Great Queens of Arthur's Court:*
Gwehywfar daughter of Cywyrd Gwent, and
Gwehywfar daughter of Gwyther ap Greidawl, and
Gwehywfar daughter of Gogfran the Giant."
— *Triad 56*

The meaning of this triad is the subject of great debate among scholars. Barbara Gordon-Wise notes that the inclusion of three Guineveres could have been a joke whose meaning has been lost over time, or despite popular opinion, it could literally mean Arthur had three wives of the same name.[50] British scholar and expert on medieval Welsh literature Rachel Bromwich argues that Celtic tradition gives us precedence for multiple siblings bearing the same name, especially if they are twins or triplets. In her book about the Welsh Triads, *Trioedd Ynys Prydein*, she writes:

> Early Irish sources provide instances in which three brothers (sometimes born together at a single birth) receive the same name, though with a distinguishing epithet; and triad 70 serves as a reminder that similar triple-births were not unknown in early Welsh narrative.

---

50 Gordon-Wise, *The Reclamation of a Queen*, 43.

Irish literature also provides examples of groups of three brothers in which the group seems to be no more than a multiplication of a single personage: one character alone acts, while the others accompany him through life, and are led by him in everything. It is apparent that this literary convention has a mythological basis, since in both Irish and Gaulish mythology there are various instances in which deities are portrayed as alternately, either in a single or triple form in which the members are incompletely differentiated.[51]

Despite this argument, few scholars take the meaning that way. Rather, it is believed to be symbolic. John Rhys says Guinevere is synonymous with the three Etains, faeries or goddess-like women of Celtic legend.[52] Arthurian and Celtic myth expert Caitlin Matthews says the three represent the triune goddess—usually called Maiden, Mother, and Crone—or perhaps "the personification of Britain as a Lady, the Land of Britain as a Mother, and the Sovereignty of Britain as a Queen."[53] Matthews and her husband John point out in their book on King Arthur that "it is not without significance that the father of the *second* Gwehywfar in this triad is one of the rival men in the primordial and eternal love triangle from *Culwch and Olwen*: Gwythyr ap Greidawl. This suggests that Gwehywfar's role in the Arthurian

---

51 Bromwich, Rachel, *Trioedd Ynys Prydein* (Cardiff: U of Wales, 2014),162-163.
52 Rhys, John, *Studies in Arthurian Legend*, 35.
53 Woodbury, Sarah, "Guinevere (in Welsh Gwenhwyfar)," accessed July 12, 2017, http://www.sarahwoodbury.com/guinevere-in-welsh-gwenhwyfar/ .

legend derives from a much earlier mythic understanding: that she shares the self-same allure as her mother, the original Flower Bride."[54]

Triad 80

In Triad 80, which appears to be an extension of Triad 56, Guinevere is listed as one of the unfaithful wives of Britain as in Traid 56, but with a new line added at the end: "One was more faithless than those three: Gwenhywfar, Arthur's wife, since she shamed a better man than any of the others."

Damning words, to be sure. Joseph Duggan argues that this triad is proof "that Guinevere was accepted as an adulteress in Welsh tradition."[55] But many scholars believe that this might have been a later addition, written after Geoffrey of Monmouth introduced Guinevere's affair with Mordred to the canon of Arthurian legend.[56]

Triad 53

"Three Harmful Blows of the Island of Britain:
The first of them Mathloch of the Irishmen struck
upon Branwen daughter of Llyr;
The second Gwennhwyfach struck upon Gwenwhyfar:

---

54 Matthews, John and Caitlin, *The Complete King Arthur*, 178.
55 Duggan, Joseph J., *The Romances of Chrétien de Troyes* (New Haven: Yale UP, 2014), 332, n 13.
56 Fulton, Helen, "Arthur and Merlin in Early Welsh Literature: Fantasy and Magic Naturalism," in *A Companion to Arthurian Literature*, ed. Helen Fulton (Chichester, England: Wiley-Blackwell, 2009), 92.

and for that cause there took place afterwards the action of the Battle of Camlan;
And the third Golydan the poet struck upon Cadwaladr the Blessed."

There is rampant speculation among scholars as to the meaning of this dolorous blow. John and Caitlin Matthews theorize that it could possibly stem from Arthur "putting aside one wife in order to marry her sister."[57] Some versions of Triad 53 have Gwenwhyfar striking the first blow. Gordon-Wise believes this may symbolize that the women of the Celts were powerful warriors whose actions determined the fate of a nation.[58] But given the information currently available from historians and archeologists, this is likely wishful, romantic thinking,[59] though women in the Celtic world had greater power and rights than many of their counterparts throughout the world.[60] Others feel that Triad 53 may show an early tradition that the Battle of Camlann came about due a dispute among women.[61] Even if this dispute didn't carry on into modern Arthurian tradition, this triad did influence the Vulgate Cycle of Arthurian legend, where the two Guineveres, one true and one false, were given much more life.

---

57 Matthews, John and Caitlin, *The Complete King Arthur*, 142.
58 Gordon-Wise, *The Reclamation of a Queen*, 91-92.
59 Much like the idea of pre-Christian Celtic matriarchal society. Although matrilineal societies, in which power is passed through the female line to men, are documented as existing.
60 MacLeod, *Celtic Myth and Religion*, 185.
61 Gordon-Wise, *The Reclamation of a Queen*, 44; Bromwich, *Trioed*, 151, n. b.

Triad 54

"Three Violent Ravagings of the Island of Britain.

- One of them (was) when Medrawd came to Arthur's Court and Celliwig in Cornwall; he left neither food nor drink in the court that he did not consume. And he also dragged Gwenhwyfar from her royal chair and then he struck a violent blow upon her.
- The second Violent Ravaging (was) when Arthur came to Medrawds's court. He left neither food nor drink in the court nor in the cantref;
- (And the third Violent Ravaging was when Aedden the Treacherous came to the court of Rhdderch Hael at Alclud (= Dumbarton); he left neither food nor drink nor beast alive.)"

Triads 53 and 54 are related in that they both tell of some kind of quarrel between Gwenwhyfar and her sister Gwennhwyfach, an argument that brought about the battle of Camlan. In Triad 53, one of the sisters strikes the other. In Triad 54, it is Mordred who strikes Guinevere. Either way, it is a serious offense. According to Bromwich, "a blow struck upon the queen was one of three forms of *sarhaed*, or insult, which demanded the payment of a heavy fine."[62] A fine may not sound overly punitive, but this was the primary vehicle by which the Celts meted out justice, even in the case of serious crimes such as rape or murder. To attach a heavy

---

62 Bromwich, Rachel, *Trioedd*, 152.

fine to striking a queen's person shows how seriously this society took the crime.

John and Caitlin Matthews believe that Triad 54 may be a small remembrance of a lost story in which Medrawd's blow upon Gwenhwyfar was symbolic of the attempted toppling of Arthur through the imagining of his virility and the taking of his wife—events that chroniclers Wace and Layamon take up and develop in the twelfth century. This would put Medrawd, as Arthur's nephew and foster son, in the place of a much older myth: nothing less than the struggle of the summer and winter rivals for possession of the Flower Bride.[63]

Whatever the meaning of is the Welsh Triads, before they were even written down, Guinevere was on the minds of the Celtic people, where she would stay for the next 1,500 years. Many see the evidence as showing that she began with a besmirched reputation, which would only get worse. To some, she was born a brat and would grow into one of the most notoriously unfaithful wives in British literature. To others, she was simply a queen who was wrongfully struck, an act which led to war.

On the other hand, Arthurian scholars Peter Korrel and Lori Walters believe that Guinevere began with a good reputation. Walters writes that "Guinevere's reputation in Welsh literature was fairly positive, although it contained some contradictions that may be the result of later additions."[64] If that is the case, she had nowhere to go but down, and she quickly did, as we will see.

---

63 Matthews, John and Caitlin, *The Complete King Arthur*, 180.
64 Walters, "Introduction," xiv.

CHAPTER THREE

THE MIDDLE AGES PART ONE: GILDAS AND GEOFFREY OF MONMOUTH

Women in the Middle Ages

Few characters in literature are as synonymous with their time period as King Arthur is with the Middle Ages. While that is not the time period in which scholars believe he would have lived—if indeed he is ever proven to be a real person, most place him in the late fifth or early sixth century—in many ways, it is appropriate because the Middle Ages was when Arthurian legend flowered and became the story most of us know.

But the attention of the bards was not evenly fixed on all characters. As Bonner writes,

> While the image of Arthur in these works of the Middle Ages is detailed and magnificent, the image of his wife created in these same works could hardly be considered thoroughly developed, much less entirely positive or negative. The reasons for Guinevere's lack of development in these works are easy to grasp. First of all, they were composed in the Middle Ages: the role of women

in medieval heroic literature is minimal and consists mainly of references to childbearing, childrearing, and domesticity. Second, Geoffrey, Wace and Layamon had the specific intention of chronicling the lives and exploits of *kings*. Third, all of these works were written by celibate church men, men who probably had little concept of the day-to-day actions or responsibilities of a female, much less her emotions or her thoughts.[65]

While all of these are true statements, there may be another dynamic at work. The Middle Ages are widely considered one of the worst times in history to be female. Jacquelyn Sweeney Johnson explains, "In this land, where the priests emphasize the superiority of men, women—recognized as descendants of immoral Eve—are relegated to low stature. They are depicted as breeders, corruptors or martyred virgins…women are used to progress the story and then are quickly discarded. In a Christian world dominated by men, the woman's role is strictly to support the life, or storyline, desired by men."[66]

While differences in age, class, religion, and location meant medieval women had a myriad of experiences, some conditions were nearly universal. "Medieval woman were classified according to their sexual status: men might be thought of collectively as knights, merchants, crusaders; women were virgins, wives or

---

65 Bonner, "Guinevere as Heroine,"13-14.
66 Johnson, Jacquelyn Sweeney, "Guenevere's Conflict: Pagan Love or Christian Ethics" (Master's thesis, Longwood University, 2003), 5-6.

widows. They were also, of course, mothers."[67] The most common occupations for peasant women were servants, laborers, brewers of ale, bakers, or spinners.[68] And of course, they were expected to keep house, with all of the washing, cooking, and other associated chores. Women could inherit land and earn and lend money, but upon marriage they forfeited any independence and turned over legal and financial matters to their husbands.[69] In towns, women often participated in their husband's businesses and sometimes even kept them running after the husband died.[70] Women in the aristocracy regularly oversaw the household, acted as executors to their wills and sometimes even defended the estates while their husbands were away.[71]

Women's lives were almost entirely dictated by the religious sensibilities of the time. In Genesis, we read that women were created second from the rib of Adam. This was frequently understood to mean that women were inferior and completely dependent on men, for Eve could not have existed without Adam. In addition, as descendants of Eve, who was responsible for original sin and mankind's expulsion from Paradise, women were seen as inherently sinful and weak, likely to lead their husbands into sin just as their foremother did.[72] Looking at the New Testament, Church authorities noted St. Paul's admonitions

---
67 Leyser, Henrietta, *Medieval Women: A Social History of England 450 – 1500* (London: Phoenix Press, 2003), 93.
68 Ibid., 144-148.
69 Ibid., 148-149.
70 Leyser, *Medieval Women*, 162-163.
71 Ibid., 165.
72 Bovey, Alixe, "Women in Medieval Society" (The British Library, 2015).

that women should be subservient to men, remain silent, and be forbidden from teaching.[73] Reinforcing the idea of women's silence was the notion that the Virgin Mary, model of all virtue, "is given only few words" in the Bible.[74]

The Virgin Mary, meek, mild, and completely obedient to God's will, was seen as the paragon of womanly virtue. She was also held up as the prime example of women's roles of wife and mother. Comer explains the role of women in society, "With such virtues as chastity, silence, obedience, and beauty, women were called on to bring men to perfection. But when seen as sexual beings, women were condemned for being weaker and easily swayed in matters of the flesh. More than that, women were thought to be 'incomplete men' because of their weaker strength as well as 'mental and moral inferiority.'"[75]

One idea that will become increasingly important as the Arthurian legend evolves is that the place women could find power in the Middle Ages was in a convent. The decision to enter a convent and become a nun is "one of the few decisions medieval women could make for themselves."[76] In so doing, Guinevere exercises a modicum of independence, regardless of her motivation. Many abbesses and prioresses reigned over their congregations like queens, and the ability to read and write was greatly prized, as were artistic skills, because they allowed the

---

73 Ibid.
74 Leyser, *Medieval Women*, 223.
75 Comer, "Behold Thy Doom is Mine," 24-25.
76 Comer, "Behold Thy Doom is Mine," 64.

convents to flourish and create valuable works that could be sold to nobility to enrich the order. Even in double religious houses where monks and nuns shared space, often it was the abbess, not the abbot, who was in charge over both. One of the reasons abbesses had such power is related to the role of the Virgin Mary. In the words of St. Bridget of Sweden, "the abbess out of reverence to the most blessed Virgin Mary to whom this order [the Brigittines] is hallowed ought to be the head and lady. For the Virgin, in whose stead the abbess is, was after Christ's ascension into heaven, head and queen of the apostles."[77]

Even though women such as Eleanor of Aquitaine and Marie de Champagne were often patrons of Arthurian literature, "within the romances' narratives, the lady's idealization and cultural privilege are often attenuated by dependent status or marginalization, just as it was for historical noblewomen from the twelfth through the fifteenth centuries."[78] For most women, life was short and difficult. They were usually married as teenagers to men they hardly knew, and quickly began having children. Maternal and child mortality rates were very high, so many women lived in fear of dying in childbed. Poverty was endemic and each new child meant more mouths to feed. If it was a girl, it meant another wedding to arrange and another dowry to pay.

As we will soon see, given the general climate of the time, it's not overly surprising when we find that Guinevere was not

---

77   Cited in Leyser, *Medieval Women*, 204.
78   Lacy, Norris J., *The New Arthurian Encyclopedia: New Edition* (New York: Taylor and Francis, 2013), 524.

treated well by the monks and scribes of the Middle Ages. As Peter Korrel asserts, "Guinevere probably received her bad reputation during the twelfth century, both by her active involvement in courtly love affairs, described in lais and romances to cater for the taste of the Anglo-Norman and French courts, and by her collaboration in the foul acts of high treason and bigamy in Geoffrey's pseudo-historical chronicle, which was taken seriously enough."[79]

Life of Gildas

> "Glastonia...was besieged by the tyrant Arthur with a countless multitude on account of his wife Gwenhwyfar, whom the aforesaid wicked king [Melwas] had violated and carried off."[80]
> —*The Life of Gildas* by Caradoc of Llancarfan

After Celtic literature, the next time Guinevere appears in the Arthurian legend is in the twelfth century. *The Life of Gildas* (c. 1130-1150) was written by the monk Caradoc of Llancarven. It is important to our study of Guinevere in that it is the first story to link her to Glastonbury and it gives us the basic outline of Guinevere's kidnapping by Melwas/Malegant and her rescue by Arthur.

According to *The Life of Gildas*, Glastonbury (or Glastonia, as it is called in the text) is where Melwas, a "wicked king,"[81] took Guinevere after raping and kidnapping her. It was thought to

---

79 Korrel, *An Arthurian Triangle*, 126.
80 Caradoc of Llancarfan, *The Life of Gildas*, Celtic Literature Collective.
81 Ibid.

be an impregnable place due to its "fortifications of thickets of reed, river and marsh."[82] But "the tyrant Arthur with a countless multitude"[83] besieged it to get her back, starting a war.

Stories of people, especially women, being carried off to faraway and/or supernatural lands are common in Celtic myth and literature.[84] Usually, this is seen as symbolic of being carried off into the realm of the faerie or a faerie leaving her Otherworldly lover in order to marry a mortal, only to be reclaimed later by her fay lover.[85] But according to Arthurian scholar John Matthews, this trope dates back to the tradition of "the rape of the Flower Bride, in which the sovereignty of the land is represented by a woman whom the would-be king or ruler must win either in combat against an adversary, or by marriage."[86] He even goes so far as to hint that this story might be the origin of Lancelot's affair with Guinevere, saying, "seen through the eyes of the medieval romancers a tale of adulterous love was a far more interesting story than a pagan story of sovereignty, though it never wholly lost touch with the more ancient theme of the queen's abduction and recovery."[87] This is certainly an interesting, if not mainstream, way of looking at Guinevere's affair and the many times she is rescued within the legend, usually by Lancelot.

Some scholars of Celtic law note that kidnapping was a

---

82 Ibid.
83 Ibid.
84 Hopkins, Andrea, *The Book of Guinevere*, 50. Even the Bretons share this myth. In it, the queen is abducted by the king of the dead and rescued by her husband.
85 Walters, "Introduction," xv.
86 Matthews, John, *Dark Age Warrior*, 33.
87 Ibid., 38.

form of legal marriage in the Celtic world. In his 1894 work, *The Brehon Laws*, Laurence Ginnell explains that the law recognized three types of wives,[88] one of which was "an adaltrach-woman of abduction,"[89] a completely legal relationship that had to have the consent of both parties to be dissolved, otherwise it had to go through the legal process.

Whatever the meaning or the veracity of the abduction of Guinevere, by the end of the twelfth century, it was firmly canonized in the tale of Camelot.

Geoffrey of Monmouth

> *"In the meantime, Mordred, that disloyal and foolish regent, began to subdue Britain for himself, and he engaged in an illicit affair with the king's wife."* [90]
> — *The History of the Kings of Britain* by Geoffrey of Monmouth

Despite its name, *The History of the Kings of Britain* (1135-1136), monk Geoffrey of Monmouth's most famous work, isn't what modern scholars would consider history. Ancient historians didn't keep to the rigorous documentation used today; it was perfectly acceptable to mix oral history, imagination, and fact and call it

---

88 Many sources on Celtic law list up to 10 types of legal marriage. One example is Peter Ellis' *Celtic Women: Women in Celtic Society and Literature*.
89 Ginnel, Laurence, "Marriage," in *The Brehon Laws* (1894), 213, and Thompson, Jack George, *Women in Celtic Law and Culture* (Lewiston: Edwin Mellen, 1996), 133, 158.
90 Monmouth, Geoffrey, *The History of the Kings of Britain* (Peterborough: Broadview Press, 2008), 267, lines 1107-1109.

history. Geoffrey claims that his history was a translation of a more ancient work unknown to his contemporaries, nor has it been proven to exist since. Because of this, many scholars don't believe this older source existed, and take the stance that his book is wholly fanciful. Other, more indulgent scholars hypothesize that he was working from oral sources.[91]

Though only a portion of *The History* relates to the study of King Arthur, it is valuable as the origin of much of the material that would later comprise Arthurian legend, including Tintagel as Arthur's birthplace, much of the myth of Merlin, the descriptions of medieval courts with their feasting, ladies, and hunts, and the introduction of Morgan as a healer, her nine sisters of Avalon, and details about Avalon.

Despite being a multi-volume work, *The History* tells us precious little of Arthur's queen, something many feminist scholars see as a reflection of women's minor roles in medieval society.[92] Gordon-Wise asserts this paucity of information is detrimental to Guinevere. "Not only is she mentioned only six times, but the queen also never speaks directly,"[93] establishing a tradition of passivity it will take hundreds of years to break. But given that Geoffrey is focused on the *kings* of Britain, perhaps we should be grateful that Guinevere is mentioned at all, even if it is only in relationship to Arthur.[94]

---

91   Peter Korell is one scholar who holds this opinion. He also says it was possible Geoffrey was influenced by is the Welsh Triads.
92   Bonner, "Guinevere as Heroine," 3.
93   Gordon-Wise, *The Reclamation of a Queen*, 11-12.
94   Bonner, "Guinevere as Heroine,"14.

From Geoffrey's account, we learn three main things about Guinevere, each of which deserves its own examination. The first piece of information about her we learn from Geoffrey is that she was the beautiful daughter of a Roman family. Susann Samples and Bonner note this small bit of information deprives her of the ability to be seen as a character in her own right. "Her worthiness to be Arthur's wife is based on ancestry and beauty"[95] with no description of her personality or character.[96] As a result, she is established as a shadow to Arthur's sun.

Next, we learn that she marries Arthur, but when Arthur leaves his government in Mordred's hands, she willingly cuckolds Arthur with him and becomes an accomplice in revolt. Geoffrey presents Guinevere's affair with Mordred as an explanation for the downfall of Arthur. In some ways, this is his way of painting himself out of the corner he created by portraying Arthur as such a model of kingly perfection. Because of Arthur's goodness, "only deception and treachery could bring down the powerful warrior king."[97] The perfect answer was a woman, sinful and weak, whom the author, as a monk, feels superior to and "sits in judgment upon."[98]

Unfortunately, this use of Guinevere as a scapegoat would taint her reputation for centuries. Scholar Peter Korrel reads in her participation in Mordred's betrayal the origin of her

---

95 Samples, Susann, "Guinevere: A Re-Appraisal," in *Lancelot and Guinevere: A Casebook*, ed Lori Walters (New York: Routledge, 2002.), 219.
96 Bonner, "Guinevere as Heroine," 14.
97 Walters, "Introduction," xvi, Samples, "A Re-Appraisal," 225.
98 Hopkins, Annette Brown, "The Influence of Wace on the Arthurian Romances of Crestian de Troies," PhD thesis, University of Chicago, 1912 (Menasha: George Banta, 1913), 37, n. 34.

bad reputation in future stories. "I think it very likely that the guilty role Guinevere played in the downfall of Britain's greatest monarch, collaborating in such a detestable crime as high treason, gave her the bad name she was to have ever after."[99]

Conversely, Barbara Gordon-Wise rejects the notion that Geoffrey blames Guinevere's affair for the downfall of Camelot, placing the blame on another famous (and long-lasting) story element. "Guinevere's infertility in Geoffrey also plays a role in the downfall of the Arthurian kingdom. Unlike in early Celtic society where the tribal king's power could be inherited by any number of male descendants, Geoffrey's England witnessed the rise of the national monarchy with its emphasis in primogeniture. Thus, Guinevere's failure to bear children partially results in the destruction of the kingdom. Without an heir, Arthur is forced to name his nephew as regent, this signaling the end of his direct line."[100] So here, whether or not Guinevere was directly at fault, society may have had a very direct effect on her storyline by its rules putting in motion the decisions that led to destruction.

Either way, she was a woman and in medieval society, anything that went wrong, whether caused by her words, actions, intentions, or even by circumstance, was her fault by association. As the descendant of Eve, she didn't stand a chance at redemption, unless—like Mary Magdalene—she repented of her sin.

Which brings us to the final unique element of Geoffrey's Guinevere: when Arthur returns, Guinevere flees to a nunnery for

---

99 Korrel, *An Arthurian Triangle*, 124.
100 Gordon-Wise, *The Reclamation of a Queen*, 46.

protection. Geoffrey writes, "When this was announced to Queen Guinevere, she gave way to despair. She fled from York to the City of the Legions and there in the church of Julius the Martyr, she took her vows among the nuns, promising to live a chaste life."[101] We are never explicitly told what "this" refers to, what Guinevere was told that causes such sorrow. It could be that she was told about Mordred's death or that Mordred was gathering men for a march into Winchester. Many believe that she was sad because of her lover Mordred's downfall, but others point out she may have finally succumbed to the hopelessness of the situation.[102]

In the same way, her motivation for flight into the convent is unclear. Was she remorseful and desiring repentance? Was she looking for a safe haven? If so, from whom—Mordred and/or Arthur, or the whole world? Did she fear punishment for her treason?[103] Tyler Tichelaar notes,

> She cannot be fleeing from Mordred because by going to the City of the Legions [Caerleon], she is moving closer to him. Mordred enters Winchester after Arthur has landed and defeated him at Richborough. Perhaps learning of Arthur's success is what makes Guinevere fearful. If this is the case, she may have fled to a nunnery as a place of clemency from fear of Arthur's wrath. Certainly, her going to a nunnery rather than joining

---

101   Monmouth, *The History of the Kings of Britain*, 259.
102   Bonner, "Guinevere as Heroine," 17.
103   Ibid., 16.

Mordred suggests she is more concerned about her own fate than Mordred's. She might also hope that if Arthur finds her in a nunnery rather than with Mordred, he might believe her innocent.[104]

This is where having not even a glimpse into her interior life makes it hard for the reader to care about Guinevere's fate.

But does it really matter? Maureen Fries would answer no. "That Geoffrey's Guinevere ends her life as a nun vowed to chastity at Caerleon, the scene of her co-coronation with Arthur, indicates her conformation to the heroine's role as reflector of the male hero's values. The performance of penitence for oneself and/or as a surrogate for a male was a function of the female in romance [literature] as it was in real life."[105] In other words, her reasons are immaterial; Guinevere was only fulfilling the role fate and society dictated for her.

The resulting Guinevere is unrecognizable from the one seen in Celtic literature. The woman who began as symbol of the changing seasons may have finally become a character (albeit a small one) with an origin, but she also has been branded with a sin she will never shake. As James Douglas Merriman writes of Guinevere's transformation, "what in pagan times had been a symbolization of primitive man's conception of natural processes became increasingly in a Christian society a matter of moral

---

[104] Tichelaar, Tyler, "While King Arthur was Away, Did Guinevere with Mordred Play?" Children of Arthur, accessed June 12, 2017.

[105] Slocum, Sally K., ed., "Popular Arthurian Traditions" in Popular Arthurian Traditions, ed.Sally K. Slocum (Bowling Green: B.G.S.U.P.P., 1992), 7-8.

concern and a question of sexual ethics."[106] In this transition we see a shift in mindset that corrupts all that was once seen as natural (sex, the turning of the year) into the basis for mortal sin that can only be absolved through repentance and turning to religion – a theme that will echo in Arthurian legend for hundreds of years to come.

---

106 Merriman, James Douglas, *The Flower of Kings: a Study of the Arthurian Legend in England Between 1485 and 1835* (Lawrence: The UP of Kansas, 1973), 24.

CHAPTER FOUR

THE MIDDLE AGES PART TWO: WACE AND LAYAMON

Eleanor as Inspiration

With the foundation of Arthurian legend established, we move into a period where authors rewrite each other, adding to and taking away from the story as they please. The pair first to be involved in this type of literary love-hate relationship were Norman poet Wace and an English priest named Layamon. Together, these two authors would go on to cement Guinevere's reputation as we know it today. Peggy Donald Gibson writes in her dissertation about Guinevere as a medieval character, "[Guinevere's] reputation is established because that is the way Wace and Layamon interpret Geoffrey's bare bones story."[107]

Eleanor of Aquitaine was thought to be the model for Guinevere for both men, regardless of how they portray her.[108] "[Wace] dedicated [*Roman de Brut*] to Queen Eleanor, who was the ardent propagator in England of the courtly ideals of

---

107   Cited in Bonner, "Guinevere as Heroine," 3-4.
108   Swabey, Fiona, *Eleanor of Aquitaine, Courtly Love, and the Troubadours* (Westport: Greenwood Press, 2014), 75.

southern France. Accordingly, Wace...partly because of his royal patroness wove into Geoffrey's narrative more pronouncedly chivalric material."[109]

Under Eleanor's rule, the power of noble women increased dramatically. Across Europe, queens educated in classical Greek and Latin encouraged literature, music, and the arts in their courts—and made sure Arthurian women were at the center of it all.[110] *Roman de Brut* is thought to have been written at the urging of Eleanor of Aquitaine[111] or at least inspired by her. According to Saux, it was written specifically for the nobility, and Layamon claimed that Wace personally presented a copy to the queen.[112] "Wace's *Roman de Brut* gives the tone of the new court: elegant, learned and sophisticated...[it's] probably to be understood as a flattering gesture towards the young monarch [Henry II]...or as a gift to Eleanor."[113]

Fiona Tolhurst draws a more direct parallel between the two queens. "The decline of Eleanor of Aquitaine's reputation in annals and chronicle histories at the turn of the thirteen century offers the most plausible explanation for the decline in

---

109 Mason, Eugene, "Introduction," *French Medieval Romances: From the Lays of Marie de France* (Auckland, New Zealand: The Floating Press, 2013), 6.
110 Day, *The Quest for King Arthur* (London: Michael O'Mara, 1999), 113.
111 Lacy, *The New Arthurian Encyclopedia: New Edition*, 524.
112 Le Saux, Françoise Hazel Marie, *A Companion to Wace* (Woodbridge: Boydell & Brewer, 2010), 81.
113 Ibid., 83.

the reputation of Guinevere as Eleanor's fictional counterpart."[114] Indeed, Eleanor, like Guinevere, was accused of adultery by clerical chroniclers,[115] but that is likely as far as the comparison goes. Most modern scholars now eschew attempts to link Eleanor and Guinevere directly, preferring to limit any connection to mere inspiration.

Another Arthurian author, Marie de France, whom we will address at length in Chapter Five, may have had ties to Eleanor. Though little is known about Marie, it is speculated that her poems may have been "written at the Court of Henry of England. From political ambition the King was married to Eleanor of Aquitaine, a lady of literary tastes, who came from a family in which the patronage of singers was a tradition."[116]

Roman de Brut

"The queen was lodged at York, in doubt and sadness. She called to mind her sin and remembered that for Mordred, her name was a hissing. Her lord she had shamed, and set her love upon her husband's sister's son. Moreover, she had wedded Mordred in defiance of right, since she was wife already, and so must suffer

---

[114] Tolhurst, Fiona, "What Ever Happened to Eleanor? Reflections of Eleanor of Aquitaine in Wace's Roman de Brut and Lawman's Brut," in *Eleanor of Aquitaine: Lord and Lady*, eds. Bonnie Wheeler and John Carmi Parsons (New York: Palgrave Macmillan, 2008), 320.

[115] Evans, Michael R., *Inventing Eleanor: The Medieval and Post-Medieval Image of Eleanor of Aquitaine* (London: Bloomsbury, 2016), 74.

[116] Mason, "Introduction," 7.

reproach in earth and hell. Better were the dead than those who lived, in the eyes of Arthur's Queen." [117]
— *Roman de Brut* by Wace

Wace took on the Herculean task of translating from Latin to French Geoffrey of Monmouth's *History of the Kings of Britain* and then transforming it into an epic poem of nearly 15,000 lines. Written in 1155, it is the first Arthurian work written in the vernacular and the first ever to mention the Round Table.[118] According to Mason, Wace's accomplishments were significant and long-lasting. "He succeeded in uniting scattered legends attached to Arthur's name, and in definitely establishing their place in chronicle history in a form that persisted throughout the later British historical annals…not only was it accepted as an authority by British historians, but French chroniclers also used it for their own purposes."[119]

In general, Wace holds faithfully to Geoffrey's material, though Wace's Guinevere is "more cultured and refined."[120] She is given a bit of personality to go with the beauty and Roman lineage with which Geoffrey endowed her, being described as "courteous, very gracious of manner…passing sweet and ready of tongue."[121] These traits are all what is expected from a woman in

---

117 Wace, *Arthurian Chronicles: Roman de Brut,* trans. Eugene Mason (Auckland: The Floating Press, 2013), 97.
118 Le Saux, *A Companion to Wace,* 81.
119 Mason, "Introduction," 4.
120 Walters, "Introduction," xvi.
121 Wace, *Roman de Brut,* 56.

a court of courtly love.

He clarifies many of Geoffrey's ambiguities, especially regarding Guinevere. For example, he is more explicit about Guinevere's willingness to have an affair with Mordred.[122] Annette Hopkins emphasizes that "Wace not only says that Arthur left the kingdom in the charge of Guinevere and Mordred, but emphasizes at length the fact that part of the regent's treachery lay in his conduct with her."[123]

Another clue comes when Wace clarifies her motivation to flee to the convent. It is clear enough that Mordred might lose the war. If he does, Arthur will be in control and she fears him because of her adultery with Mordred, which is clearly described as both a "trespass" and "sin." As she thinks upon her relationship with Mordred, she thinks of how she "shamed" Arthur by "wed[ding] Mordred in defiance of right, since [she] was wife already."[124]

The language, and Wace's changes in translation, also point to deep guilt for Guinevere. Le Saux explains, "Whereas in the Latin [Geoffrey's *History of the Kings of Britain*] Guinevere takes the veil out of despair ('desperans,' both versions), in the French text [Wace's *Roman de Brut*], it is out of shame—ostensibly shame at her sexual lapse, but in reality, shame at Mordred's cowardice."[125] As Annette Hopkins points out, the language used "implies that

---

122 Korrel, *An Arthurian Triangle*, 191. In some versions she is Mordred's sister so that would have been incest – if so, this could have been the seeds of that part of the story.
123 Hopkins, Annette, "The Influence of Wace," 36.
124 Wace, *Roman de Brut*, 97.
125 Le Saux, *A Companion to Wace*, 142-143.

she went [into the convent] merely for the reason that her cause was lost. Wace dwells on her recognition of her guilt, and we can imagine that he saw the end of Guinevere not without feeling."[126] Later, Hopkins adds, "W[ace], imbued with the ideas of chivalry, treats her as one to be pitied rather than condemned."[127] A kind thought for the author, but it still does nothing to rehabilitate Guinevere's ruined reputation, which, while it looks bad now, is about to get worse under a Norman's pen.

Layamon

> *"That was evilly done, that they [Guinevere and Mordred] were (should have been) born; this land that they destroyed with numerous sorrows; and themselves at the end Worse gan [sic] disgrace (or destroy) so that they there lost their lives and their souls, and ever afterwards became odious in every land, so that never any man would offer a good prayer for their souls."*
> —*Brut* by Layamon[128]

Layamon's *Brut*, written sometime between 1191–1205, was an English adaptation of Wace's *Roman de Brut* in alliterative verse. Layamon, a country priest who was fascinated by the Saxons and their warrior lifestyle,[129] made some changes, resulting in a story

---

126 Hopkins, Annette, "The Influence of Wace," 8.
127 Ibid., 37, n. 34.
128 Layamon, *Roman de Brut* (Auckland: The Floating Press, 2013), ebook loc 2030.
129 Mason, "Introduction," 8.

that is much harsher and is thought to be more like the chronicle sources of Wace and Geoffrey. Tyler Tichelaar succinctly sums up Layamon's changes: "In writing of Arthur in English, Layamon was reclaiming Arthur from the somewhat romantic embellishments Wace had added."[130]

In this version of the tale, Arthur clearly loves Guinevere (or Wenhaver, as she is called), but she clearly loves Mordred, setting up a triangle of unrequited love. Unlike in Wace, there is no mention of Guinevere's barrenness.

"Layamon is much more specific in describing the affair of Mordred and Guinevere and in describing Arthur's reaction to their horrible deeds. Because of Layamon's additions in these areas, his Guinevere is almost entirely unsympathetic and villainous,"[131] notes Bonner. Layamon implies Guinevere willingly became Mordred's queen. Some scholars go so far as to say that Layamon hinted that Mordred and Guinevere were together even before Arthur left, using this passage as proof: "It was all kept very quiet in parliament and at court,/Because nobody realized this could be going on."[132]

But realize it Arthur did, with a little Otherworldly aid. He had a prophetic and terrifying dream in which Guinevere pulled down the roof of his hall and Mordred hacked at its beams with an axe—symbolizing their roles in the fall of the kingdom of Camelot. In retaliation, he cut her to pieces with his sword for

---

130   Tichelaar, "While King Arthur was Away," accessed June 12, 2017.
131   Bonner, "Guinevere as Heroine," 24.
132   Cited in Bonner, "Guinevere as Heroine," 26.

her suspected infidelity and dropped them into a "black pit."[133]

When he finds out Guinevere and Mordred's betrayal isn't just in his mind, Arthur is so outraged that he says he intends to "kill Mordred and burn the queen to death,"[134]—the first, but certainly not the last, time that punishment is meted out in Arthurian legend—"reveal[ing his] certainty of her guilt and need for punishment."[135]

Many scholars agree that this nightmare is "the most significant change Layamon makes to the narratives of Geoffrey and Wace."[136] It shows an unusually cruel and brutal side to Arthur that is in keeping with some early Celtic depictions of the famous king. Bonner argues this element was added to evoke pity for Arthur, the victim of the destructive and evil pair.

As in Geoffrey and Wace, in this version Guinevere ends her days as a nun, alive "only because nobody knows where she is or even whether she lives or died."[137] Given Arthur's earlier threat, her anonymity is merited. There is a slight implication that she may have drowned by her own hand or another's in the line, "Then men knew not of the queen, where she were gone, nor many years afterward man knew it in sooth, whether she were dead, or whether she herself were sunk in the water."[138]

So the woman who began the century as a name without

---

133 Layamon, *Roman de Brut*, loc 2438.
134 Gordon-Wise, *The Reclamation of a Queen*, 76, 80-81. This could have been an early medieval punishment for adultery, but is more likely linked to witchcraft and heresy.
135 Bonner, "Guinevere as Heroine," 29.
136 Ibid., 26.
137 Korrel, *An Arthurian Triangle*, 152.
138 Layamon, *Roman de Brut*, Loc 2505.

a true personal identity is now little more than an adulterous, traitorous wife. Bonner summarizes Guinevere's transformation: "The overall contribution these authors [Geoffrey, Wace, and Layamon] make concerning Guinevere is negative. She is painted a woman with power, beauty and a noble background. These qualities fail to stop the demise of the kingdom, of the king and of Guinevere herself. She is portrayed as villainous and immoral. These three authors have her enter a convent at the close of her story. Whether they intended to show her desire for refuge or remorse in this action, they mold her into a queen of cowardice, deception and evil."[139]

And this is just the beginning of the changes to her character.

---

139 Bonner, "Guinevere as Heroine," 29-30.

CHAPTER FIVE

THE MIDDLE AGES PART THREE: CHRÉTIEN DE TROYES AND MARIE DE FRANCE

"Come through the garden to-night and speak with me at yonder window, when everyone inside has gone to sleep. You will not be able to get in: I shall be inside and you outside: to gain entrance will be impossible. I shall be able to touch you only with my lips or hand, but if you please, I will stay there until morning for love of you." [140]
— *Lancelot, or The Knight of the Cart* by Chrétien De Troyes

Lancelot or The Knight of the Cart

Ah, yes, where would the great romance of Arthurian legend be without the French? Chrétien was a twelfth-century poet who gave the legends a softer side that would have the ladies swooning for centuries by adding in the love affair between Guinevere and Lancelot, and he was the one who first gave them these names (as

---

140 De Troyes, Chrétien, *Lancelot, or The Knight of the Cart* (Herklion Press 2013), 67.

opposed to the Welsh Gwehywfar or Latin Guanhumara).[141] His poetry also contains the first incidence of Guinevere being falsely accused of a crime she didn't commit[142] and of the love triangle between Arthur, Lancelot, and Guinevere.[143]

Given all these "firsts," one would think Chrétien wrote about Guinevere extensively, but he really only focuses on her in the romance *Lancelot*, also known as *The Knight in the Cart*. She is quite a minor character in his other poems, many times only called "the Queen." When he does mention Guinevere, his treatment of her is wildly inconsistent, making her almost seem like different people. Peter Noble enumerates them: "Chrétien treats Guinevere in three ways. There is a marked contrast between the warm, capable and sympathetic queen of *Erec and Enid* (1170), (1176), and *Yvain* Chrétien de Troyes (1177-1181), the colorless and irreproachable queen of Perceval, and the calculating adulteress of *Lancelot*."[144]

In *Erec and Enid*, Guinevere is "a model consort and an inspiration to young knights of the court."[145] She is kind and generous, warm and friendly, playing matchmaker to lovers and intermediary between warring companions. Noble sees this as a type of role modeling or wish fulfillment. "Her role is no doubt an idealization of the role aspired to by many women of the

---

141 According to John and Caitlin Matthews, Chrétien did not invent the character of Lancelot, but he was the first to make him Guinevere's lover and he's the one who made Lancelot the most popular of Arthur's knights. See their book, page 246.
142 Hopkins, Andrea, *The Book of Guinevere*, 56.
143 He also introduced the search for the Holy Grail.
144 Noble, Peter, "The Character of Guinevere," 534.
145 Ibid., 203.

period, as she is admired, respected and influential."[146]

It is only in *Lancelot/The Knight of the Cart/Charette*[147] that Guinevere becomes a main character, likely at the behest of Marie de Champagne, Chrétien's patroness. In this story, Guinevere is kidnapped by Kay, who gives her to Malegant. When Lancelot is on his way to rescue her, he hesitates for just a moment before riding in the back of a cart, which at the time was only used to transport criminals.[148] When Guinevere hears of this, she berates him, accusing him of the sin of pride. "Did you not hesitate for shame to mount the cart? You showed you were loath to get in, when you hesitated for two whole steps. That is the reason why I would neither address you nor look at you."[149]

But not long after it is she who is prideful and self-centered. She coldly rebuffs Lancelot's attempts to see her after his fight with Malegant, saying, "He cannot please me. I care nothing about seeing him…I shall never deny that I feel no gratitude toward him,"[150] and blatantly disregards Lancelot's safety and reputation in her manipulations of him at the tournament. Comer explains,

---

146 Ibid., 535.
147 *Charette* is French for "cart."
148 De Troyes, *Lancelot, or The Knight*, 8. The text itself gives a good indication of why Lancelot would fear for his reputation by riding in a cart: "Whoever was convicted of any crime was placed upon a cart and dragged through the streets, and he lost henceforth all his legal rights, and was never afterward heard, honoured, or welcomed at any court. The carts were so dreadful in those days that the saying was first then used 'When thou dost see and meet a cart, cross thyself so that no evil may befall thee.'"
149 Ibid., 67.
150 Ibid., 59.

Guinevere's repudiation of Lancelot has more to do with the rules that govern courtly love than it has to do with her feelings for him. It seems like her behavior is erratic but in reality she has shifted priorities...Part of her duty [as a courtly lover] is to correct any behavior in her lover that does not follow the rules of courtly love, which Guinevere does.... The rules of courtly love suggest that in order to be a nurturing queen to her lover, she must be wanton and jealous. Guinevere is therefore vilified by the very rules of narrative that she is following.[151]

In Chrétien's poetry, Lancelot is almost obsessively in love with Guinevere, falling into religious-like swoons and forgetting his own safety because he is thinking of her. By her spell-like thrall over him, Guinevere "reveals the potential dangers of a man's unquestioning devotion to a woman,"[152] something to be both simultaneously admired according to the tenets of courtly love, yet avoided at all costs in the reality of the male-dominated medieval period. Roberta Krueger notes, "[Woman's] privilege as a literary figure is less an indication of 'real' power than a male mystification of femininity, one that obscures the reality of her historical decline."[153] Women were given a lofty ideal to aspire to, yet most were lucky if they survived the horrors of abuse, childbirth, and poverty.

---

151 Comer, "Behold Thy Doom," 16, 22.
152 Walters, "Introduction," xix.
153 Krueger, Roberta L., "Desire, Meaning and the Female Reader," in *Lancelot and Guinevere: A Casebook*, ed. Lori Walters (New York: Routledge, 2002), 232.

"Intentionally or not, Chrétien illustrates the destructive power of love for Guinevere; it both stuns and brainwashes a previously capable and astute knight,"[154] writes Bonner. The implied lesson here is that men must guard their hearts, for if they fall too deeply for a woman, she will unman them. So male readers were warned to take heed, while female readers were exhorted to guard themselves against spreading their inherent lust.

Guinevere and Lancelot as Models of Courtly Love

One interesting point about Chrétien's treatment of the now infamous love affair is that it doesn't contain the stain of sin that will later mar the stories for generations. Guinevere and Lancelot's love is one of bliss and joy with no hint of remorse, which is Marie de Champagne's ideal of courtly love. Bonner notes, "Where Wace and others expel Guinevere from their narrative following her indiscretions, Chrétien lets her go totally free, never making the affair known to Arthur."[155]

If the story is to be read as an allegory of courtly love, then this makes perfect sense. While the definition of courtly love is greatly debated by scholars, we can look to the twelfth century Rules of Courtly Love as defined by Andreas Capellanus

---

154 Bonner, "Guinevere as Heroine," 37.
155 Bonner, "Guinevere as Heroine," 39-40.

for guidance.[156] His rules help explain Guinevere's jealousy[157] and Lancelot's swooning.[158]

Guinevere and Lancelot's love fulfills all four attributes of the ideal of courtly love, as defined by Gaston Paris, a nineteenth century scholar who is credited with being the person to coin the term, and refined by DePaul University professor David Simpson:[159]

1. **Aristocratic** - That is, happening within the nobility at the royal court. Guinevere is queen and Camelot is her royal court.

2. **Ritualistic**[160] - The man makes grand gestures and woos his love with songs, poems, and other favors. In return the woman only needed to hint at her approval. This may be the best explanation for Guinevere's haughty thoughtlessness. In addition, the woman was the mistress of the affair and the man her submissive slave of love. His love for her has an almost religious tone to it.[161] We see this played out

---

156 Capellanus, Andreas, "De Arte Honeste Amandi [The Art of Courtly Love], Book Two: On the Rules of Love," Medieval Sourcebook, accessed July 17, 2017. Applicable rules will be quoted in the following footnotes. For a full listing of the rules, see http://sourcebooks.fordham.edu/source/capellanus.asp.

157 From Capellanus' "Rules:" "He who is not jealous cannot love," "Real jealousy always increases the feeling of love," "Jealousy, and therefore love, are increased when one suspects his beloved," and "A slight presumption causes a lover to suspect his beloved."

158 From Capellanus' "Rules:" "Every lover regularly turns pale in the presence of his beloved," "When a lover suddenly catches sight of his beloved his heart palpitates."

159 Bumke, Joachim, *Courtly Culture: Literature and Society in the Middle Ages* (London: Duckworth, 2004), and Simpson, David L., "Chivalry and Courtly Love," The School for New Learning, DePaul University. Accessed July 14, 2017. http://condor.depaul.edu/dsimpson/tlove/courtlylove.html

160 As Capellanus' "Rules" state: "The easy attainment of love makes it of little value; difficulty of attainment makes it prized."

161 One example is Lancelot's actions after he bends the bars to get into the queen's room. "He comes to the bed of the queen, whom he adores and before whom he kneels, holding her more dear than the relic of any saint." 69.

in the often melodramatic effect Guinevere's love has on Lancelot. Courtly love also has its own set of rules that lovers must learn and observe.

3. **Secret**[162] - The affair must only be between the two lovers. Note that it is always when their affair is discovered that Guinevere and Lancelot's love ends. Putting aside how it likely would have made Arthur feel, this convention explains why the revelation of their affair has such serious effects.

4. **Adulterous**[163] - Their love happens outside of marriage. This is different from the modern connotation of adultery, which usually implies extramarital sex. Courtly love allowed for physical contact, but it was about romance, not sex. In a world when most marriages were for political or economic gain or only to produce children, this was the real love that resulted in the sublime. Since Guinevere is married and the author gives us little hint of affection between her and Arthur, as opposed to the great passion between her and Lancelot, this criterion is fulfilled.

As Peter Noble points out, Guinevere was written specifically for this type of court: Chrétien took very little of his material for [Guinevere] from his predecessors, with the result that she is very largely his own creation, made necessary by the type of society for which he was writing and by the demands of the stories themselves. As Chrétien was writing during at

---

162 As Capellanus' "Rules" state: "When made public love rarely endures."
163 As Capellanus' "Rules" state: "Marriage is no real excuse for not loving."

least part of his career for the sophisticated court of Marie de Champagne at which women played a considerable social role, it would be only realistic to portray a character fulfilling such a role, even if idealized, in the romances.[164]

Comer goes one step further, arguing that "Guinevere as a character is not important; Guinevere as a symbol is…any other married noblewoman could just as easily play the part [of Lancelot's lover]…Guinevere's personality is ancillary and expendable."[165] It was Guinevere's job to bring out the best in the knight in her service; in exchange, he would be her servant.[166] "Starting with the French tradition of courtly love, noble women occupied a space that was both public and private…. She was also to be something of an icon—a figure for the knights to swear fealty to and for their ladies to imitate. As a wife, she was expected to follow her husband's direction, and bear an heir, as well as perform that most courtly and impossible of tasks, bring her lover to perfection."[167]

The melodramatic actions and reactions of Arthurian characters, especially Lancelot and Guinevere, are part and parcel of courtly romances. Comer notes that this drama has caused confusion among critics and scholars. "Th[e] manner of courtly love is so extreme that critics still do not know whether writers

---

164 Noble, Peter, "The Character of Guinevere in the Arthurian Romances of Chrétien De Troyes," *The Modern Language Review*, 67, no. 3 (1972), 524.
165 Comer, "Behold Thy Doom is Mine," 23.
166 Ibid., 24.
167 Ibid., 2.

like Chrétien were treating the subject seriously or mockingly."[168] So deep is Lancelot's passion for Guinevere, it even fuels him to perform feats of superhuman strength, as evidenced when he removes the iron bars leading to her chamber so that they might become lovers. Bonner notes that Guinevere is an equal actor and willing partner in this scene of seduction. She concludes that "Guinevere's willingness and carelessness in this scene indicate that love has also debased her."[169]

Is that true, or is Guinevere's abandon a sign of her independence? Here she is acting against the morals of society by using her free will to take a lover. Samples writes, "It is noteworthy that in *Charette*, Guinevere's independence is sexual, which is revolutionary because this affair challenges the existing institution of marriage and enhances the role of women. The lovers choose each other, and Guinevere enjoys an equal status in the relationship."[170]

And therein lies the rub. Because this Guinevere, unlike Chrétien's portrayals of her in his other poems, dares to act on her own accord, she is punished with the personality of a harpy. Walters says, "Her treatment...is an example of the distrust that surrounds the actions of a strong woman."[171] It is only when she becomes a major character in *The Knight in the Cart* that Guinevere becomes unlikable and, in the words of Lori Waters,

---

168 Ibid., 27.
169 Bonner, "Guinevere as Heroine," 39.
170 Samples, "A Re-Appraisal," 222.
171 Walters, "Introduction," xix.

"downright unattractive."[172]

So Guinevere acts independently of society, but does that mean she has true agency? Most scholars, including Maureen Fries, say no. "In *Lancelot*, Guinevere would at first appear to be the dominant character, especially in terms of courtly love, which informs the romance.... But only on the surface, as further analysis discloses.... Guinevere exists, like other heroines of Arthurian and other romance, to get into trouble the hero must get her out of. The incentive to heroic action, she is at the same time it's reward. Functionally, Guinevere is unable to act on her own."[173]

Chrétien's Motivations

Unlike many scholars who believe Chrétien's personal opinion of Guinevere—outside of the influence of Marie de Champagne—was neutral to favorable, Bonner argues that "while Chrétien intends his Guinevere to be more than a pretty face, his low aspirations for her become clear in a careful analysis of her brief roles.... Her only control lies in matters of manners....Chrétien confines her actions to the inconsequential and...tells readers very little about her motivations or emotions."[174]

While we may not know Chrétien's opinion of her, there is a widely-held belief that Guinevere's affair with Lancelot was likely forced on him by Chrétien's patroness, Marie de

---

172   Ibid., lxi.
173   Fries, "Female Heroes, Heroines," 8.
174   Bonner, "Guinevere as Heroine," 36.

Champagne. Comer notes "there is also a certain inconsistency in Guinevere's character...that does not exist in the [works of later authors]. Chrétien acquiescing to his patroness's wishes and the influence of literary trends of the time can explain the incongruity. These forces as well as the theme of courtly love that pervades Chrétien's *Knight of the Cart* transform Guinevere from Arthur's good and faithful wife to Lancelot's jealous and fickle mistress."[175] Later on, Comer elaborates, noting "Guinevere is almost two different characters—one with Arthur and one with Lancelot. When seen with Arthur, she is a good queen and a supportive wife; when seen with Lancelot, she is a demanding and jealous lover."[176]

This makes sense when one considers that sexual adultery is rare in courtly romances,[177] and when it does occur, it is not glorified; in fact, it is looked down upon.[178] "Was it the poet's intention to glorify courtly love, which was stronger than all injections of morality?" asks Bumke. "Or did he intend to take a stance of ironic aloofness from this kind of love?"[179] We likely will never know the answer, but Chrétien's handling of the subject of adultery shows how uncomfortable he was with the idea. As a poet, he would have known that such a storyline was not commonly accepted, yet he had to please his patroness, however reluctantly.

---

175 Comer, "Behold Thy Doom," 12.
176 Ibid., 71.
177 But emotional adultery is common. Most nobility were married for political purposes, rather than love.
178 Bumke, *Courtly Culture*, 397.
179 Ibid.

Another theory for the change in Guinevere's demeanor takes the exact opposite argument, positing that Marie de Champagne "forced Chrétien to portray the queen as a calculating adulteress in order to illustrate the code of 'courtly love' popular at the time."[180] If we follow this line of thinking, then it seems Marie might have been using a bit of reverse psychology here; it could be that she wanted Chrétien to point out the affair *because* it is the exact opposite of what is commonly accepted in such circles. By pointing out the offending behavior, Chrétien would be enforcing the desired end: a pure, spiritual love that transcended the urges of the flesh—the ideal of courtly love.

Barbara Gordon-Wise takes yet another tack in trying to explain the abrupt about-face, by arguing Chrétien "was trying to avoid the French tradition of 'an insipid Guinevere' but the price was that she was even more deeply linked to adultery and seduction."[181] It's possible that because Guinevere was a kind, nurturing character in Chrétien's other stories, that this is how he really saw her and the "calculating adulteress"[182] we meet in *The Knight of the Cart* is his way of registering a complaint while still doing as Marie de Champagne asked.

Regardless of authorship or intent, Chrétien's poetry forever changed the fabric of Arthurian legend, anchoring it firmly in the tradition of courtly love espoused by Marie de Champagne and her nobility. He gave us a more well-rounded

---

180 Walters, "Introduction," lxi.
181 Gordon-Wise, *The Reclamation of a Queen*, 64.
182 Comer, "Behold Thy Doom," 18.

Arthur and Guinevere, a king who "does more than wage war and conquer other nations, but also a more detailed and more active Queen."[183] Guinevere in some ways appears strong—she holds Lancelot in her sway with her love and is unabashedly sexual—but she is really only a symbol of the beauty idolized by a romantic court. As Walters notes, "Woman's 'power' is a fiction of the male subject who needs her to resist so that he can desire her."[184] For all her seeming power, Guinevere is still very much "dependent upon the actions and desires of men.... Chrétien develops little more than her unhealthy love for Lancelot,"[185] writes Bonner. But again, that is to be expected under the egis of courtly love where "[beauty] is more important than any real virtue and even supersedes the usually important one of chastity."[186]

Marie de France

> "I say this truth to you, my queen,
> and you had better understand—
> some servant girl she has at hand,
> the poorest in her retinue,
> is, Lady Queen, worth more than you."
> — *Lanval* by Marie de France[187]

---

183 Bonner, "Guinevere as Heroine," 31.
184 Walters, "Introduction," 238.
185 Bonner, "Guinevere as Heroine," 32.
186 Fries, "Female Heroes, Heroines," 9.
187 De France, Marie, *Marie de France: Poetry*, International Student Edition (New York: W.W. Norton, 2015).

Around the same time Chrétien was writing, a type of poetry called a "lai" (or "lay") was being composed by Marie de France[188] and her court, which viewed Guinevere from a completely different perspective. Here she was not held up as an ideal woman; rather, she was condemned as lustful and evil. "[The] sketch of Guenevere in 'the Lay of Sir Launfal' is a character one does not recall with pleasure," writes Mason in his introduction to Marie's works.[189]

Andrea Hopkins elaborates, "Parallel to the descriptions of Guinevere as a noble lady was from an early date a strong tradition of a bad Guinevere. This is a queen whom power has corrupted and she uses her feminine wiles to manipulate Arthur, throwing tantrums, crying or sulking to get her own way. Portrayals of her love affair with Lancelot here show that she is capable of extreme jealousy, and worst of all, she does not flinch at scheming to harm those who have thwarted her desires out of spite. The first occasion on which we meet this Guinevere is in one of the twelfth century's Breton lays of Marie de France, 'Lanval.'"[190]

In this lai, Guinevere attempts to seduce a young knight named Sir Lanval. When he rejects her, she accuses him to others of trying to seduce her, while at the same time suggesting to him that his lack of desire for her is because he is homosexual. This

---

188   Not to be confused with Marie de Champagne, Chrétien's patroness. Very little is known of Marie de France, not even when she lived or where. There is debate as to whether, since she wrote in the French dialect of Northern France, she was a Frenchwoman, or if as tradition dictates, she was an English subject from Pitre, Normandy. See Mason, the introduction to *French Medieval Romances* p. 3 for more.
189   Mason, "Introduction," 5.
190   Hopkins, Andrea, *The Book of Guinevere*, 66.

is a motif that dates back to Potiphar's wife in the Bible, a story popular in the Middle Ages,[191] though David Chamberlain argues Guinevere is worse than the Biblical woman "given her motive, haste and virile husband."[192] John and Caitlin Matthews argue that Guinevere's motivation is that she "fears him because he sees through her many infidelities...here there is no doubt of the queen's infidelities and she is presented as a scheming and promiscuous woman."[193]

Lanval is not the only lai in which Guinevere is portrayed in a negative light, again having to do with sex. *Du Cor* and *the Conte du Mantel* both contain tests of chastity, which Arthur's queen (though unnamed) fails. A similar English ballad called *The Boy and the Mantle* gives almost the exact situation, naming Guinevere, who fails the test. It is claimed that she slept with fifteen men and she is called "a bitch and a witch/and a whore bold."[194]

So what did Marie de France have against Guinevere? Obviously, something to do with sex, a sensitive subject for both men and women in the Middle Ages. In this work, Marie uses Guinevere to invoke two of the most taboo sexual subjects of her (and almost any) time: homosexuality and adultery. But her beef with Guinevere was not likely personal. Then, as now, Guinevere likely represented more than just a character. In this

---

191 Gordon-Wise, *The Reclamation of a Queen*, 63.
192 Chamberlain, David, "Marie de France's Arthurian Lai: Subtle and Political," in *Culture and the King: The Social Implications of Arthurian Legend* (Albany: State U of New York P, 1994), 23.
193 Matthews, John and Caitlin, *The Complete King Arthur*, 258.
194 Korrel, *An Arthurian Triangle*, 125.

case, she represented Arthur's court and its values, turning them upside down by her actions.[195] Logan Whalen sees Marie's poetry as pushing the envelope of her society. "Marie's brief foray into Arthurian fiction...exemplifies the ambivalent capacity of courtly fiction both to reflect erotic fantasies and social desires and to probe the darker forces that subtend courtly society, where competition, sexual humiliation, and treachery threaten to undermine chivalric identity."[196]

In the lai of *Lanval*, women are shown as their two generally accepted polarities: seductive like Guinevere or pure and Otherworldly like the Fairy Queen.[197] It may be that this poem is calling attention to what would later be called the virgin/whore approach to viewing the feminine.

Or the intent could be the exact opposite, and Marie de France really is the early feminist some proclaim her. "An age so feminist in its sympathies as ours should be attracted more easily to Marie de France," writes Mason. "To deliver oneself in any medium is always difficult. For a woman in the Middle Ages to express herself publicly by any means whatever was almost impossible. A great lady, a great Saint or church-woman might do so very occasionally. But the individuality of the ordinary wife was merged in with that of her husband."[198]

Several scholars see the lais as Marie de France's way of

---

195 Thomas, Alfred, *Reading Women in Late Medieval Europe: Anne of Bohemia and Chaucer's Female Audience* (New York: Palgrave Macmillan, 2015), 142.
196 Whalen, Logan, *A Companion to Marie de France* (Boston: Brill, 2011), 67.
197 Thomas, *Reading Women*, 142.
198 Mason, "Introduction," 2.

fighting back against the rules of the society in which she lived, arguing that she reverses traditional gender roles by having the knights depend on their maidens. Jessica Medeiros praises Guinevere's comfort with her sexuality:

> Guinevere's villainous nature can be viewed as yet another gender role reversal thrown in by bad ass Marie. Throughout history, women have been portrayed as innocent and pure, characteristics which are widely equated with femininity. Usually, women in stories are the damsels in distress, not the hero or in Guinevere's case, the villain.... Guinevere...attempt[s] to seduce Lanval simply because she finds him sexually attractive [not because she loves him]. This is further evidence of a woman owning her sexuality instead of shying away from it.[199]

As we have seen, the twelfth century has given us an interesting mix of perspectives on Guinevere. She began the century cemented in history as an adulterous traitor and then Chrétien de Troyes wrestled her already sullied reputation into the confines of courtly love. While he did Guinevere a favor by making her a main character in *The Knight of the Cart*, he also presented a confusing, often contradictory view of her, one that would be darkened over the next several centuries. Marie

---

199 Medeiros, Jessica, "Why Marie De France Was A Medieval Bad Ass," *The Odyssey*, August 22, 2016.

de France, while lesser known, was merciless on Guinevere, perhaps as a way of railing against the mores of her society. The combination of these two portrayals means that deep into the Middle Ages, Guinevere is tainted by both confusion and a stain that is seemingly impossible to remove.

CHAPTER SIX

THE MIDDLE AGES PART FOUR: THE VULGATE CYCLE

> *"They agreed at last that they would speak to the nurse of King Arthur's betrothed, and they would be so generous toward her that, on the night when Guenevere was to lie down with her husband, the old woman would put the seneschal's daughter [the False Guinevere] with the king instead of her; and she would take Guenevere to play in the garden that evening and 'then we will seize her and take her to such a place that he will never hear news of her.'"*[200]
> — Lancelot from the Lancelot-Grail Cycle

Importance of the Vulgate Cycle

The Vulgate Cycle (also known as the Lancelot-Grail Cycle) is comprised of five interconnected tales that tell the story of King Arthur from his birth to his death. It is believed to have been written in early thirteenth century and to be the work of several authors, likely Cistercian monks and clerics. It is a very

---

[200] Lacy, Norris, J., *The Lancelot-Grail Reader: Selections from the Medieval French Arthurian Cycle* (New York: Garland Pub., 2000), 83.

important piece of Arthurian literature, as it marks the shift from verse to prose, and its more famous cousin, Malory's *Morte d'Arthur*, couldn't exist without it. It was the first Arthurian story to include Arthur's incest with his sister (in this version Lot's unnamed wife, not Morgan) and Mordred being his son. It was also the first to associate Guinevere with witchcraft (through a poisoned apple), tell the story of the true and false Guineveres, and give Guinevere "hypnotic" power over Lancelot.[201]

The True and False Guineveres

In Chapter Two, we examined the idea that Arthur had three wives, all named Guinevere, as well as the episode where one of the Guineveres struck the other in Triads 53 and 54. By the thirteenth century, this idea had morphed into there being Guinevere the False and Guinevere the True. Their story is told in the book *Merlin*.

Guinevere the False is the identical half-sister of the real Guinevere, fathered by Leodegan (or Leodegrance) and the wife of Cleodalis, his seneschal. Both Guineveres are conceived the same night, born the same day and look exactly alike, except the true Guinevere has a birthmark of a crown on her back.

Leodegan's enemies scheme to replace the true Guinevere with the false Guinevere on Arthur's wedding night, but Merlin learns of the plan and commissions two knights to stop it. Years

---

201 Gordon-Wise, *The Reclamation of a Queen*, 77.

later, Guinevere the False forms an alliance with Bertholai, an old knight who had been banished from Leodegan's court for murder. They send a message to Arthur proclaiming that Guinevere the False is the true queen, and that Arthur has been living with an impostor since his wedding night.

Bertholai and his knights capture Arthur and give him a love potion which makes him fall in love with Guinevere the False and reject Guinevere the True. He accuses the True of being the False and demands she be stripped of the skin on her head, cheeks, and palms before she is exiled.[202]

Lancelot acts as champion to Guinevere the True against three of Bertholai's knights to prove her innocence. This is where the story diverges into two possible endings. According to the Vulgate *Lancelot*, Lancelot and the true Guinevere flee Arthur's court for Sorelois, where they live for several years before Guinevere the False perishes of an illness, confessing on her deathbed. But in the non-cyclical, Post-Vulgate Lancelot *du Lac*, Bertholai and the False Guinevere immediately admit their guilt and are burned.[203]

As Jane Burns points out, it is interesting that "the Old French text never labels one Guinevere 'true' and the other 'false.' In fact, the narrator's initial distinction between the pretender to

---

[202] Gordon-Wise, *The Reclamation of a Queen*, 77. The head, cheeks, and palms are the traditional places a queen was anointed. Some scholars say this was an act of disfigurement or that it was a way of making her no longer tempting to men, or of taking her power and sexual control.

[203] Bruce, Christopher W., "Guinevere the False," *The Arthurian Name Dictionary* (New York: Garland, 1999).

the throne [is] 'Genievre, las fille le roi Leodagan de Tarmelide" [Guinevere, the daughter of King Leodagan of Tarmelide] and King Arthur's wife as 'la roine' [the queen]."[204] But yet the True and the False are how the two women have been known for centuries.

This strange insertion into Arthurian legend is thought by some to be representative of the "tendency of medieval writers to polarize the female figure"[205] into good/bad, Madonna/whore, true/false. This theory would certainly fit with the way women were generally portrayed by men in medieval society. Also fittingly for the time, we see here Guinevere punished for acting too independently, even though Arthur sinned with Guinevere the False just has she did with Lancelot. Burns explains,

> In her adulterous liaison with Lancelot, Guinevere oversteps [her] role as Arthur's queen and royal consort to become too thoroughly and independently the lord herself.... Guinevere's behavior is deemed unacceptable in this instance because it defies legal statutes and social codes. But her adulterous act is equally threatening to courtly society because it crosses proscribed gender boundaries. 'How dare she, a woman, pursue an adulterous passion in defiance of her spouse?' this text seems to ask.

Adultery was acceptable for men, not women, in the

---

[204] Burns, E. Jane, "Which Queen?: Guinevere's Transvestism in the French Prose Lancelot," in *Lancelot and Guinevere: A Casebook*, ed. Lori Walters (New York: Routledge, 2002), 249.
[205] Gordon-Wise, *The Reclamation of a Queen*, 11.

Middle Ages; the province of lords, not ladies. That Guinevere pursues her adulterous liaison with such resolve smacks inappropriately of male prerogative. This feme [woman] and roine [queen] has taken the liberties of a man.[206]

Guinevere in *The Vulgate Cycle*

Guinevere figures the most prominently in the third book of the cycle, *Lancelot*. When the story begins, Arthur and Guinevere have a loving relationship. Lancelot meets Guinevere at court and is captivated by her beauty. She bestows the sword of knighthood on Lancelot, a role usually played by Arthur.[207] He goes on many adventures and over time falls more in love with Guinevere, who secretly returns his feelings. Guinevere initiates their first kiss. Their love is chaste at first, but when Arthur is kidnapped by an enchantress named Camille, Guinevere and Lancelot become lovers. Lancelot comes to the Grail Castle where he is tricked into sleeping with the Fisher King's daughter, Elaine, whom he believes to be Guinevere. Guinevere finds out and berates Lancelot, who goes mad and wanders in the forest for a long time.

In the fifth book, *Morte le Roi Artu*, the story takes a darker turn. Lancelot returns to his affair with Guinevere, who is petty

---

206 Burns, E. Jane, "Which Queen?: Guinevere's Transvestism in the French Prose Lancelot," 254.
207 Walters, "Introduction," xxi. Walters claims this symbolizes Guinevere's true allegiance to Lancelot.

and jealous when she suspects Lancelot of having an affair with Elaine. Agravain, Morgan, and others suspect Guinevere and Lancelot are having an affair. Guinevere is accused of murdering the brother of Sir Mador de la Porte and is given forty days to find a champion, as recommended by law. Lancelot, who has been recovering from wounds, saves her.

After her acquittal, the lovers become reckless, but Arthur refuses to believe they are having an affair, so Agravain, Mordred, and Guerrehes hatch a plot to catch the lovers together. They do and Lancelot escapes, but Guinevere is not so lucky and is sentenced to death at the stake. Lancelot rescues her, but in the process, he kills Gaheriet, angering Arthur. In retaliation, Arthur attacks Lancelot's castle of Joyous Gard.

At the urging of the Pope, Arthur takes Guinevere back after months of fruitless fighting, but at Gawain's suggestion, follows Lancelot to Brittany, leaving Mordred alone with Guinevere. Guinevere becomes a nun, possibly to escape Mordred's advances, and dies shortly after hearing of Arthur's death. Lancelot sees Guinevere die in a vision and becomes a hermit. Later, he dies while stretched out on Guinevere's tomb.

It is notable that unlike in Chrétien's story, this version of Arthurian legend introduces tremendous guilt on the part of the lovers, to the point where Guinevere and Lancelot never know a moment's peace, and they are punished for their adultery. None of this is really too surprising given that the story was written by monks, but it is still a striking departure from previous legend. According to Meredith Ross, this is also in keeping with literary tradition. "In the tradition of French prose romance—especially in the Vulgate Cycle—the main characters are destroyed not by external enemies but by internal flaws."[208] So despite the punishment Arthur later metes out, the lovers' true undoing is their inescapable guilt.

The Vuglate Cycle's Guinevere, while she does a lot more than many of her earlier counterparts, doesn't have much personality. She exists, especially in *Lancelot*, only as an object of affection for the men in her life. Some scholars believe she isn't meant to be seen as a person in her own right, but as a symbol of Lancelot's fatal flaw[209]—it is loving her that costs him the Grail and brings about the fall of Camelot. Here again we see her not as a person in her own right, but as a person beloved by Lancelot.

It very well could be that the monks who penned this version of Guinevere, being chaste and cloistered away from the outside world, simply didn't have the experience with women necessary to craft a convincing female character. Or, it could be that they were more interested in getting across their religious message of the evils of woman and the importance of repentance than in representing Guinevere accurately. After all, she was nothing more than a tool to them.

In the Vulgate Cycle, we witness Guinevere becoming Eve, the cause of the fall of Camelot just like Eve was to Paradise.

---

208 Ross, Meredith, "The Sublime to the Ridiculous: The Restructuring of Arthurian Materials in Selected Modern Novels" (PhD diss., University of Wisconsin–Madison, 1985), 167.
209 Kennedy, Edward Donald, "Introduction," *King Arthur: A Casebook* (New York:Routledge, 2013), xxv.

Gordon-Wise explains the implications of this idea: "Riddled with clerical misogyny, this work emphatically associates the figure of Guinevere with the devil, thus echoing the medieval acceptance of the notion of woman as demonic temptress."[210] Given this—and the other overt religious messages of the tales—it's only fitting that Guinevere and Lancelot can only find peace, and maybe even salvation, in the religious life they both turn to after their affair is exposed.

The Vulgate Cycle is the last of the major works of Arthurian legend to be penned by monks and clerics; after this, lay people take over telling the story. But the condemnation and religious symbolism they (Gildas, Geoffrey of Monmouth, Layamon, and the Cistercians who wrote The Vulgate Cycle) threaded into the story remain, casting a long shadow of guilt that will become more prominent as the popularity of the Arthurian legend soars at Thomas Malory's hands.

---

210 Gordon-Wise, *The Reclamation of a Queen*, 14.

CHAPTER SEVEN

THE MIDDLE AGES PART FIVE: ALLITERATIVE MORTE ARTHURE AND THOMAS MALORY

"It was my darling dainteous and full dere holden,
Keeped for encrownmentes of kinges annointed;
On dayes when I dubbed dukes and erles
It was burlich borne by the bright hiltes;
I durst never dere it in deedes of armes
But ever keeped clene because of myselven.
For I see Clarent uncledde that crown is of swordes,
My wardrope at Walingford I wot is destroyed.
Wiste no wye of wonne but Waynor herselven;
Sho had the keeping herself of that kidd wepen,
Of coffers enclosed that to the crown longed,
With ringes and relickes and the regale of Fraunce
That was founden on Sir Frolle when he was fey leved."[211]
— *The Alliterative Morte Arthure*

Alliterative Morte Arthure

Not to be confused with Thomas Malory's *Morte d'Arthur* or the *Mort Artu* that is part of the Vulgate Cycle, *Morte Arthure*,

---

[211] Krishna, Valerie, The Alliterative Morte Arthure: A New Verse Translation (Washington, D.C.: UP of America, 1983), lines 4196-4208.

sometimes called *The Alliterative Morte Arthure* to distinguish it, is a 4,346-line Middle English alliterative poem, retelling the latter part of the legend of King Arthur. It was written around the year 1400 by an unknown author (possibly a poet named Huchoun) and there is only one manuscript of it still extant. It's one of the lesser-known works of Arthurian literature and all but unknown to non-academic audiences.

The Alliterative Morte Arthure draws from Geoffrey of Monmouth and Wace/Layamon as main sources, but there are other parts that appear to be original to its author. Tichelaar explains, "The Alliterative Morte Arthure, unlike the slightly earlier Stanzaic Morte Arthur, rejected French additions [by Chrétien] by returning to the plot of Guinevere willingly marrying Mordred…. The poet first deleted the French romantic additions. Then he added new details to Guinevere and Mordred's relationship to make the queen's guilt more substantial. Like Layamon and Wace, the poet was largely clarifying Geoffrey of Monmouth's statements."[212] With Mordred as Guinevere's groom, *The Alliterative Morte Arthure* eliminates the relationship between Lancelot and Guinevere. Thomas Malory appears to have heavily drawn on this alliterative version for the second part of his famous work of a similar name, with the only major change being turning the tragedy of the poem into a story of triumph in the end.[213]

Guinevere plays a very small role in the poem, in which, as

---

212 Tichelaar, Tyler, "While King Arthur was Away," accessed June 12, 2017.
213 Ibid., and Benson, C. David, "The Ending of the Morte Darthur," in *A Companion to Malory*, ed. Elizabeth Archibald (Woodbridge: D.S. Brewer, 2000), 221-222.

we shall see, she is portrayed as a terrible mother and a treasonous queen. One of the most unique additions that this poem makes to the character of Guinevere is that it shows her "bear[ing] Mordred's children as a sign of her and Mordred's love for each other. No other text makes Guinevere the mother of Mordred's children."[214]

In general, Guinevere's depiction in this work is largely negative, and according to Beal, she functions mostly as a symbol of grief.[215] Fries summarizes Guinevere's reduced role: "Guinevere, developed in the *Prose Vulgate* from Chrétien's characterization in the *Charette* into a subtle female portrait in the *Lancelot* and *Mort Artu* and Malory's *Morte*, is diminished in the alliterative poem. Her warmth and her grandeur, her jealousy and her capriciousness, are here reduced to two briefly described scenes."[216]

The first time Guinevere appears in the poem, she is weeping over Arthur leaving for war, which Beal believes makes her a symbol of all war widows.[217] At first, this interpretation might seem odd, but looking at the text, it becomes a strong possibility. Here she certainly sounds like every woman across the centuries who has had to send a beloved boyfriend or husband off to war: "Guinevere, softly weeping, embraces him/And speaks to him tenderly, with tears without measure/ 'I could curse the man has caused this war/That denies me the honor of/And robs my

---

214   Tichelaar, "While King Arthur was Away," accessed June 12, 2017.
215   Beal, Rebecca S., "Guenevere's Tears in the Alliterative Morte Arthure: Doubly Wife, Doubly Mother, Doubly Damned," in *On Arthurian Women*, ed. Bonnie Wheeler and Fiona Tolhurst (Dallas: Scriptorium Press, 2001,), 1.
216   Fries, "The Poem," 40.
217   Beal, "Guenevere's Tears," 2.

right to serve my wedded lord/All my life's joy is departing the land/And I am left in desolation, believe me, forever."[218]

Guinevere's second appearance has her weeping as she leaves to become a nun, which Beal says makes her a symbol of women who have lost children.[219] "Guenevere weeps as she goes to take the veil, dressed as for death—facing the loss of her second husband and their children…[her] mourning recalls the episodes in the poem that recall the slaughter of children."[220]

It is not without significance that Guinevere enters the convent out of fear that either Arthur or Mordred will kill her, leaving her children victim to Arthur's anger, rather than out of repentance as in previous stories.[221] Beal explains, "Again Guenevere weeps, then goes to Caerleon in garments signifying death or mourning, and the mention of Guenevere's children elides into their loss."[222] So in leaving them behind, she has condemned them to near certain death, the actions of a selfish woman rather than a caring mother. When all is said and done, Beal argues, "the poem has no sympathy for Guenevere, at the end left without any honor,"[223] or as the text tells us, "but all in falseness and fraud and fear of her lord."[224]

However, Tichelaar argues Guinevere has a much more

---

218 Krishna, *A New Verse Translation*, 19, lines 697-702.
219 Beal, "Guenevere's Tears," 2, 4.
220 Ibid., 1, 2.
221 Fries, "The Poem," 40.
222 Beal, "Guenevere's Tears," 4.
223 Ibid., 6.
224 Stone, Brian, trans., "Alliterative Morte Arthure," in *King Arthur's Death* (London: Penguin Books, 1988), line 3918.

active and important role in the poem than Beal sees. He says the passage quoted at the opening of this chapter shows "Guinevere as aggressively committing treason against Arthur by giving Mordred Arthur's sword, Clarent, which she has in her keeping. Guinevere is the only one Arthur trusted with his sword, so when she gives it to Mordred, she is actively betraying Arthur's trust. There is no more traitorous act she could commit than to use Arthur's own sword against him."[225] Tichelaar appears correct; even if not, Guinevere is most certainly guilty of treason by way of her marriage to Mordred while she was still wed to Arthur.

Thomas Malory

Malory's *Le Morte d'Arthur* is one of the most famous works of Arthurian legend, routinely taught in high schools and colleges in the United States and Britain. Of all of the works discussed in this book, it is the one most people probably know. Thanks to this 1470 work, which spans twenty-one volumes, we have a popular notion of King Arthur as the greatest Christian King ever to rule England. Malory firmly placed Arthur in the Middle Ages, which is one reason why a lot of people have a hard time thinking of him as a historical Celt. He is also responsible for popularizing Guinevere's kidnapping by Malegant, making Morgan a shape-shifter, and giving generations of readers the hope that Arthur may come again when Britain most needs him. T. H. White,

---

225 Tichelaar, "While King Arthur was Away," accessed June 12, 2017.

the musical *Camelot*, and frankly anyone else who dabbles in the legends, owe him and his forebears a lot.

The Poisoned Apple

> *"Then, as the book saith, sir Lancelot began to resort unto queen Guenevere again, and forgot the promise and the perfection that he made in the quest."*[226]

Most people are familiar with Book Eight of *Le Morte d'Arthur*, "The Death of Arthur," but Guinevere also figures into Book Seven, which begins with the story of "The Poisoned Apple." It opens by telling us that after the quest of Sakgreall (Sangreall or the quest for the Holy Grail), Lancelot and Guinevere resumed their affair. As is usual in these stories, Mordred and Agravain spread evil rumors about them throughout the court. Because of this, Lancelot stays away. Guinevere accuses him of no longer loving her, claiming she will never love him. In a fit of anger, she banishes him from the court to Brittany.

While Arthur and the others are grieved by Lancelot's absence, Guinevere feigns indifference and spends much time in the company of the other knights. She personally prepares a great feast for them, but in the midst of the revelry, Sir Patrise of Ireland collapses dead from one bite of a poisoned apple that had been on Gawain's plate.

---

226 Malory, Thomas, *The Morte Darthur, Parts Seven and Eight*, ed. Derek Brewer (Evanston, IL: Northwestern UP, 1987, 1968), 47.

When Guinevere is accused of murder by Sir Mador, Arthur has to uphold his own law, so Guinevere is given fifteen days to find a knight to defend her or she will be burned at the stake. The rumors spread by Mordred and Agravain work so well that no one will defend her. Eventually, Sir Bors reluctantly agrees. But on the fifteenth day, an unknown knight comes to defend Guinevere. He defeats Sir Mador, who recants his accusation. The Lady of the Lake appears and declares Guinevere innocent, revealing the real killer, who is linked to Mordred and Morgan. When the knight reveals himself to be Lancelot, some people are joyful, but others see this as confirmation that Mordred's rumors about Guinevere and Lancelot are true.

In addition to the role this story plays in *Le Morte d'Arthur*, "The Poisoned Apple" shows who was loyal to Guinevere and who was not, as well as the differing opinions and lack of trust surrounding Guinevere.[227] Arthurian enthusiast Morgause of Orkney elaborates: "The fact that not one of the knights believes her to be innocent (with the exception of Bors), and their refusal to support her for fear of dishonouring themselves, is a far cry from their earlier readiness to defend the queen at all costs. This is more than just another tale of Lancelot's bravery and nobility—there is a real distrust of the queen amongst the knights of the Round Table…Guinevere's near brush with death shows that not even the knights' respect for Arthur will persuade them to champion her cause."[228]

---

227 MorgauseofOrkney, "'The Poisoned Apple'- Thoughts," *In My Defens* (2014).
228 Ibid.

The titular apple is seen as a symbol of many things, not the least of which are the Round Table and Camelot itself (the poison being what brings about the end of Camelot). According to Kenneth Hodges, "Guinevere's actions, particularly in 'The Poisoned Apple,' show her struggling to hold together the unity of the Round Table, threatened by the rivalries among the affinities (factions of Arthur's knights)."[229] C. David Benson, in his article about the end of *Le Morte*, notes the immediate sense at the beginning of the story that "these are indeed the final days of the Round Table."[230] The Grail Quest is over, but not all of the knights are still with them. The end is near; all that remains is to wait for the final tragedy to unfold.

The apple can also be related to Guinevere. Morgause of Orkney sees it as being symbolic of Guinevere and Lancelot's relationship. "It might seem like another poisoned apple is Lancelot and Guinevere's relationship, both through the fact that the affair is in the spotlight throughout the chapter, and that it will eventually have a corrosive effect on the unity and bonds of trust between the knights of the Round Table. It's also a good opportunity for Malory to point out, yet again, that Lancelot is the Ultimate Sinner because of his renewed love for Gwen in defiance of God's wishes."

Sin is a common theme with the apple, for obvious reasons. David Day believes it is an allusion to Eve and original sin, thus

---

229 Hodges, Kenneth, "Guinevere's Politics in Malory's 'Morte Darthur,'" *The Journal of English and Germanic Philology*, 104, no. 1, (2005): 54.
230 Benson, "The Ending," 222.

hinting at Guinevere's affair with Lancelot. He notes that "it also implies comparison with Troy, whose downfall was the result of a poisonous curse placed on a golden apple and a beautiful queen's adulterous love affair."[231]

Interestingly, at least one scholar sees a connection between this story and its more famous cousin, which we will examine shortly. David C. Benson writes, "Malory moves the story [of the *Knight in the Cart*] to a much later point in the Arthurian saga and uses it both to explore the love of Guinevere and Lancelot and to replay the themes of 'The Poisoned Apple' in a darker mode."[232]

Le Morte d'Arthur

> "*Guinevere, learning of the battle*
> *And the deadly ruin done,*
> *Took five ladies and went away*
> *To Amesbury as a nun,*
> *And there remained in holy prayer,*
> *Weeping evermore.*
> *She never would be happy again:*
> *Yes, white and black she wore.*"[233]
> — *Le Morte d'Arthur* by Thomas Malory

After several centuries on the periphery, Guinevere is finally a key character. In fact, Ann Howey sees her as the cornerstone of

---

231 Day, David, *The Quest for King Arthur* (London: Michael O'Mara, 1999), 112.
232 Benson, "The Ending," 226.
233 Malory, Thomas, "Le Morte d'Arthur," in *The King Arthur Collection* (Rochester: Maplewood Books, 2014), 301, lines 3566-3573.

Le Morte d'Arthur, writing that Guinevere "inspires the plot of the work as a whole. First, she is often the mechanism by which Lancelot is sent from court on different adventures....Second, she provides the framework for more examples of Lancelot's prowess....Third, the revelation of their love set in motion the feud that will take Arthur from England, allowing Mordred to usurp the throne."[234]

Before analyzing this on a deeper level, a quick plot summary of the parts of the story concerning Guinevere is in order.

Guinevere is kidnapped by Melegraunce and rescued by Lancelot. Though Morgan twice attempts to poison Arthur's mind that the two are having an affair, they are still chaste. But Arthur and Morgan are not, and she conceives his child. In a move that harkens back to the more brutal, tyrannical Arthur found in the earliest Arthurian legend, the King, like the Biblical King Herod, orders all newborn males killed in an effort to rid himself of his unwanted newborn son.

When Guinevere hears Lancelot has gotten Elaine pregnant, she scorns him for being unfaithful to her, but then she believes his explanation that he thought he was lying with her and forgives him. However, she is still jealous when Elaine comes to court. After Lancelot is again tricked into Elaine's bed, Guinevere banishes him from her sight.

Lancelot goes mad and disappears into the forest. Despite paying high sums of money to try to find him, Guinevere fails

---

[234] Howey, Ann, "Once and Future Women: Popular Fiction, Feminism and Four Arthurian Rewritings," (PhD thesis, University of Alberta, 1997), 28.

for fifteen years. When Lancelot returns in time to see his son knighted and go on the Grail Quest, Guinevere weeps for joy. Lancelot cannot achieve the Grail because of his past love for Guinevere, even though it was chaste.[235] They love each other even more now, but despite frequent intimate conversations in public, they are not yet lovers.

Again, Mordred and Agravain spread rumors that Lancelot and the queen are having sex. Lancelot avoids Guinevere and pays attention to other women to stave off scandal. As in Chrétien, they talk through iron bars leading to her chamber. He asks to come in and she says yes, so he pulls out the bars through the strength of his desire. But Malory does not explicitly tell us if they had sex. They are trapped by Mordred and Agrivane, though they are not guilty on that night.

Guinevere is sentenced to the stake and Lancelot rescues her. He keeps her safe while Arthur attacks Joyous Gard, but then he returns her to Arthur. She becomes a nun at Amesbury after Arthur and Mordred's deaths as penance for her sin. One day, she unexpectedly runs into Lancelot in the town surrounding the convent and faints at the sight of him. Lancelot wants to take her with him to France, but she advises him to go and take a wife. He asks her to kiss him one final time, but she refuses.

She returns to the nunnery having taken responsibility for her sins and her role in the downfall of Camelot. Later, Lancelot has a vision of Guinevere's impending death and goes to take her

---

[235] His sin was not having an affair but loving her, rather than God.

body to be buried beside Arthur's at Glastonbury.

Like the story, Malory's Guinevere is complex, and often contradictory, which can make it difficult to get a handle on exactly who Malory intended her to be. Bonner notes that Guinevere's abrupt repentance without noticeable motivation "leaves readers puzzling over the route from point A, Guinevere as noble figure, to point B, Guinevere as conniving adulteress, to point C, Guinevere as repentant nun. Guinevere's change is too undocumented to be believable…Therefore, readers still face a dilemma concerning sympathy for her character and her enduring positive image."[236] It is possible that Malory, like Chrétien, was not comfortable with the affair, but by the time he was writing, it was such an important part of the story, he couldn't leave it out.[237] Ross agrees, noting, "The English and French traditions disagree on whether chivalry is heroic or merely sinful and on the characterization of Arthur, Gawain, Guinevere and Lancelot. Most importantly, ambiguity results from ironic disjunction between Malory's materials and his own views."[238] This would explain the abrupt changes in Guinevere's personality, as Malory grappled with a sin he was forced to include, but then had to find a way to redeem.

Malory is known to have drawn on a number of sources for this work – this is sometimes seen as the reason for his inconsistency when it comes to Guinevere. Ross believes that

---

[236] Bonner, "Guinevere as Heroine," 47.
[237] Comer, "Behold Thy Doom," 72.
[238] Ross, "The Sublime to the Ridiculous," 193.

"the widely varied sources and Malory's inexperience as an author (or historian, as he saw his role) mean that Guinevere suffers from a bi-polarity within her characterization. She blows hot and cold in her dealings with Lancelot, so much so that her instability becomes part of her character in later Arthurian retellings (Tennyson in particular uses this to his advantage)."[239]

Walters agrees, but notes Malory's watering down of the total denouncement of her in other texts. "Malory portrays Guinevere as a beautiful, courageous lady and an effective queen who assumes the function of judge and teacher of chivalry to young knights. Her rashness, however, calls down destruction on her own head; when she undergoes three public accusations of adultery, the other knights come to see her as a destroyer of men. Malory, however, does not go so far as the full condemnation of her found in previous versions of the story."[240]

Malory may not be as hard on her as some of his predecessors but many readers are more than happy to disparage her characterization. Hodges writes, "Although Sir Thomas Malory says Queen Guinevere 'was a trew lover, and therefor she had a good ende,' many critics have found her 'jealous, unreasonable, possessive and headstrong.'"[241] Indeed, Malory imputes great pride, lack of trust, and jealousy to Guinevere, especially in relation to Elaine.[242] However, Benson notes that

---

239 Ibid., 35.
240 Walters, "Introduction," xxx.
241 Hodges, "Guinevere's Politics," 54.
242 Wyatt, Siobhan, *Women of Words in Le Morte Darthur: The Autonomy of Speech in Malory's Female Characters* (London: Springer International Publishing, Palgrave

despite her fickleness, extreme unreasonableness, and being quick to take offense, this Guinevere possesses "a force and dignity… that is not in Malory's two sources and that will enable her to respond to the coming storm."[243] Likewise, Norris Lacy finds a middle ground, calling Guinevere "the epic Queen of history and chronicle, bounteous of her gifts to the knights of the Round Table, and she is also the tragic heroine of romance, deserving our pity for having been given in marriage to a man she must respect but cannot love, and fated to love a man she cannot marry."[244]

Guinevere as Symbol

Another way to look at the conflicting character of Guinevere is that she is really meant to be viewed as more than simply a character; as in earlier works, she and her actions can also be seen as symbolic. Ross notes that Malory does this with many of his characters. "Individuality is peripheral in Malory. What matters in *Le Morte D'arthur* is how much a knight possesses chivalric traits: Malory is interested not in Lancelot but in *Sir Lancelot*."[245] If that is the case, might it not also be true that he is not interested in Guinevere, but *Queen* Guinevere—how well she lives up to the example of the ideal queen? If that is the case, her contradictions begin to make sense since she both fulfills and fails in her duties as a queen. On one hand, she is a capable supervisor

---

Macmillan, 2016.), 134-135.
243 Benson, "The Ending," 223.
244 Lacy, *The New Arthurian Encyclopedia: New Edition*, 215.
245 Ross, "The Sublime to the Ridiculous," 162.

and helpmate to Arthur, yet she fails to produce an heir, which is her most important duty.[246] In succumbing to her feelings for Lancelot, Guinevere also fails in her fidelity to her king, which is the supreme duty of any subject, especially the queen.

But out of her failings comes something good. Several critics see Guinevere as a savior figure both to herself and those in her world, especially Lancelot—through her penance and embracing of Christianity.[247] Indeed, in becoming a nun, she takes on the role of repentant sinner like Mary Magdalene, one who has given up earthly sensuality for the joys of heavenly holiness. Fries sees deep meaning in this symbolism.

> In both the stanzaic *Morte* and Malory, Guinevere's taking of the veil emerges even more specifically than in Geoffrey of Monmouth as a rejection of the worldly heroine's role: Guinevere refuses Lancelot's love in an attempt at salvation for them both. Her spurning of his offer of marriage and even of a final kiss casts her into a heroic mold, but it is a male-inspired one: that of the repentant worldly woman, on the model of Mary Magdalene, Mary of Egypt and other formerly sexual females.[248]

---

246 Jillings, L. G., "The Ideal of Queenship in Hartman's Erec," in *The Legend of Arthur in the Middle Ages : studies presented to A.H. Diverres by colleagues, pupils, and friends*, eds. P. B. Grout et al. (Cambridge: D.S. Brewer; Torowa N.J., U.S.A.: Biblio Distribution Services, 1983) 123.
247 Bonner, "Guinevere as Heroine," 7.
248 Fries, " Female Heroes, Heroines," 11.

In her sin and repentance, Guinevere acts as the guardian of morality for both the female sex and the court of Camelot, and by extension, as a warning for the women of the Malory's time. "[In the Middle Ages] woman exists to bring man to perfection," writes Walters. "[The] underlying message for woman is that for civilization to flower, she must keep tight hold on her sexual proclivities."[249] And if she is weak and sins, she must repent; by doing so, she can save not only herself, but those around her. Wyatt notes that while Lancelot's sin may have deprived him of the Grail, Guinevere "tries to repair Lancelot's flaws, and that is an important distinction in Malory's work."[250] Moreover, as Comer points out, by refusing the final kiss with Lancelot, Guinevere is in effect ensuring salvation for them both. "In a society of almost constant competition, where battle determines rank, wealth, and even guilt, Guinevere's refusal of Lancelot and a worldly outlook is her effort to ensure salvation for both her and her lover. Yet Malory makes the claim that it is the fact that she was faithful to Lancelot that ensured her salvation.... That is the great irony of Malory's work and more importantly of Guinevere's role: she is simultaneously condemned and praised by all those around her,"[251] just like women in the Middle Ages, who were problematic in a masculine world. And just as medieval men would have liked to have locked away all women—and by extension their polluted sinfulness and temptation—in a nunnery, Guinevere's

---

249 Walters, "Introduction," xxxi.
250 Wyatt, "Women of Words," 135.
251 Comer, "Behold Thy Doom is Mine," 49-50.

only choice was seclusion. Elizabeth Edwards eloquently shows how for Malory sadness, tragedy, and pity are part and parcel of being a woman. "Pathos is the condition of the individual isolated from community, and it has also become, for Malory, the new condition of femininity."[252]

For Guinevere, the Middle Ages weren't so much a straight march through time, as a gradual and continuous decline. She began as a minor, perhaps even throwaway, character in Gildas and Geoffrey of Monmouth, and then was branded a traitor by Wace. Chrétien de Troyes tried to redeem her, but the insistence of his patroness on including Guinevere's affair with Lancelot negated his attempts. The monks and clerics who got hold of her in the twelfth century seized on the affair to turn her into an example intended to encourage women to be chaste, and a warning to men against the evils of the female sex. *The Alliterative Morte Arthure* abandoned all pretense of making Guinevere a likable character, once again reducing her character to a pittance of a role who symbolized grief and treason. Drawing on this source, Malory then turned her into a repentant sinner, which in some ways was a positive step—she gave sinful people hope for salvation—but it also reinforced the negative light in which she has been seen for centuries. And so Guinevere was destined to remain in the state of shame for several hundred years while the Arthurian legend fell out of favor.

---

[252] Edwards, Elizabeth, "The Place of Women in the Morte Darthur," in *A Companion to Malory*, ed. Elizabeth Archibald (Woodbridge: D.S. Brewer, 2000), 54.

CHAPTER EIGHT

THE RENAISSANCE TO THE NINETEENTH CENTURY

After Malory, the Arthurian world—especially when it came to Guinevere—went into something of a drought until the nineteenth century. As Peter Korell notes, the queen was virtually written out of the legend at this point in history. "In spite of Malory's partial whitewashing of Guinevere, she could not find favor with many later authors dealing with the Arthurian legend. In the first three centuries following Malory's *Le Morte D'Arthur*, she is almost completely ignored."[253] One of the few Arthurian plays of the Elizabethan age, Thomas Hughes's *The Misfortunes of Arthur* (1587), was based on the work of Geoffrey of Monmouth and concentrated on the revenge Arthur takes on Mordred for seducing Guinevere, rather than on the possible culpability of Guinevere herself. Even Edmund Spenser's famous *The Faerie Queen* (1590-1596) made Arthur a bachelor, eliminating Guinevere altogether.

Many scholars and critics believe this was due to shifting morality. As Walters points out, "The new moral consciousness that developed after the Reformation viewed Lancelot and

---

253 Korrel, *An Arthurian Triangle*, 274.

Guinevere's love with disfavor.... The historical tradition that had become increasingly popular typically depicted Guinevere as a woman of questionable virtue and had no knowledge of a character named Lancelot. Consequently, even though Malory had done much to improve Guinevere's reputation, writers largely ignored her for three centuries after his epic."[254]

The country's religious shift from Catholicism to Protestantism also had a heavy influence. "Protestantism itself recoiled from Arthur's Catholic ambience, especially the Grail story, and Puritan moralism found the cheerful violence and sexual awareness of romance unappealing,"[255] explain Rob Gossedge and Stephen Knight.

According to Ross, politics can also be blamed. "In the seventeenth century, the legend became closely associated with the Royalist cause in the Civil Wars—James I claimed descent from Arthur and was even hailed as 'Arthur's self returned'—while the historical existence of Arthur was increasingly suspect."[256] James I was also associated with Arthur because he united England, Wales, and Scotland, which was prophesied to occur when Arthur returned. But his commonalities with the legendary king ended there, especially since he espoused the divine right of kings, whereas Arthur was a symbol of equanimity for all.[257]

---

[254] Walters, "Introduction," xxxviii.
[255] Gossedge, Rob and Stephen Knight, "The Arthur of the Sixteenth to Nineteenth Centuries," in *The Cambridge Companion to the Arthurian Legend*, eds. Elizabeth Archibald and Ad Putte (Cambridge: Cambridge UP, 2009), 103.
[256] Ross, "The Sublime to the Ridiculous," 32.
[257] Merriman, *The Flower of Kings*, 35.

This sour mood reigned until the Victorians revived the interest in Arthuriana. As the Industrial Revolution choked the air with soot and changed the pace of life irrevocably, the Middle Ages began appearing to people as "an idyllic time when life was simpler and people lived in closer contact with the universe and their natural impulses."[258] So great was their longing for this time that Malory's *Le Morte d'Arthur* was republished three times in the 1820s alone. Walters believes this proliferation of Malory's story had a positive effect on other writers. "Taking their primary inspiration from Malory, writers looked to the Middle Ages for models of ethical conduct to help improve the present."[259] Yet, as in all other time periods, they found it impossible to write about the past without consciously or unconsciously infusing it with a bit of their present views. "Ironically, it seems that although Tennyson, Arnold, Morris and other Victorian writes may have turned to chivalric romance to escape from the strains and drudgery of modern industrial society, they invariably injected a modern consciousness and modern concerns into their writing,"[260] writes Ross. But perhaps they shouldn't shoulder too much blame, as this is a sin committed by every generation, as further analysis will show.

---

258 Walters, "Introduction," xxxix.
259 Walters, "Introduction," xxxix.
260 Ross, "The Sublime to the Ridiculous," 64.

CHAPTER NINE

TENNYSON, IDYLLS OF THE KING

> *She like a new disease, unknown to men,*
> *Creeps, no precaution used, among the crowd,*
> *Makes wicked lightnings of her eyes, and saps*
> *The fealty of our friends, and stirs the pulse*
> *With devil's leaps, and poisons half the young.* [261]
> — *"Guinevere," Idylls of The King* by Alfred Lord Tennyson

About the Idylls

Other than Malory, one of the best known, or at least easily recognized, works of Arthurian literature is Tennyson's *Idylls of the King*.[262] It rose to bestseller status in the midst of Victorian Arthurian mania and has retained its top status for more than a century. "It was Alfred, Lord Tennyson, who brought the Arthurian tradition to the forefront of literature and art in the

---

261 Tennyson, Alfred Lord, "Guinevere" *Idylls of a King* (Public domain book, 2012), 319.
262 John and Caitlin Matthews assert "Tennyson had debated calling the collection The True and The False, a title that reflected his desire to contrast the various kinds of love described in the poems" (328). This title could also have been a reference to the tradition of the True and False Guineveres, which would have been especially apt, given that Victorian women were given two main roles, as we shall explore further in this chapter: the angel in the house or the fallen woman.

form of his *Idylls of the King*,"²⁶³ asserts Comer.

Idylls is a series of twelve poems about the court of Camelot. Guinevere either appears in or is mentioned in almost all of the poems, although she plays a significant role only in "The Coming of Arthur" (where she and Arthur marry), "Lancelot and Elaine" (which is Elaine of Astolat's tragic story), and "Guinevere" (which is Guinevere and Arthur's last meeting at the Amesbury convent).

Rumors about Lancelot and Guinevere's alleged affair are part of the story even before the reader actually meets her. Therefore, Comer asserts, "the queen has negative connotations attached to her before she has appeared on the scene in any significant role."²⁶⁴ This point is significant given the role that rumors play in the Arthurian legend and as a signal of the way Guinevere is later characterized.

When Tennyson introduces Guinevere, she is already with the nuns at Amesbury, anonymously in hiding because of the affair with Lancelot and the ensuing war. The first part of the poem is her reflection upon the events that have led up to her disgrace at Camelot and in the eyes of her husband, the king. Unlike in other versions of the legend, she falls in love with Lancelot when he first escorts her from her home to marry Arthur, whom she is repelled by.²⁶⁵ Early in their relationship, she and Lancelot have many close calls that lead to fear and guilt. Interestingly, no actual details of the relationship between Lancelot and Guinevere are

---

263   Comer, "Behold Thy Doom," 6.
264   Ibid., 54.
265   Bruce, "Guinevere the False," 245.

given in this poem. There is no indication or even implication that they may have engaged in sexual intercourse. The lovers try to swear that they will never see one another again, but their love is too great to resist, so they make secret plans to meet, and are caught by Mordred. This leads to war between Arthur and Lancelot, and Guinevere flees to the convent.

When Arthur arrives at Amesbury, Guinevere is overcome by repentance and cries on her knees as Arthur tells her of his woes and eventually grants her his forgiveness. According to Comer, this harsh insertion is one of Tennyson's additions to Arthurian lore. "The scene between Guinevere and Arthur at the nunnery is original to the *Idylls*... The king, in essence, berates her for destroying Camelot and his dreams, telling her, 'For thou hast spoilt the purpose of my life.'"[266] Afterwards, Arthur leaves, and Guinevere repents of all she has done. "At this point, the fallen woman has utterly accepted that she will remain shamed in the eyes of the world forever,"[267] argues Bonner. There will be no public redemption for this queen.

Guinevere as a Character

It is significant that, as Gordon-Wises writes, "Tennyson is one of the first writers to acknowledge the significance of the Guinevere figure by allotting her an individual idyll."[268] Many scholars note

---

266 Comer, "Behold Thy Doom," 65.
267 Swanson, Kelsey, "Guinevere: Victorian Gender, Sexuality and Nature" (Literature 330: Romancing Arthur, Harlaxton College, 2010), 16.
268 Gordon-Wise, *The Reclamation of a Queen*, 49.

how he built upon the tradition begun by Malory and Chrétien, from whom Guinevere received her core personality of a "self-absorbed, scheming manipulator."[269] It is Tennyson who "reveals the Queen's own insecurities and, perhaps, the actual motivation behind her angry outburst"[270] at Lancelot regarding his relationship with Elaine. But Bonner points out that knowing her motivation doesn't mean the reader will sympathize with Guinevere. "This implication does not necessarily represent Guinevere in a more positive light than that of Chrétien or Malory, for she is still wrathful and scathing in her words. However, Tennyson does create a more believable reaction in his Guinevere"[271] through her jealousy of the younger and more beautiful Elaine, with whom she is vying for attention.

This possibly one-sided competition affects Guinevere's relationship with Lancelot. Comer observes, "Tennyson's Guinevere is never as exuberant or expressive in her love for Lancelot as either in Malory or Chrétien. Tennyson's Guinevere mostly shows her love in fits of jealousy over his relationship with Elaine… Guinevere's love for Lancelot is not pure but always tempered by another emotion—generally guilt or jealousy,"[272] hinting at an immature nature that is "always just under the surface."[273]

In her dissertation, Comer notes that Tennyson's additions to the character are significant, especially in that Guinevere is

---

269 Bonner, "Guinevere as Heroine," 51, Comer, "Behold Thy Doom," 53.
270 Bonner, "Guinevere as Heroine," 51.
271 Ibid., 52.
272 Comer, "Behold Thy Doom," 57.
273 Ibid., 53-54.

more well-rounded with clear internal conflicts that give a her life outside of the actions of men around her. "Tennyson may have consulted previous texts for the basis of Guinevere, but as David Staines says, she is a 'creation, not a re-creation'... Guinevere is more consistent than in Malory but she is also a more pitiable character, continually chastised for living her life in a way antagonistic to Arthur's idealistic plans for Camelot."[274] A few pages later, Comer continues, "Tennyson's Guinevere is a character torn between her duties to a man she does not love and the love she feels for a man she cannot be with. Malory hints at this internal conflict, but it comes to fruition in Tennyson."[275]

Much of this conflict stems from the strict set of rules Tennyson created for her and tied her up in so tightly that she couldn't win for losing.[276] Not only is Guinevere bound in an impossible situation, but the expectations of her are higher than any person could hope to achieve. "Arthur and his knights exploit the women of Camelot for their own ends," writes Stephen Ahern. "This exploitation follows a common trajectory: the knight idealized his female counterpart, and when the woman does not live up to the demands such a role dictates, she is blamed for his failure to succeed in the world."[277]

In the *Idylls*, Arthur is a godlike figure who is presented as an example of perfection. Therefore, those around him can

---

274 Ibid., 53.
275 Ibid., 55.
276 Ibid., 69.
277 Ahern, Stephen, "Listening to Guinevere: Female Agency and the Politics of Chivalry in Tennyson's 'Idylls,'" *Studies in Philology* 101, no. 1 (2004): 90.

only be seen as inferior by comparison. Guinevere, for example, is highly judgmental. She is critical of Arthur for his spotless reputation and his insistence on seeing only the good in others, saying he needs to be brought down to earth in order to love her. She is critical of Lancelot as well and constantly exploits him, "demonstrating the very power the Victorians feared to tempt and control men through their weaknesses,"[278] writes Swanson. Guinevere is a woman of contradictions, whose weakness is her humanity, which pales in comparison to Arthur's supernatural perfection. Walters argues she is fighting two opposing polarities at the same time, so she is bound to lose. "Torn between regal dignity and a passionate nature, Guinevere is a creature of extremes whose tragic flaw is her inability to appreciate the highest of human values, which find their ultimate incarnation in her husband, Arthur."[279]

In Tennyson's fictional world, women were believed to be the forces that made the men in their lives—kings, knights, and nobles—better men. Ahern cites a specific example: "The interior monologue [Arthur] delivers when first captivated by Guinevere's beauty exemplifies the kind of Victorian rhetoric that proffers refuge in woman as the palliative to a life spent tossed about by the storms of fortune."[280] In this monologue, Tennyson has Arthur say:

> What happiness to reign a lonely king,
> Vext—O ye stars that shudder over me,

---

278   Swanson, "Guinevere: Victorian Gender," 10.
279   Walters, "Introduction," xi.
280   Ahern, "Listening to Guinevere," 92.

> O earth that soundest hollow under me,
> Vext with waste dreams? for saving I be joined
> To her that is the fairest under heaven,
> I seem as nothing in the mighty world,
> And cannot will my will, nor work my work
> Wholly, nor make myself in mine own realm
> Victor and lord. But were I joined with her,
> Then might we live together as one life,
> And reigning with one will in everything
> Have power on this dark land to lighten it,
> And power on this dead world to make it live.[281]

In other words, Arthur believes that if he could only marry the fair maiden, he could live up to his full potential, both as a man and as a king, and the world would be better for it. Because, in Tennyson's view, Arthur is godlike in character, it stands to reason he would expect Guinevere to be a goddess. As Arthur's strength, she should embody the Victorian ideals of the blameless, angelic noblewoman by being fertile, pure, supportive, and true. Instead, she is barren, vain, demanding, and jealous. "Codified initially by the medieval courtly love tradition, the myth of romantic love permeated western literature with a conviction that union with the beloved will enable sexual, emotional, and spiritual fulfillment. The ideal of woman as ennobling influence gained especial force in Tennyson's ear, which saw a revival of interest in the culture of chivalry,"[282] explains Ahern.

---

281 Tennyson, Alfred Lord, "Guinevere,", 3-5.
282 Ahern, "Listening to Guinevere," 89-90.

In short, Guinevere is a sinner like all other mere mortals, but she commits the grave sin of betraying the Christ-like figure of Arthur and, therefore, must take upon herself "most of the blame and the pain for her downfall"[283] and that of those around her. Gordon-Wise explains this shift in guilt: "Guinevere becomes responsible for Lancelot's inability to find the Holy Grail and his inability to marry the chaste Elaine; thus she becomes the destroyer not only of Camelot but also of family values and religion."[284] Tennyson implies the queen's sin is the reason for the destruction of the realm. In fact, she admits as much to Lancelot, saying, "Mine is the shame, for I was wife and thou/ unwedded."[285] By making her so clearly fallible in comparison to the spotless Arthur, Tennyson "turns the story from a tragedy to a melodrama, and turns Guinevere from a good and shrewd queen to a pitiful and pitiable woman."[286]

Comer clearly sees Guinevere's blood on Tennyson's pen. "Tennyson had a great love of Arthur and elevated the character to, if not a godlike level, then at least one of an impeccable man and ruler. Consequently, Guinevere is vilified both for not loving the highest of men and for destroying his proverbial city on the hill. It is Tennyson's interpretation of Guinevere that haunts our contemporary culture, but each interpretation brought her one step closer to the character we recognize: an intricate character

---

[283] Ellis, Kimberly, "Lancelot and Guinevere: The Love Affair through the Ages" (Hanover, December 12, 2000).
[284] Gordon-Wise, *The Reclamation of a Queen*, 65.
[285] Tennyson, "Guinevere," lines 118-119.
[286] Comer, "Behold Thy Doom," 65.

condemned by the roles she is forced to enact."[287] Arthur is clearly the hero of *Idylls*, with everyone else playing a secondary role and fulfilling the same basic function: glorifying Arthur. Comer writes, "These supporting characters are pawns, both for Tennyson and Arthur: for Tennyson, they are placed in the same way that mirrors are placed in a room to maximize light and to focus the eye, and for Arthur, they are used to achieve his goals and his dreams. Guinevere, in particular, is used in this way. She is an ancillary figure, berated for her failure to live up to her husband's impossible standards."[288]

Being a trespasser on so grand a scale, the only possible redemption open to Guinevere would come only after she has suffered greatly for her sins and been moved to sincere and deep remorse. So important was this idea to Tennyson that he devotes more space and details to her life as a nun than we've seen thus far, even in the stories written by monks and clerics. Bonner notes that unlike previous authors, Tennyson shows Guinevere getting the reward for her repentance. "[He] awards her with a visible and outward sign of her redemption as she becomes Abbess because of 'her good deeds and pure life,' [an] ending distinctly different from those of the narratives where she is never heard from again after disappearing behind convent walls."[289]

---

287 Ibid., 10-11.
288 Ibid., 52.
289 Bonner, "Guinevere as Heroine," 60.

Guinevere as a Reflection of Victorian Society

There is some debate among critics about whether *Idylls* is meant to be read as "an allegory on the struggle between the soul and the flesh, or whether Tennyson meant it to be a commentary on Victorian society."[290] Comer argues it was Tennyson's obvious need to imbue his Arthuriana with the morals of his time that turned Guinevere into "a tragic character, condemned by the very conventions she is forced to enact."[291] His fictional world was both "medieval and Victorian—taking elements of both but never properly fitting in either."[292]

Elizabeth Brewer puts it more bluntly. "In the *Idylls of the King*, Tennyson humiliated his Guinevere as only a Victorian male writer could." We can almost hear Brewer's sarcasm as she continues, "Of course, he had the good of the nation at heart: as Laureate, he felt it his duty to do what he could to uphold moral standards."[293]

Victorian society in both Britain and America was one of contradictions, especially when it came to sex and morals. On one hand, women were expected to behave like angels, being chaste, silent supporters of their fathers, husbands, and brothers. Yet the nineteenth century is when both nations saw women stand up in the streets for the first time and demand surety in the courts for married women's property, a fair divorce law, reform in women's

---

290   Comer, "Behold Thy Doom," 6.
291   Ibid., 53.
292   Ibid., 74.
293   Brewer, Elizabeth, *T. H. White's The Once and Future King* (Cambridge: D.S. Brewer, 1993), 287.

education, women's suffrage, and a woman's right to work outside the home.[294] On the other hand, it was considered perfectly normal for men—even married ones—to visit prostitutes, while those women were denied even the basic respect of a Christian burial.[295] Adultery was decried from the pulpit and the judges' bench, yet it was the most rampant open secret of Victorian society.

Debra Mancoff argues Guinevere's treatment in *Idylls* is a direct reflection of Victorian society. "The harsh light Tennyson turns on Guinevere illuminates the King, whose fury at betrayal seemed justified in a time when marital stability and service were so central to the social order."[296] Umland takes this idea one step further, noting that although Guinevere has had every privilege and opportunity in life, she "has betrayed both her public duty of assisting Arthur in his creation of a moral atmosphere that would encourage the prorogation of his ideals, and her private vows to the husband who deserves her love and fidelity."[297]

Arthur may have been justified in his actions by the morals of the time, but Guinevere certainly was not. Bonner notes that Guinevere was in many ways the opposite of the ideal Victorian lady. "Guinevere can, on the other hand, be seen as very

---

294 Gordon-Wise, *The Reclamation of a Queen*, 66.
295 Goldsmith, Barbara, *Other Powers: The Age of Suffrage, Spiritualism and the Scandalous Victoria Woodhull* (New York: Alfred A. Knopf, 1998), 153.
296 Mancoff, Debra N., "To Take Excalibur: King Arthur and the Construction of Victorian Manhood," in *King Arthur: A Casebook*, ed. Edward Donald Kennedy (New York: Routledge, 1995), 268.
297 Umland, Rebecca, "The Snake in the Woodpile: Tennyson's Vivien as Victorian Prostitute," in *Culture and the King: the Social Implications of the Arthurian Legend*, eds. James P Carley, Valerie M Lagorio, and Martin B Shichtman (Albany: New York State U of New York P, 1994), 283.

not Victorian because of her adultery, [which was] one of the most unpardonable, but common, sins of the Victorian age."[298] Tennyson condemns Guinevere for her adulterous relationship with Lancelot time and again: "this is all woman's grief,/That she is woman, whose disloyal life/Hath wrought confusion in the Table Round;"[299] "so glad were spirits and men/Before the coming of the sinful Queen."[300] Even Arthur, who claims to love her still, condemns her:

> Well is it that no child is born of thee.
> The children born of thee are sword and fire,
> Red ruin, and the breaking up of laws.[301]

Victorian society had no patience for female adulterers and even the legendary Guinevere could not escape their judgment.[302] Women who dared to express their sexuality were roundly condemned as plagues upon their society. Guinevere should be included in this group, Swanson argues. "The blame is placed on Guinevere for Lancelot's failure to find the Holy Grail, further enforcing that Guinevere has become an infection to her society. Sexually manipulative and the ultimate temptation to lead a man astray, she is equated with harlotry and prostitution, eventually bringing everyone down with her rapidly spreading disease."[303]

---

298 Bonner, "Guinevere as Heroine," 7.
299 Tennyson, Alfred Lord, "Guinevere," lines 214-216.
300 Ibid., lines 265-266.
301 Ibid., lines 557- 560.
302 Ellis, Kimberly, "Lancelot and Guinevere: The Love Affair through the Ages," Hanover College (2000).
303 Swanson, "Guinevere: Victorian Gender," 12.

This is because such actions disrupt the stability of the family and institution of marriage, upon which Victorian society relied to keep their sense of moral balance.[304]

Just as in Tennyson's poetry, to be a woman in the Victorian era was to be subject to contradictions on a daily basis. Women were at once indispensable because they brought forth life, and utterly perplexing in a male-dominated world, especially once they showed a willingness to go against cultural norms and began, for the first time in history, to demand their rights. "The dichotomy of the feminine which we see in the *Idylls*...reflect the patriarchal nature of Victorian society and its concern with the 'woman question,' certainly a key issue in the last half of the nineteenth century,"[305] writes Gordon-Wise.

The woman question was brought about by a flawed model in which women were expected to be submissive models of physical and spiritual purity,[306] argues Bonner. Ahern explains how this idea relates to Tennyson's work: "The *Idylls* candidly depicts the problems that result from subscribing to a model of feminine nature that pervaded Victorian thinking...The problem with such rhetoric becomes evident when abstract qualities are projected onto an actual person,"[307] illustrating the impossibility of the demands this society placed on women. Comer concurs. "The Victorian version of a trophy wife [is] useful only in so far

---

[304] Comer, "Behold Thy Doom," 59.
[305] Gordon-Wise, *The Reclamation of a Queen*, 66.
[306] Bonner, "Guinevere as Heroine," 8.
[307] Ahern, "Listening to Guinevere," 89.

as she can fulfill a prescribed role, that of the 'angel in the house' or the ideal woman."[308]

As in other time periods, those who do not conform are condemned and named as the purveyors of all evil in society, and Ahern reminds the reader that Guinevere must suffer the same fate. "Because [Guinevere] has refused to conform to the submissive wifely role her husband and her society prescribe, she has become not only a threat to social order, but the signifier of all threat to that order. Guinevere's assertion of free will represented by her choice of lover is an example of behavior that shakes the foundations of her patriarchal culture... Because she is 'taken everywhere for pure' such a woman will spread moral contagion to the entire population."[309]

When such rigorous restraints are placed on a society, a kind of morbid fascination develops surrounding what is forbidden. People became fascinated by illicit love[310] and the idea of the fallen woman, especially as embodied by Guinevere. Ahern calls her "the kind of Magdalen figure that fascinated a Victorian reading public eager for tales of sin punished and virtue rewarded."[311]

According to Comer, few of these characters were written by women, and therefore their experiences are of limited value. "The 'fallen' woman in literature has long been a topic

---

308 Comer, "Behold Thy Doom," 60.
309 Ahern, "Listening to Guinevere," 105-106.
310 Comer, "Behold Thy Doom," 51.
311 Ahern, "Listening to Guinevere," 111.

of discussion, curiosity, and analysis. Deborah Ann Logan, in her article on fallen women in Victorian texts, notes that male writers write about fallen women, and not from the perspective of fallen women, the result being that the characters 'remain one-dimensional, talked about but not developed, objectified in euphemistic terms that fail to establish the social contexts leading to fallenness.'"[312]

So after Tennyson had his way, one of the most famous literary queens was reduced to little more than a miserable failing, a secondary citizen who finds redemption only after much pain and suffering. His Guinevere may show more depth than previous incarnations, but overall little good has been done for her character in this retelling. While Tennyson "examines a more complex Guinevere [than the medieval one], we are uncomfortable with her 'groveling' and his Victorian moralizing,"[313] both of which alienate modern readers.

---

[312] Comer, "Behold Thy Doom," 75.
[313] Falsani, Teresa Boyle, "Parke Godwin's Guenevere: An Archetypal Transformation," *Quondam Et Futurus* 3, no. 3 (1993): 55.

CHAPTER TEN

WILLIAM MORRIS, THE DEFENCE OF GUENEVERE

'All I have said is truth, by Christ's dear tears.'
She would not speak another word, but stood
Turn'd sideways; listening, like a man who hears

His brother's trumpet sounding through the wood
Of his foes' lances. She lean'd eagerly,
And gave a slight spring sometimes, as she could

At last hear something really; joyfully
Her cheek grew crimson, as the headlong speed
Of the roan charger drew all men to see,
The knight who came was Launcelot at good need.[314]
— The Defence of Guenevere by William Morris

Defense or Deception?

Published in 1858, William Morris' 295-line poem, *Defence of Guenevere*, is controversial, both in interpretation and what it means for the character of Guinevere. Among non-scholars,

---

314 Morris, William, *The Defence of Guenevere and Other Poems* (New York: Longmans, Green and Co., 1908), 8-10.

it is not well-known and is often overshadowed by the works that came before it (Tennyson) and after it (White). But "The Defence of Guenevere" is important in that it was the first work to give Guinevere a chance to speak for herself; up to that point, her story always had been told from a narrative distance. "Very much differing from the authors who made it their intention to depict the lives of 'kings,' William Morris, in his poem 'The Defence of Guenevere,' directly strives to show Guinevere's side of the Arthurian conflict,"[315] notes Bonner.

The poem finds Guinevere accused of treason, standing before a jury of the knights who used to serve her. It progresses as her trial does, allowing her to tell the reader and the jury at the same time of her actions and motivations. She is strong and unafraid to speak up for herself, "not submissive or shamefaced in her words. She is bold and persuasive, possessing the same powers of manipulation that enabled her to reduce Lancelot to catatonia in the tales of Chrétien."[316]

At first glance, this poem appears to be the work all Guinevere fans have been waiting for, the opportunity for her to redeem herself; however, that is not exactly what transpires. Generations of critics have questioned whether or not Guinevere's testimony can be believed. Bonner lays out the case against her: At first, "her words make her appear almost as pitiful as the begging Guinevere of Tennyson."[317] But "this Guinevere is not disabled

---

315 Bonner, "Guinevere as Heroine," 8.
316 Ibid., 61.
317 Ibid., 62.

by remorse. Further, [her words] could indicate a lack of real remorse on her part. Morris' Guinevere is an actress, playing to the crowd, coaxing and seizing its sympathies."[318] Making several excuses for her actions, Guinevere falls into the trap of "methinks the lady doth protest too much," losing the reader's sympathy. Silver sees this as Guinevere's downfall. "It is Guenevere herself who, in seeking our sympathy, reveals too much about herself for us to believe her innocent; it is her plea of moral confusion, the high point of her argument, that convinces us of her culpability."[319] Silver's analysis continues, noting that what Guinevere says she will say, and what she ends up saying, are often two different things.[320] "She informs us that in internal chaos she has moved beyond the normal riles of human behavior. Even her marriage vow has become 'a little word/Scarce meant, at all' for she has forgotten the significance of her marriage."[321]

Her situation is pitiable, yes. Like so many women throughout history, she is stuck in a loveless, arranged marriage that she had little say in and which she yearns to break free of with Lancelot. But she cannot even look outside of marriage for her happiness because the law, as well as cultural morality, forbids it. Rebecca Umland reminds the reader that here, as in Tennyson, "as presiders over hearth and home, women who violated their duties or disrupted the domestic order by sexual indulgence were

---

[318] Ibid., 63.
[319] Silver, Carole G., "'The Defence of Guenevere': A Further Interpretation," *Studies in English Literature*, 1500-1900, vol. 9, no. 4 (1969): 696.
[320] Ibid., 701.
[321] Ibid.

perceived as the worst possible threat."³²² Morris' Guinevere knows this, yet she is not afraid to bring up her situation in open court, something Laura Struve praises as previously unthinkable. "Guenevere's speech is radical because it places a woman's desires before her husband's and before society's interest in enforcing morality."³²³

Guinevere attempts to defend herself by saying she was just a woman playing the part dictated to her by courtly love and the mandate that a knight must fulfill the requests of a lady, for better or for worse.³²⁴ She is still proud, deceptive, and defiant like in earlier versions of the legend, but she leaves readers with more questions than answers,³²⁵ especially in regard to her sincerity. According to Gossedge, Guinevere's words should be taken with a grain of salt. "Morris makes her speak her own defence but it is no defence at all, just defiance. She denies the charges, says she has made her choice, that she enjoys and invites onlookers to enjoy her own sensual athleticism, and waits for Lancelot's rescue."³²⁶

Lest Guinevere's reputation be left in any doubt, her closing words seal how she is seen. With a frustrated sneer, she cries, "By God, I will not tell you more today,/Judge any way you will—what matters it?"³²⁷ According to Bonner, this "leaves the reader with a picture of the upturned nose and rolling eyes of the Queen. She

---

322 Umland, Rebecca, "The Snake in the Woodpile," 276.
323 Struve, Laura, "The Public Life and Private Desires of Women in William Morris's 'The Defence of Guenevere,'" *Arthuriana*, vol 6.3, (October 3, 1996): 21.
324 Bonner, "Guinevere as Heroine," 64.
325 Ibid., 8-9.
326 Gossedge, "Sixteenth to Nineteenth Centuries," 116.
327 Morris, *The Defence of Guenevere*, lines 277-278.

believes this trial and the concerns of its members to be beneath her...she does not seem concerned about 'setting things right' by reuniting with the King and obtaining forgiveness."[328] Bonner goes on to say, "The final vision of Guinevere portrayed by Morris is of a woman who is evil to the core."[329]

Indeed, this is a queen who is not so much defending herself, but manipulating the jury (and thereby the reader) to believe a version of events that best suits her. Her actions are deliberate, meant to evoke drama. As Silver writes, "The very point of the poem is that Guenevere's defense is not to be fully believed.... In this sense, Morris' title is ironic."[330]

Is the title meant to indicate that the poem is Morris' defense of Guinevere or that it is Guinevere's defense of herself? This is a question many critics ask. The answer may lie somewhere between the two. Some scholars suggest that the ambivalence perceived in Morris' poem was reflected in the thoughts of the author. Beverly Taylor and Elizabeth Brewer note that the poem "allowed Guinevere to tell her own story, in making her own defense...[because] Morris makes use of an Arthurian theme to give expression to (his own) inner conflict."[331] She also cites Florence Boos' assertion that Morris' Guinevere wants "'liberation—from the crippling social and sexual constraints that closed in on Victorian women like a vise' as well as for a 'heroine's

---

328   Bonner, "Guinevere as Heroine," 65.
329   Ibid.
330   Silver, "A Further Interpretation," 702.
331   Cited in Falsani, "Parke Godwin's Guenevere," 55.

right of self-determination.'"[332] Ross agrees, writing that "Morris' portrait of Guinevere is much more sympathetic than Tennyson's, presenting her as a romantic individualist rebelling against society's hypocrisy."[333]

That may be, but he doesn't give his audience any reason to cheer for Guinevere, instead having her fall back on well-established, negative aspects of her character that are by this time becoming clichéd. Morris' Guinevere relies upon manipulation and clever lies in order to get her way, a stereotypical portrayal of the female, but one that Laura Struve argues actually gives her strength. "The Queen does more than merely elude the law; she also announces its potential for manipulation."[334] In this way, she can be seen as a role model for other Victorian women who might wish to follow in Guinevere's footsteps and circumvent the attitudes and conventions that restrained women.

Regardless of whether or not the poem is meant to mirror larger societal issues, Morris does break the mold in the ending he assigns to Guinevere. "Morris concludes his poem in an entirely novel way. Guinevere is not locked away to do repentance for her sins. She does not grovel before her king. Moreover, instead of shunning Lancelot and telling him to leave her to her penance as Malory's Guinevere does, she apparently will welcome him, and, with his help, will escape the condemnation that is planned for

---

332 Falsani, "Parke Godwin's Guenevere," 55-56.
333 Ross, "The Sublime to the Ridiculous," 62.
334 Struve, "The Public Life and Private Desires," 25.

her,"[335] notes Bonner. In this way, the poem is revolutionary. Not since Chrétien have we seen someone willing to let Guinevere and Lancelot have happiness as a result of their affair. Morris's poem is groundbreaking and ahead of its time—a harbinger of the relaxing moral standards to come in the twentieth century.

---

[335] Bonner, "Guinevere as Heroine," 65-66.

CHAPTER ELEVEN

GUINEVERE IN THE EARLY TWENTIETH CENTURY AND T. H. WHITE

Arthuriana for a New Age

After Tennyson and the Victorians reignited the obsession with the Arthurian legend, interest in it only grew. Muriel Whitaker explains why: "The Victorian interest in Arthurian legend persisted into the twentieth century, thanks to lingering Pre-Raphaelitism and an attachment to social and moral values expressed through the image of the medieval knight. Sir Thomas Malory's *Mort D'Arthur* remained the chief source for writers and artists, but the Protestant ethic of Tennyson's *Idylls of the King* also affected their treatments until mid-century."[336]

According to *A Bibliography of Modern Arthuriana (1500-2000)*, 162 Arthurian novels were published between 1884 and 1983 and nearly 40 short stories. If we dig deeper into each decade, the steady growth is even more apparent, especially from 1950 through 2000. From 1900-1950, less than 50 new Arthurian

---

[336] Whitaker, Muriel, "Unifying Makers: Lancelot and Guinevere in Modern Literature and Art," in *Lancelot and Guinevere: A Casebook*, ed. Lori Walters (New York: Routledge, January 4, 2002), 159.

novels were released, but from 1950-1980, that number more than doubled. Ann Howey breaks it down by decade: "Bibliographies record 23 Arthurian novels published from 1950-59; from 1960-1969, there were 33; from 1970-79, there were 71. This adds up to 127 total in 36 years...For the years 1980-89, bibliographies list 120 examples of long prose fiction and a further 39 short stories. From 1990-1996, the number of short stories has already more than doubled (to 83), while the number of novels stands at 97, about 80% of the total previous decade."[337]

The number of Arthurian books by women also increased sharply in the latter half of the twentieth century. Howey gives the details: "Surveying bibliographies, one finds nine in the 1950s, 13 in the 1960s, then 31 and 48 in the 1970s and 1980s respectively. Since 1990, 38 Arthurian novels have been published by women, 79% of the total of the previous decade."[338] Why this trend is important and what cultural factors may have influenced it will be explored later on when the second half of the twentieth century is examined.

Maureen Fries, in 'Trends in the Modern Arthurian Novel' calls the prevalence of Arthurian prose fiction 'the most surprising development in the last hundred years' of the legend's history."[339] To what should we attribute this rise in popularity? There are many possible explanations, including a post-Tolkien fantasy

---

337 Howey, Ann and Stephen R. Reimer, *A Bibliography of Modern Arthuriana 1500-2000* (Cambridge: D.S. Brewer, 2006), 15.
338 Ibid.
339 Ibid., 14.

boom, but one of the strongest is the human desire to use fantasy to escape a negative reality. Between the world wars, the advent of nuclear war, and the sheer number of revolutionary changes that took place in the twentieth century, it stands to reason that people might have been looking to Camelot as a utopia or to King Arthur and Guinevere as heroes who might save them in times of peril. As Raluca Radulescu, professor of medieval literature and English literature at Bangor University, writes in a February 2017 *Newsweek* article, "In this confusing and sometimes frightening world, audiences seek reassurance in the models of the past. They want a standard of moral integrity and visionary leadership that is inspirational and transformational in equal measure. One that they cannot find in the world around them, but will discover in the stories of King Arthur."[340]

The timeless universality of the themes in the Arthurian legend might also account for the continuing attraction. No matter the year, love, loyalty, might versus right, betrayal, and equality are part of our lives. Radulescu explains this concept:

> The Arthurian revival of the late 19th century...helped put [Arthur] back on the international cultural map by removing the historical aura, and emphasizing the values he stood for.... Moral integrity, loyalty to one's friends and kin, abiding by the law and defending the weak, form the cornerstone of how Arthurian fellowship has been

---

340 Raluca Radulescu, "Why the Legend of King Arthur Still Resounds Today," *Newsweek*. February 3, 2017.

defined through the centuries. They offer the reassurance that doing the morally right thing is valuable, even if it may bring about temporary defeat.[341]

Moreover, the appeal of a boy who came from nothing (or so he thought) to become king mirrors the struggle to find and better oneself, always a popular theme, but especially so in the twentieth century. As unions began to protect the interests of workers and the birth of the middle class[342] gave rise to the concept of upward social mobility, more and more people saw Arthur as an example of successful advancement. Mancoff explains: "For the upper middle and upper-class male, hero worship was a potent constructive force; it taught virtue through example. To admire a hero incorporated the desire to strive for heroic belief and action, wedding practical energy to romantic association. The man who could recognize a hero in society could recognize the heroic in himself. And as recognition of the hero is inseparable from identification with the hero, it was central to the construction of contemporary manhood."[343]

---

341 Ibid.
342 Though the middle class had begun to form in the 1800s along with the Industrial Revolution, it wasn't until after The Great Depression and World War II in United States and the fall of the Edwardian country house power system in England after World War I, that our modern definition of "middle class" living began to congeal, helped along in great part by the G.I. Bill in the United States and the rise of a fourth class of professionals in England. See Roth, Mark. "The Historic Roots of the Middle Class." *Pittsburgh Gazette*. November 20, 2011, for more information on this topic in the United States, and Perkin, Harold, *The Rise of Professional Society: England Since 1880* (Routledge, 2016) for information pertaining to England.
343 Mancoff, "To Take Excalibur," 259.

Plus, the twentieth century was a time of great archeological discovery in the realm of Arthurian legend, as the plausibility of a historical Arthur gained steam in academic circles. Archeologists such as Leslie Alcock and Geoffrey Ashe kept discoveries consistently in the news and churned out publications that kept all things Arthurian top of mind for authors and the general public alike.[344]

As the popularity of the Arthurian legend grew, so did interest in Guinevere. "Both in medieval and modern fiction, the figure of Guinevere personifies the feminine ideal, and in so doing indicates our changing attitudes to women and to sexual morality. In the last hundred years in particular, her character has undergone many changes, some of them startling,"[345] writes Brewer. We'll examine many of these changes in great detail in the coming pages, but for now, it will suffice to note that in the first half of the twentieth century, Guinevere was not treated well at all—perhaps even worse than she was by the Victorians. Whitaker bluntly affirms this notion. "Between 1900 and 1940, most authors and editors exculpated Lancelot by diminishing or denigrating the queen."[346]

In the period of the mid-1950s through the mid-1970s, Arthurian legend went through what is known as the "anti-

---

344 Higham, N.J., *King Arthur: Myth-Making and History* (London: Routledge, 2009), 26-27.
345 Brewer, Elizabeth, "The Figure of Guenevere in Modern Drama and Fiction," in *Lancelot and Guinevere: A Casebook*, ed. Lori Walters (New York: Routledge, January 4, 2002), 279.
346 Whitaker, "Unifying Makers," 159.

romantic tradition"[347] of historical fiction, a movement that emphasized darkness and the brutality of reality in the Dark Ages. Three examples of popular Arthurian works from this time are Henry Treece's *The Great Campaigns* (1956) and *The Green Man* (1966), as well as Peter Vansittart's *Lancelot: A Novel* (1978). In these works, Guinevere is a prostitute, who is vain, deceitful, lustful and proud.[348] In creating her thus, the authors debase her about as much as a woman can be and give her a personality that is easy to hate, a tradition carried on by one of Arthuriana's most famous modern authors, T.H. White.

T. H. White—The Once and Future King

> "Guenever...dressed like a gipsy, entertained like a lodging-house keeper, and kept her lover a secret. On top of this, she was a nuisance. She had no sense of style. She was growing old ungracefully, and she cried or made scenes like a fishwife."[349]
> — *The Once and Future King* by T. H. White

Even if people who know next to nothing about the Arthurian legend likely have heard of T. H. White's 1958 book *The Once and Future King*. It is the source of the Broadway musical and the Hollywood movie *Camelot*, as well as the Disney movie *The*

---

347 Thompson, Raymond M., *The Return from Avalon: A Study of the Arthurian Legend in Modern Fiction* (Westport: Greenwood Press, 1985), 41.
348 Ibid., 43.
349 White, T. H., *The Once and Future King* (London: HarperCollins, 1994), 478-479.

Sword in the Stone. It is, in many ways, a retelling of Malory. Guinevere and Lancelot appear in Book Three of the story, "The Ill-Made Knight," which is primarily about Lancelot. Guinevere is also in Book Four, "The Candle in the Wind," but is portrayed at a distance.

The influence of cultural and mindset shifts of the time are reflected in the story. As James Noble points out, writers like T. H. White and his contemporaries like Godfrey Turton often strove "to depict Guenevere with the psychological realism of the modern novel."[350] Brewer credits these novelists with creating a Guinevere who is psychologically complex, albeit neither as physically nor as emotionally appealing as the Guinevere who is to be found in the more recent novels of the 1970s and 1980s.

Ross notes that "White takes a fairly standard Freudian approach toward his characters."[351] When applied to his female characters, the result is brutal. Brewer puts it bluntly: "White, for all the brilliance of his psychological analysis, belittles Guinevere as only a modern realist writer could."[352] While there is no explicit sex between Guinevere and Lancelot in this version, according to Brewer, there is a bit of Freudian influence to the relationship between Guinevere and Arthur—who functioned as a type of father-figure—and Lancelot, who is representative of the son the aging Guinevere couldn't have.[353]

---

[350] Noble, James, "Guinevere, the Superwoman of Contemporary Arthurian Fiction," *Florilegium* vol 23.2 (2006): 197.
[351] Ross, "The Sublime to the Ridiculous," 327.
[352] Brewer, "The Figure of Guenevere," 287.
[353] Brewer, "T. H. White," 84-85.

In addition, the love between Lancelot and Guinevere reflects the psychological realism of the modern era, with Lancelot experiencing internal conflict and Guinevere tormented by jealousy. "Tender scenes between the lovers often end in the disharmony of misunderstanding,"[354] Brewer notes. In keeping with the modern idea of psychoanalysis, White spends most of the story analyzing the motivations behind his main characters and the choices they make, which Brewer sees as part of the reason they can be seen in a negative light. "White, by contrast with Malory, sees the love of Lancelot and Guinevere as unfortunate rather than intrinsically virtuous. His main interest is in trying to understand and to explain the motivation and the relationships of the three participants in the love triangle…nor is there any redemptive power in their love; that is to come only from Arthur's generosity and affection."[355]

White may have broken the physical mold of Guinevere (or Guenever, as he spells it) by giving the traditionally blonde-haired, blue-eyed woman dark hair and making her obsessed with aging, but otherwise, she is still the same weak woman who is dependent on the men in her life.[356] Or, stated more strongly by Bonner, "White portrays her as incapable and idiotic, a clown-like figure at best."[357]

Many critics praise this portrayal as being the first

---

[354] Ibid., 77.
[355] Ibid., 221.
[356] Bonner, "Guinevere as Heroine," 74.
[357] Ibid., 68.

where Guinevere is well-rounded enough to stand on her own as a character, and giving her a strength and intelligence not previously seen, but they still note the lack of internal insight into her character, especially at key moments like the three times she is threatened with death at the stake.[358] One would think that at terrifying times like those, the reader would get a glimpse into Guinevere's thoughts and emotions, but none is given, making her hard to relate to.

As a result, this Guinevere is not a likeable character. She is petty, temperamental, and utterly devoid of sympathy for Lancelot's intense spirituality, and prone to outrageous hissy-fits and exaggerations.[359] In Bonner's analysis, "Unlike the graceful and noble Guineveres of the past, White's Guinevere is without manners. Her temper is not simply volatile as it was in Malory; it is extremely unbecoming. Furthermore, White clearly delineate [sic] Guinevere's role in Arthur's world as a subservient woman."[360] According to Bonner, White transferred all of his mother's worst qualities on to Guinevere, especially her melodrama.[361] White himself describes Guinevere in conflicting terms in his own journal from October 10, 1939:

> What sort of person was Guenever? She must have been a nice person, or Lancelot and Arthur (both nice people) would not have loved her.... And Guenever hardly seems

---

358 Ibid., 9.
359 Brewer, "T.H. White," 79.
360 Bonner, "Guinevere as Heroine," 66.
361 Brewer, "T.H. White," 91.

to have been a favorite of Malory's whatever Tennyson may have thought of her. She was insanely jealous of Lancelot: she drove him mad. She was suspected of being a poisoner: she made no bones about being unfaithful to Arthur; she had an ungovernable temper. She did not mind telling lies. She was hysterical, according to Sir Bors. She was beastly to Elaine. She was intensely selfish....

Guenever had some good characteristics. She chose the best lover she could have done, and she was brave enough to let him be her lover. She always stuck to Arthur, although unfaithful to him, possibly because she really liked him. When finally caught, she faced the music. She had a clear judgment of moral issues, even while defying them, a sort of common sense which finally took her into a convent when she could quite well have stayed with Lancelot now that her husband was dead.

Was this a piece of clear-sightedness or was it cowardice? One way to put it would be to say that she grasped the best of two men so long as she profited by it, but afterwards betrayed them both. When there was no more to be got out of the Arthur-Lancelot situation, she preferred the convent. The other way to put it would be to say that she finally recognized her ill influence and shut herself up.

She was brave, beautiful...she had very little control over her feelings, which were often generous.... It is plain that Guenever was a woman of character. She must have been a passionate lover.[362]

Elsewhere he writes, "She [Guinevere] is an Anna Karenina, but her trouble is that she has no children.... Guenever is one of the realist women in literature: not a Dresden shepherdess or any stereotyped figure, but somebody with a frightful temper, enormous reality, etc. She was beautiful, sanguine, hot-tempered, demanding, impulsive, acquisitive, charming...but...she was not promiscuous. She must have been generous too. It is difficult to write about a real person...."[363]

It is interesting to note that in this quote White blames Guinevere's personality failings on her barrenness. As Whitaker puts it, "He has found a motivation for the queen's jealousy, boredom, and irritability in her childlessness and the menopause."[364] Because, of course, all a woman—even a queen—could ever want is to bear children. And when she can't, she will be miserable because she missed her chance to fulfill her role as a woman. This smacks of the highly misogynistic attitude toward women prevalent in the late 1950s and early 1960s when White was writing. Ross argues that it should, because it was that very societal attitude White was railing against. "The narrator

---

[362] Cited in Brewer, "T.H. White," 87-88.
[363] Cited in Brewer, "T.H. White," 89, 92.
[364] Whitaker, "Unifying Makers," 163.

attributes Guenever's demanding, erratic behavior to...a social code which does not allow a woman to be active, but forces her to stay at home weaving while her lover can wear out his passion on a quest."[365] However, it is hard to believe that White, a self-professed woman-hater, would use his story to speak out against society's repression of women; it is more likely he was espousing the status quo.

It's not just Guinevere that White denigrates. He's not particularly adept at handling female characters, making Elaine, Morgause, and Guinevere "man-eaters."[366] Brewer notes that White never found love himself, had "a mother he detested," and very few female friends, so perhaps he could not positively relate to women.[367] His mother issues were definitely relevant to his portrayal of Guinevere, which some critics, such as Ross, say he "overc[a]me in his loathing for women in order to create."[368] But in-depth analysis seems to show that Guinevere ended up worse off at White's hands than she was in the Middle Ages under the pens of the Cistercian monks, Malory, and the moralizing Victorians. By the time White was done with her, Guinevere was reduced to a histrionic, bitter shrew of a woman who was jealous of anyone younger than her.

White's ham-handed handling of Guinevere was not only a sign of times; it was a warning of things to come. A hint of

---

365 Ross, "The Sublime to the Ridiculous," 328.
366 This is White's own word. See Brewer, "T.H. White," 78, and Ross, "The Sublime to the Ridiculous," 301.
367 Brewer, "T.H. White," 79-80, 85, 88.
368 Ross, "The Sublime to the Ridiculous," 301.

a soon-to-be-recurring theme in Arthurian legend appears in Chapter Nine of "The Ill Made Knight" when White goes to great lengths to try to explain Guinevere's behavior as being in part due to a "made marriage." As Bonner writes, "He indicates that 'the system' was first at fault. Guinevere was a victim of patriarchal society; she was never consulted about her emotions or ideas."[369] A few pages later, Bonner continues, "Underneath all her hot temper and her other trappings, she is a meek and subservient woman who wants only to satisfy and please Arthur and Lancelot."[370] Enter Guinevere, victim of the patriarchy, who will be with us through the early 1980s when the feminists finally pull her out from the shadows to shine light upon her character in its own right.

---

[369] Bonner, "Guinevere as Heroine," 70.
[370] Ibid., 73.

CHAPTER TWELVE

GUINEVERE, VICTIM OF THE PATRIARCHY
(1960'S—EARLY 1980'S)

Beginning in the 1960s, the women of the United States and Britain started to advocate for their rights, to demand equality with their male counterparts in the bedroom and the boardroom. Like all of the cultural shifts before it, this focus on women seeped into the Arthurian legend produced from the 1960s to the 1980s. Bonner shows how this affected the stories of this period: "After the women's movements of the 1960's [sic]...a different species of Arthurian legend was required. Not only are the female characters of the legends more fully, and some say more realistically, developed, but also some of the legends are now written by females."[371]

Female authors and scholars of the period, who for the first time had formalized women's studies programs at colleges and universities to aid them,[372] began to raise questions about

---

371 Bonner, "Guinevere as Heroine," 75.
372 Cornell University held the first women's studies course in America in 1970. It was called "The Evolution of Female Personality." For more information, see Ju, Anne, "Women's Studies at Cornell Evolves over 40-year History to include Sexual Minorities," *Cornell Chronicle*, 2009.

traditional interpretations of gender roles and how they affect women's potential for leadership, both in literature and in the real world. They began to realize that prevailing cultural attitudes toward women in the time periods in which Arthurian legend is set had a direct effect on how Guinevere, Morgan, Elaine, and the other women of Camelot are portrayed. According to Cooley, this affected not only the literary aspects of the stories, but the historical as well. "A secondary factor that plays into women's leadership is the author's interpretation of sub-Roman British society, because a general trend across contemporary Arthurian literature shows that the more heavily the new society of Camelot relies on Roman standards of gender (instead of ancient Celtic ones, whatever they were), the less likely it is that women will be accepted into any leadership roles."[373]

However, even if the novelists set their Camelot in Celtic rather than Roman Britain, that doesn't mean women were treated as equals. Hoberg shows that many of them were still shown as subservient. "Like Tennyson's Guinevere, these contemporary ladies are emphatically subordinate characters, competing unsuccessfully for Arthur's attention—and the reader's—with Merlin or Lancelot, or Arthur's vision of a new world order. Bereft alike of political influence and personal magnitude, each of them is consigned to cloistered seclusion when Arthur casts her off, and narrative oblivion thereafter."[374]

Two very famous female authors of the period wrote

---

373 Cooley, "Re-vision from the Mists," 16.
374 Hoberg, "In Her Own Right," 68.

surprisingly un-feministic portrayals of Guinevere in Arthurian legend: Rosemary Sutcliff and Mary Stewart. "These early women writers still spoke in the voice of male protagonists,"[375] explains Roberta Davidson, implying this might be a reason for their lack of compelling female characters. Creating a strong Guinevere was not the intent of these authors, says Lori Walters. Rather, Guinevere's reputation in these books "began with a desire to find excuses for her faults."[376]

Rosemary Sutcliff's 1963 classic *Sword at Sunset* is groundbreaking in that it delves deep into Guinevere's feelings and motives, especially around her more controversial choices, but it doesn't show her as a strong woman, nor a particularly pleasant one. Hoberg and Gordon-Wise characterize her as a "sullen and neglected chattel bride"[377] who tells her husband she's "more likely to knife him in his sleep" than to become a clingy wife.[378]

Sutcliff's Guinevere (Guenhumara) is a lonely, often isolated woman[379] who has very little chance at happiness, at least within the bounds of her marriage. Hoberg believes this contributes to her eventual infidelity. "Sutcliff develops numerous motives for Guenhumara's adultery, beginning with Arthur's reluctance to marry, his neglect of her emotional needs, and his

---

375 Davidson, Roberta. "When King Arthur Is PG 13." *Arthuriana*, vol. 22, no. 3 (2012), 6.
376 Walters, "Introduction," xlv.
377 Hoberg, Tom, "In Her Own Right: The Guenevere of Parke Godwin," in *Popular Arthurian Traditions*, ed. Sally K. Slocum. (Bowling Green: Bowling Green State U Popular P, 1992), 68.
378 Gordon-Wise, *The Reclamation of a Queen*, 99.
379 Walters, "Introduction," xlv.

absence during the birth and later the death of her child."[380] One has to wonder whether Guinevere's marriage is a reflection of many at the time, which often were equally lonely and often emotionally distant due to societal conceptions of masculinity and traditional gender roles.

Written roughly a decade later, Mary Stewart's Merlin trilogy (1970-1979) was a bit more overt in its feminism, even though Stewart's Guinevere is a "winsome but passive nonentity."[381] Despite Guinevere's bland personality, Howey notes "Stewart's novels tend to awareness of feminist issues through the representation of some of the female characters of the legend."[382]

Stewart plays with the Vulgate Cycle's concept of the two Guineveres, making the women more than cardboard characters, yet not quite fully rounded. Howey explains, "Arthur's first wife, Guenever, has been groomed for her role as Queen by Ygraine herself, and she demonstrates intelligence and political astuteness. Bedwyr describes her as 'delightful. She is full of life…and she is clever…When she dies while miscarrying his child, Arthur grieves…Stewart makes Arthur's second Guinevere share some of her predecessors' positive traits. She is also full of life and spirit; she possesses 'a sort of outgoing gaiety and a way of communicating joy.'"[383] In contrast, the second Guinevere's position forces her "to create a public image to hide harsher realities."[384]

---

[380] Gordon-Wise, *The Reclamation of a Queen*, 98.
[381] Hoberg, "In Her Own Right," 68.
[382] Howey, "Once and Future Women," 30.
[383] Ibid., 44-45.
[384] Ibid., 46.

Those realities are that she is in fact a victim of both her husband and his society. As Walters writes, "Stewart attributes the queen's major flaws of shyness and insecurity to the sense of dependency fostered by the patriarchal society in which she was raised."[385] At one point, Arthur even says, "Why even royal ladies are bought and sold and are bred to lead their lives far from their homes and their people, as the property of men unknown to them,"[386] reflecting a clearly misogynistic and long-held idea that women are owned by their husbands and fathers.

It is interesting that both of these writers approach their Guineveres with clear acknowledgment that they are living in a male-dominated world, yet neither of them seems to feel there is anything they, as the authors, or Guinevere, as a character, can do about it. Neither of them give Guinevere the agency to fight against or change her fate.

That is left to future authors, who will challenge the patriarchal concepts these two pioneers had internalized. Inspired by the feminist movement and determined to reject traditional notions of patriarchy, female authors would soon begin writing what author Sara Cooley calls in her thesis "feminist Arthuriana." She explains, "[it] is distinct from works in both the historical genre of Arthurian literature and the increasingly popular genre of feminist fiction because it usurps a pre-existing literary tradition and reclaims the canon for feminist ends."[387]

---

385 Walters, "Introduction," xlv.
386 Stewart, Mary, *The Merlin Trilogy* (New York: Eos, 2004), 273.
387 Cooley, "Re-vision from the Mists," 6.

They would do this by reinventing Arthurian legend yet again. As Amy Richlin "declares in her essay on feminist interpretations of ancient stories, women 'can appropriate; we can resist. The old stories await our retelling: they haunt our language anyway.'"[388]

But before these authors could allow Guinevere to triumph, there would be one more weak characterization, albeit in a book of strong women.

---

[388] Ibid.

CHAPTER THIRTEEN

MARION ZIMMER BRADLEY
—THE MISTS OF AVALON

> "'If all goes as I plan, you'll wed the High King himself.' Guinevere shrinks away, saying, 'I'd be afraid to be High Queen.'
>
> 'You're afraid of everything, anyway...that's why you need a man to take care of you.... You must trust me to know what's best for you. That's what I am here for, to look after you and make a good marriage with a trusty man for my pretty featherhead.'"[389]
> — *The Mists of Avalon* by Marion Zimmer Bradley

Women in the Fore

Marion Zimmer Bradley was the first author to attempt a major feminist reinvention of Arthurian legend in her groundbreaking 1983 novel, *The Mists of Avalon*. It was different from any work that came before it in its clear intent to tell the stories of the women in King Arthur's court. *The Mists of Avalon* resonates

---

[389] Bradley, Marion Zimmer, *The Mists of Avalon* (New York: Random House Publishing Group, 2001), 256.

because Bradley has reinvented "the underlying mythology of the Arthurian legends,"[390] writes Meredith Ross in her dissertation on the restructuring of Arthurian legend in modern novels. The original *New York Times* review of *The Mists of Avalon* says almost the same thing verbatim, adding, "Nor is it a surprise to find at this time a rewriting of the 'matter of Britain' from the female perspective, as Jean M. Auel's *Children of Earth* series has begun to rewrite prehistory the same way. Looking at the Arthurian legend from the other side, as in one of Morgaine's magic weavings, we see all the interconnecting threads, not merely the artful pattern."[391]

In addition, *The Mists of Avalon* shifts the setting from the Malory-influenced medieval Christian court that so informs earlier iterations of the legend to a semi-historical pagan Britain that is very different from prior cultural-religious contexts, subtly changing the emphasis from the male members of the court to the female. Because of this, Johnson notes the book "immediately shocks the reader of traditional Arthurian legend with a startling change in setting....In Bradley's heretofore pagan England, women were held in the highest esteem and even venerated as the embodiment of the Goddess. This idea complemented the growing neo-paganism that was emerging in the latter twentieth century, as well as the general awareness of female potential and equality."[392]

---

390 Ross, "The Sublime to the Ridiculous," 447.
391 Quilligan, Maureen, "Arthur's Sister's Story," *The New York Times*, January 30, 1983.
392 Johnson, "Guenevere's Conflict," 6.

As with so many other things in Arthurian legend, this is in keeping with the trends of the times. By the early 1980s, Wicca[393] was taking hold among a certain segment of the population as an alternative to the oppression of Christianity, especially among women who sought power and acceptance in religion. One of its myriad traditions, Dianic Wicca, was a goddess-only religion that sought to remove the power of the patriarchy by removing men from its worship and consideration completely. Cooley explains how this religious movement may have influenced Bradley's writing: "The introduction of Goddess-worship, paganism, the 'Old Ways,' or any other female-centric pre-Christian religious practice...is a direct result of the combination of the resurgence of Goddess worship as a feminist spiritual reclamation and Celtic Reconstructionism, which makes it possible to incorporate a 'realistic' portrayal of sub-Roman British religious practice."[394] Ironically, Bradley's novel would go on to inspire several branches of Arthurian, Avalonian, and Celtic Wicca in the decades after the book's publication.[395]

Guinevere: Christian in a Pagan World

During this period, Arthurian legend was slowly moving from the realms of myth and legend into the genre of historical fiction, which provided its own set of problems. Historians and

---

[393] Wicca's founder Gerald Gardner claimed the religion had ancient roots despite the fact that it was established as a neo-pagan religion in the 1960s.
[394] Cooley, "Re-vision from the Mists," 17.
[395] One of which is the Sisterhood of Avalon, founded by Jhenah Telyndru.

archeologists were advancing theories that placed a historical Arthur, if such could ever be proven to exist, in post-Roman Britain, a time period for which little hard evidence is available, even less so about women. It was difficult to write about "pseudo-historical women living in a period from which there is little solid historical evidence about the nature of women's lives," but Cooley notes this provided female writers with a great creative opportunity. "Rather than restricting Arthurian feminist authors to 'historically accurate' portrayals of their female characters, however, the lack of unbiased historical evidence provides these authors the perfect opportunity to re-envision the lives of Guinevere, Morgan, Lynett, and others in ways that were relevant to twentieth century women but remained in a speculative sub-Roman British society."[396]

That is exactly what *The Mists of Avalon* did. "Bradley focalizes her narrative through several women; her writing is one of the most often identified by commentators as feminist,"[397] notes Howey. However, it wasn't the raging feminist manifesto a reader might expect, at least not where the character of Guinevere is concerned. Bonner pointedly calls out the misleading nature of the promotional copy of the novel: "The cover of [Bradley's] paperback novel reads, 'The magical saga of the women behind King Arthur's throne.' One might thus expect Bradley's novel to introduce a very different Guinevere... However, Bradley's

---

396 Ibid., 7-8.
397 Howey, "Once and Future Women," 30.

Guinevere is the antithesis of the liberated woman."[398] Serving as an example of what powerful men make women into, this Guinevere is shy, always panicking and fearful. She is wracked by guilt, consistently feeling that she is never good enough. This docile, weak personality was likely influenced by her upbringing in a thoroughly Christian convent education, where she learned little but the womanly skills of cooking, herbs, and healing, and most of all, a fear of God. In case Guinevere's tepid personality doesn't shine through strongly enough, Bradley gave her the twin afflictions of myopia and agoraphobia, branding her "narrow-sighted and by extension, narrow-minded."[399]

This Guinevere has no desire to rule, nor has she any self-esteem. She seeks only to please the men in her life, even going so far as to speak in a soft voice because a loud one offends her father.[400] Her father clearly has no expectations for or confidence in her, calling her "my pretty little featherhead."[401] Any thoughts of moving against the patriarchal society in which she lives are stifled by fear of her father,[402] which Johnson sees as consistent with Guinevere's larger purpose in the book: "Lee Ann Tobin suggests that Guinevere's primary role in *The Mists of Avalon* 'is to show how women lost their power in Western civilization. In Guinevere, Bradley describes a woman whose upbringing has been traditional in that she is trained to be submissive by

---

398 Bonner, "Guinevere as Heroine," 75-76.
399 Cited in Bonner, "Guinevere as Heroine," 10.
400 Gordon-Wise, *The Reclamation of a Queen*, 143.
401 Bradley, "The Mists of Avalon," 256.
402 Ibid.,144.

her family and her Christian church.' Accordingly, Guinevere is meek and acknowledges her father's decision as if he were, in fact, speaking the words of God."[403] A timid girl, a shrewish wife and lover, a religious fanatic, and a queen who has no interest in ruling, Gwenhwyfar is, for all intents and purposes, "the villain of Bradley's novel and a character with whom few readers find it easy to empathize."[404]

Like so many medieval women before her, Guinevere's main duty is to provide an heir. In keeping with Arthurian tradition, she has trouble in this area. Howey explains: "Gwenhwyfar is desperate to have a son. She wishes to bear Arthur's heir in order to give herself more power, knowing that Arthur has promised to do anything for her, should she bear him a son. This is ironic since he offered her joint rule of the kingdom when they were first wed and she refused"[405] out of fear.

It is Arthur who suggests she might wish to sleep with someone close to him in order to have a child, resulting in the ground-breaking threesome the book is remembered for. However, as Johnson notes, the scene is not there for shock value; it helps drive the growth of Guinevere's character. "Arthur's proposal sends Guinevere into a moral quandary. The same religion that says she should obey her husband also says the act he wants her to commit is a sin, and she wonders: 'How could she, a

---

403 Johnson, "Guenevere's Conflict," 22.
404 Noble, James, "Guinevere, the Superwoman,", 199.
405 Howey, "Once and Future Women," 96.

woman, make that decision?'"[406] Though we know she eventually takes her husband's advice, it is not out of obedience to him, as we would expect. Rather, Guinevere chooses to ask Morgaine for a charm "so that she had no choice but to love Lancelot, then she would be freed of that fearful choice."[407] Just as she is scared of everything, she fears taking responsibility for her actions. Johnson points out that despite her fear, Guinevere's decision ends up being freeing for her. "Guinevere decides that since neither God nor her husband rescued her from the devastating experience with Melegrant, she will not feel guilty being with the man who does save her." She willingly has sex with Lancelot, choosing never to hide her love for him ever again.[408]

This is one of the few controversial acts of Guinevere's life. For the most part, and even in this case, she goes along with what the men in her life, most notably Arthur, wish for her. According to Bonner, "Guinevere is merely part of Arthur's domestic backdrop; he exists and acts in the world without her say or even her knowledge."[409] Though the scandalous ménage à trois may seem a subversive act on her part, Guinevere is really just once again obeying her husband by living out his idea.

Guinevere only twice attempts to act independently, and both end in tragedy. Her choice to return to Caerleon during the Saxon invasion eventually results in her miscarriage and her

---

406 Johnson, "Guenevere's Conflict," 31.
407 Bradley, "The Mists of Avalon," 336.
408 Johnson, "Guenevere's Conflict," 36.
409 Bonner, "Guinevere as Heroine," 82.

attempt to negotiate with Malegrant on her own ends in him raping her. Johnson sees a definite correlation between Guinevere's choices and the repercussions she suffers. "Guinevere is literally beaten and defiled for daring to step out of the submissive mold demanded by her church. The Queen realizes after the rape that her religion, with its abhorrence of women, has so poorly equipped her to deal with life without the benefit of man that she is incapable of making decisions based on sound judgment. This episode becomes a defining moment for Guinevere as she contemplates what she feels is an injustice forced on her by virtue of her gender, her God and her marriage."[410]

In the end, it is Guinevere's stubborn clinging to her Christian upbringing that causes her undoing. According to Johnson, "Throughout the novel, Guinevere struggles to do what is right as determined by her upbringing and church, all while inwardly resenting her loss of self."[411] While some critics praise her iron will in this regard as well as her success in converting Arthur to Christianity,[412] Gordon-Wise sees it as questionable at best. "In this revisionist treatment, it is not her love for Lancelot that causes the downfall of Camelot; instead it is her powerful will which has embraced patriarchal Christianity."[413] She convinces Arthur to turn his back on Avalon and give up the rites of the Goddess. Later she reveals Arthur's illegitimate son and forces

---

410 Johnson, "Guenevere's Conflict," 27.
411 Ibid., 23.
412 Noble, James, "Guinevere, the Superwoman," 202.
413 Gordon-Wise, *The Reclamation of a Queen*, 147.

Arthur to confess to a priest who gives him a public penance.[414]

Even when Bradley takes the unusual step of giving Guinevere the chance to run away with Lancelot, Guinevere ultimately succumbs to the martyrdom expected by her patriarchal Christian culture. She experiences happiness at her possible freedom with Lancelot for less than a page before changing her mind and deciding to sacrifice herself for the good of Arthur and Lancelot. Instead of being pushed off the page by her author, as earlier Guinevere's were, Bonner points out that she "willingly ushers herself out of the story. She does not attempt to seize her own desires; instead she steps aside to create peace in the world of men."[415] By not fleeing with Lancelot, Guinevere chooses to live out her days in a nunnery, even though the idea terrifies her, becoming a willing sacrifice for the good of Arthur and others.

Feminist or Feminot?

Why is there such a weak Guinevere in an otherwise feministic book? It seems to be a function of Guinevere's being Morgan/Morgaine's antithesis. Howey argues that "Bradley's portrayal of the unfairness of Gwenhwyfar's position is compromised…by the implicit comparison between Morgaine and Gwenhwyfar."[416] Whether Ms. Bradley wrote her that way consciously or not is impossible to say, but Guinevere clearly is everything Morgaine

---

414 Ibid., 146.
415 Bonner, "Guinevere as Heroine," 83.
416 Howey, "Once and Future Women," 62.

is not. She is weak whereas Morgaine is strong; agoraphobic whereas Morgaine takes on the world; simpering whereas Morgaine is bold; not to mention Christian and dutiful whereas Morgaine wields the powers of Avalon and answers to no one. Gordon-Wise writes that Bradley "offers her female readers two alternatives—be independent of men, as Morgaine is, or be ruled by them, as Guinevere is."[417]

To the reader, this contrast can feel as though Bradley thought she had to make the two women diametrical opposites in order to get her point across that Morgan has been wronged through the centuries and to give her the redemption she deserves. Gordon-Wise has another theory: that Bradley is making a statement on the relationship between gender and power in history. "By contrasting the figure of Gwynwyfar to that of Morgaine, Bradley has created a powerful foil who makes telling comment on the patriarchal versus the matriarchal vision of life…In this way, Gwynwyfar carries a significance never even hinted at in earlier Arthurian material."[418] Whereas Morgaine is the feminist ideal, this Guinevere brings to light the type of women all females would be if no one had rebelled against the long-held belief that men were superior; while she may not be the modern woman's role model, Bradley's Guinevere is a warning, the image that causes the female reader to whisper, "there but by the grace of God go I."

---

417 Bonner, "Guinevere as Heroine," 76.
418 Gordon-Wise, *The Reclamation of a Queen*, 142, 144.

CHAPTER FOURTEEN

PARKE GODWIN AND GILLIAN BRADSHAW

"I've learned and unlearned all my life; it's helped me to survive. There are no constants, nothing is immutable, only random circumstance from which our experience builds a coherent arc of life. And for that arc you have only to be truly done with one thing before moving to another. There's an art in letting go."[419]

— *Beloved Exile* by Parke Godwin

A New Type of Guinevere

Around the same time that *The Mists of Avalon* was published, two other authors were tackling the subject of Guinevere in very different ways. They gave readers a fresh perspective by having something positive to say about Guinevere. First came Parke Godwin's early 1980s novels *Firelord* (1980) and *Beloved Exile* (1984), in which Guinevere is shown for the first time as Arthur's equal. She is a woman with agency, intelligence, and a willingness to act according to her own whims. It is likely not coincidental

---

419 Godwin, Park, *Beloved Exile* (Avon Books, Reprint edition: 1994), 72.

that this is the same time period when women were beginning to enter the workforce en masse and take responsibility for their place in business and society as well as in the home.

Godwin's *Firelord* is mostly about Arthur and Morgan, who is a Pict, but Guinevere is there, representing and mirroring in many ways Arthur's ambition to fulfill his destiny to become Emperor of Britain. The young, unmarried Guinevere is intelligent. She has suitors, but she rejects those who want her only as a brood mare, keeping an interested eye on Arthur, both as a man and potential future king. When it appears that he will become Ambrosius' successor, Guinevere defies her father and sides with Arthur. When wed, they are equals as they attempt to piece together a united kingdom.[420] This is a Guinevere quite different from those who have come before, a woman who is Arthur's equal in education, experience, and will. As Howey writes, "This Guinevere does not exist to inspire knightly deeds, for she can fight for herself. Nor does she fit the stereotype of woman as ruled by emotion; she believes she must 'think first, act, and then feel.'"[421]

However, Guinevere shares one damning trait with her previous literary incarnations: her hatred of Arthur's former lover, Morgan (or Morgana, as she is called in this story) both for coming before her in Arthur's affections and in her ability to bear a child to Arthur, which Guinevere cannot do. "As Arthur's queen and wife, she has no intention of sharing him with even

---

420 Hoberg,, "In Her Own Right," 69.
421 Howey, "Once and Future Women," 123.

the memory of a former beloved,"⁴²² notes Howey. So she takes what appears to the reader as a drastic step but is in fact in keeping with the war-like nature of her time: Guinevere arranges for the deaths of Morgana and her people, the Pryden, leaving only Mordred and Arthur alive. She does not deny her role in the crime, but justifies it as protection against a horde of Pryden that would invade Camelot, in a defense Hoberg characterizes "as remarkable as [the one] Morris' Guinevere makes to the charges of adultery."[423] Understandably upset, Arthur exiles Guinevere for Morgana's death. But instead of fleeing, she raises an army against Arthur, threatening war until he reinstates her in her proper place as queen.

In giving Guinevere strength and determination, "Parke Godwin has fashioned a Guenevere of equal status and strength with Arthur, who was his friend and his lover, and if necessary, his adversary, a fit consort for this greatest of legend's kings.... [She] stands equal with Arthur during his life and, after he dies, perseveres in her own right and shapes her own arduous but ultimately triumphant future," [424] writes Hoberg.

Firelord's sequel, *Beloved Exile*, tells of Guinevere's life after the death of Arthur. The story begins with her hearing the news of Arthur's passing. There is no last great battle; it is clear Morgana and Mordred are responsible for Arthur's death.[425] Arthur names Guinevere his successor. She must then fight Constantine, who

---

422 Ibid.
423 Hoberg, "In Her Own Right," 70.
424 Ibid., 68.
425 Gordon-Wise, *The Reclamation of a Queen*, 120.

also seeks the throne. On her way to deal with Constantine, she is kidnapped and enslaved by the Saxons, eventually falling in love with her owner and being freed after many years of captivity. In the end, Guinevere reaches a compromise with those who wish to have power in Britain. She goes into exile in Constantinople as advisor to the Emperor Justinian, ending her life as powerful as she was in her youth.

Beloved Exile was the first story to explore a non-cloistered life for Guinevere after Arthur's death. Gordon-Wise notes, "In middle age, when the traditional Guinevere retires to a convent, this Guinevere struggles to survive and to regain her freedom."[426] While many critics, have noted that Saxon captivity seems an odd fate for Guinevere, Falsani argues that the slavery was necessary in order for Godwin's overly-proud Guinevere to learn compassion; it brought about her personal and political self-awakening.[427] "Guinevere's adventures, her trials, awaken in her the ability to empathize with her subjects, to understand and identify with their needs and to desire to help them."[428] In this way, one could read the story as an attempt to correct the personality defects written into Guinevere's character by previous authors.

Interestingly, Guinevere's Saxon captors, who do not know her true identity, speak of the queen Guinevere as "most notorious with these family-minded folk as a depraved wanton with an insatiable sexual appetite, whose reputed exploits were

---

426 Ibid., 122.
427 Falsani, "Parke Godwin's Guenevere," 59.
428 Ibid., 62.

the subject of much interest—and the object of much awe—as the martial achievements of her consort."[429] One cannot help but wonder whether this is a wink and a nod to the character's traditional reputation throughout the rest of Arthurian legend.

To completely change his Guinevere, Godwin did away with what he called in 1989 "'the 'medieval cliché' of her retreat to a nunnery after Arthur's death. Such a 'totally devout and submissive Christian ending' he notes in a letter to [Teresa Boyle Falsani] would 'make [Guinevere] something utterly insupportable in context of the legend,' for he contends that she was 'rendered astride both pagan and Christian traditions."[430] Falsani goes on to write, "Parke Godwin's revisionist characterization of Guinevere…is remarkable because it makes of Guinevere a female archetype capable of heroic independence, dignity and strength,"[431] completely at odds with the meek, jealous, temperamental woman of previous legend. This is a Guinevere for the modern age, one who will rule alongside her husband and claim her worth in her own right rather than allowing others to define it for her. She is a fitting symbol of the time when women were beginning to come into their own as people, both in the workplace and in the home, demanding an end to the sexual harassment that plagued them for so long and speaking up for equal rights. As Gordon-Wise notes, "In the final analysis, our discussion of the revisionist view of Arthur's queen in modern

---

429   Hoberg, "In Her Own Right," 74.
430   Falsani, "Parke Godwin's Guenevere," 56.
431   Ibid., 63.

fantasy indicates the transformational potential of the Arthurian mythos as it continues to reflect changing societal values."[432]

Gillian Bradshaw

> "I am old now. If I see my reflection, in water or a cup of wine—there are no mirrors in the convent, I can scarcely believe that I am the same Gwynhwyfar whom Arthur and Bedwyr loved. The face I see is an old woman's, lined with use. Much use: many tears, hour upon hour of a grief which can never be eradicated, never be forgotten. Lined with laughter, too."[433]
> — *In Winter's Shadow* by Gillian Bradshaw

Gillian Bradshaw's Arthurian trilogy (1980-1982) makes Guinevere a central character in the final book, *In Winter's Shadow*. "Narrated in the first person by Gwynwyfar (Guinevere), this novel is one the first of the Arthurian worlds to give the queen a central and active role in the events of Arthur's kingdom,"[434] Gordon-Wise points out. This highly involved queen has her own agency and her own agenda, which she is not afraid to promote. Gordon-Wise highlights Guinevere's role in reversing the male-dominated focus of past authors: "No longer on the pedestal of courtly love or veiled by the misogyny of the medieval church,

---

432   Gordon-Wise, *The Reclamation of a Queen*, 139.
433   Bradshaw, Gillian, *In Winter's Shadow*, 1981 (Naperville: Sourcebooks Landmark, 1981, 2011), 405.
434   Gordon-Wise, *The Reclamation of a Queen*, 133.

Bradshaw's Guinevere serves as a vehicle to dispel masculine myths of honor and valor."[435]

According to Gordon-Wise, she is a strong woman in her own right, with none of the "vanity, jealousy or weakness of medieval tales; instead she is educated and realistic in her emotions, be they sexual or maternal."[436] This freedom may well come from the fact that she has no men attempting to control her; her father dies early on and his successor, her cousin, attempts to punish her by levying excessive demands for land, which cut her off from the tribe.[437] Gordon-Wise notes that by having Guinevere suffer losses and face conflict in her back story, "Bradshaw creates a character who is an emotional, private person, and who accepts the responsibilities and obligations of her political role as well."[438] This is especially clear toward the end of the book when Guinevere accepts that becoming a nun is the only path open to her. When Taliesin suggests she might marry Lord Sandde and become Empress, a mature, clear-headed, realistic Guinevere replies, "I would not last a year. We do not have the warband to enforce such a rule, and the kings of Britain would not permit the unfaithful wife of a usurper to claim the purple...I will go north and join a convent."[439]

Gordon-Wise argues that Guinevere is the true leader and hero of the novel because she serves as Arthur's seneschal

---

435   Ibid., 150.
436   Ibid., 134.
437   Ibid., 136.
438   Howey, "Once and Future Women," 79.
439   Bradshaw, *In Winter's Shadow*, 403.

and steward.[440] She fulfils the typical female role of managing Arthur's fortress, but she is also involved in all aspects of his campaign.[441] She works hard, pulling her own weight to keep the country together.[442] Brewer notes that in addition to ruling in partnership with Arthur, Guinevere navigates policy to outwit Mordred, tends the sick, and fundraises for Arthur's campaigns.[443] In so many ways, Arthur would not be who he is without her by his side. Howey explains: "By often extolling Gwynhwyfar's abilities and responsibilities, Bradshaw emphasizes throughout the series the ways in which the Queen is important to Arthur's dream; Gwynhwyfar is not just a figure-head, but gives Arthur practical assistance in running the kingdom."[444] Gone is the fading wallflower or damsel in distress of previous legend. As Gordon-Wise points out, "This Gwynwyfar may occasionally be aided, but she is never just rescued."[445]

The old aphorism "all work and no play makes Jack a dull boy" can be applied to Guinevere's affair, which in this book is with Bedwyr, not Lancelot. By the time she takes Bedwyr as a lover, Guinevere needs some time away from Arthur and all the responsibilities that come with being his queen; she needs to remember who she is again outside of her throne, as a woman in her own right. Howey notes, "The affair with Bedwyr is

---

440 Gordon-Wise, *The Reclamation of a Queen*, 134-135.
441 Howey, "Once and Future Women," 54-55.
442 Knight, Stephen, "Queen Guinevere," *The Politics of Myth* (Strawberry Hills, NSW: ReadHowYouWant, 2015), 82.
443 Brewer, "The Figure of Guenevere," 286-287.
444 Howey, "Once and Future Women," 55.
445 Gordon-Wise, *The Reclamation of a Queen*, 137.

Gwynhwyfar's one instance of selfishness.... Bedwyr allows her to be a person instead of a role, woman instead of empress.... Her love for Arthur does not diminish: she insists that she "loved [Arthur] even when [she] was unfaithful."[446]

Despite this, Bradshaw refuses to lay the guilt for the downfall of Camelot at Guinevere's feet, perhaps reflecting the growing tolerance for infidelity, especially on the part of women, in society in the early 1980s. "Gwynhwyfar articulates the traditional verdict of her actions: her adultery destroys the kingdom. Yet the events of Bradshaw's novel and the opinions of its other characters contradict that verdict,"[447] argues Howey. For example, even King Arthur forgives Guinevere her sin. He "even blames himself for not realizing that Gwynhwyfar, like a strong warrior 'need[s] rest sometimes,'" Howey explains. "His understanding and acceptance of her actions reinforces our empathy for the queen while his comparison of her to a warrior prevents any suggestion of the 'weak woman' stereotype. Others of Arthur's supporters also forgive her because they admire her courage for returning to take Arthur's side in the standoff with Mascen."[448]

One of the most unique choices Bradshaw makes with her Guinevere is to give her a new reason for becoming a nun, and imbuing that role with power. After Arthur's death, Guinevere's options are not many: live as a doomed Empress or join the convent. She realizes that the end has come for Camelot, saying,

---
446 Howey, "Once and Future Women," 78.
447 Ibid, 79.
448 Ibid.

"there is nothing left of the empire, and nothing remaining from which we could build again, and nothing to show for our lives' effort but guilt, shame and a few lying songs."[449]

In her wisdom, Guinevere sees a better end in trading her title for religious life where the skills of her old life are still very applicable. Over time, Guinevere becomes an abbess and is responsible for nearly 100 people. Her duties include overseeing the varied activities that keep a busy convent running: "The local people come to me with their problems, the sisters copy books and look after orphaned children."[450] Here we see a glimmer of the power of the medieval women who used this life choice to its best advantage, taking what it offered and transforming their convents into small religious kingdoms that they governed just like the queens of the secular world.

The maturity and wisdom this Guinevere has gained throughout the course of the book also enable her to see that in order for progress to continue, sometimes one has to look beyond what is expected and trust those willing to help, even if they are former enemies whose way of life is very different. Toward the end of the book she says, "I had begun to fear that the ability to read would die out and the world would truly be confined to the present. But this Irish abbot is wild about books.... [The future is in the hands of] a handful of monks on a little island called Iona.... They are not Roman, have no understanding of what Rome was and meant. Yet they are as set to change the world

---

449 Bradshaw, *In Winter's Shadow*, 401.
450 Bradshaw, *In Winter's Shadow*, 406.

as I was when I rode south to Camlann many years ago."[451] By her willingness to set aside her own pride and allow the monks to continue what she and Arthur started, Bradshaw's Guinevere shows more depth and reason than her previous counterparts.

Godwin and Bradshaw gifted the Arthurian-loving world with something it sorely needed—a Guinevere who lives up to, if not surpasses, the until-now dormant potential in her character. In turn, this uplifting of Camelot's queen brought hope to a generation of female readers who were coming of age reading about her alongside the flowering of second-wave feminism. In writing about these admirable portrayals, Gordon-Wise expresses her wish that "perhaps through her revision in modern fantasy novels, Guinevere may now help to shape a more positive image of the feminine."[452] If the next several Guineveres created by feminist authors as the 1980s progress are any indication, that is exactly what took place.

---

451 Bradshaw, *In Winter's Shadow*, 409.
452 Gordon-Wise, *The Reclamation of a Queen*, 6.

CHAPTER FIFTEEN

SHARAN NEWMAN

Guinevere as Superwoman

By the time second-wave feminism was making its way into the workplace in the mid-1980s, Guinevere had evolved into a character with greater depth and agency than ever before. As Walters writes, "Since the new focus on Guinevere's feelings corresponded to the development of the feminist movement, it ultimately led to her treatment as a being with desires and ambitions different from those dictated by a patriarchal society."[453] In many ways, she became an example of all the feminist movement hoped to achieve, just like she had been a symbol of proper female behavior in (more submissive) years past. Howey points to the opportunity this created: "Guinevere…provides contemporary writers with a female character whose importance to the legend's events is established, yet she can be used to elaborate her own story or psychological motivation in new ways, or she can supply a new perspective on the traditional events or characters of the legend."[454]

---

453 Walters, "Introduction," lvx.
454 Howey, "Once and Future Women," 28.

Just like the women for whom she was now being written, Guinevere was an "I-can-do-it-all" type woman. Feminism changed work for women irrevocably. It gave women economic clout for the first time and at least the possibility of equaling their husbands. They demanded equal treatment with men in the workplace as well as at home, and no longer stood for the sexual harassment that used to be considered par for the course for the rare working woman.[455] Consequently, Arthurian authors gave Guinevere a greater say in the rule of Camelot and dared to change the sexist traditional portrayals of her. "Written during an era when women were experiencing sexual freedom and demanding equal rights within the workplace, the authors empower female characters, who prevail in spite of masculine ministrations to keep them in check and provide readers with a readily identifiable conflict,"[456] notes Johnson.

During this time, Guinevere comes into her own, a being with her own identity, thoughts, and desires. Bonner summarizes how this happened: "Some female authors have attempted to 'free' Guinevere from the strictures of patriarchal society: they have tried to portray her as more than just a tool to man's action, as more than an ornament of the King, as more than a submissive and pleasing lover. They have given Guinevere more actual action and autonomy than she is given by authors of previous years."[457]

In keeping with this trend, suddenly the previously barren

---

455 Cooley, "Re-vision from the Mists," 35.
456 Johnson, "Guenevere's Conflict," 69.
457 Bonner, "Guinevere as Heroine," 75.

queen began having children and ruled beside her husband. Brewer notes this is unusual in the Arthurian tradition. "In the nineteen-eighties, Queen Guenevere seems to have become a superwoman, a successful executive and administrator whose role is not merely to attend state functions as a graceful consort, but to rule... The Arthurian superwoman must also have experienced pregnancy and childbirth."[458]

One interesting theory on Guinevere's sudden fertility after hundreds of years of barrenness – put forth by Gordon-Wise – is directly tied to the culture of the time: "The treatment of this problem [Guinevere's barrenness] in these current Arthurian fantasies suggests an ongoing debate, perhaps centered on the issue of career versus children, within the feminist community."[459] According to this theory, Guinevere's fecundity serves a larger purpose. Her previous inability to have children is seen as a symbol of the stifling nature of patriarchal control where women could not live up to their full potential, whereas her newfound ability to bear babes is tied to the fruitfulness of the feminist movement. If she can at least be pregnant, she is seen as taking on the responsibility of the modern woman by "having it all"—a successful queenship in which she actively participates (a.k.a. a job outside the home), children, a thriving marriage (with Arthur), and a satisfying sex life (presumably with Lancelot, if not with Arthur).

But yet, this fully-formed life may not be quite the liberation

---

458 Brewer, "The Figure of Guenevere," 286-287.
459 Gordon-Wise, *The Reclamation of a Queen*, 152.

it is cracked up to be. "Increased attention to the Arthurian ladies, has not, for the most part, liberated fictional women from traditional feminine roles," Lacy argues.[460] Cooley agrees, adding, "[T]he duties of Arthurian women [still] fall under traditional feminine gender roles, such as home-keeping and child-bearing and -rearing: the only differences between noble and peasant women are the management aspects of running a household and the understanding that their marriage will be based on the political advantage of men before all else."[461]

In some ways, this is an obvious and unnecessary argument to make, primarily because most Arthurian fiction is set in the past, when women were expected to perform these duties. It would be very odd for a reader to encounter a semi-medieval or quasi-Celtic Lancelot saying he will clean up the dishes after a feast so Guinevere can go and rest, or Arthur demanding equal parenting time with Mordred from Morgan. Second, the argument rings false because—transgender literature aside—Guinevere will always be female. While in the 1980s and beyond, men began doing more of the household chores and child-rearing,[462] women

---

460   Lacy, *The New Arthurian Encyclopedia: New Edition*, 526.
461   Cooley, "Re-vision from the Mists," 36.
462   The 2015 American Time use survey commissioned by the U.S. Bureau of Labor Statistics shows that even in 2015, thirty-five years after the period we are discussing, women spent on average one hour more a day performing household activities than men. When that was broken down into specific activities, "women spent more than twice as much time preparing food and drink and doing interior cleaning, and over three times as much time doing laundry as did men." See "American Time Use Survey," Bureau of Labor Statistics, United States Department of Labor. December 20, 2016. Accessed August 15, 2017. https://www.bls.gov/tus/charts/household.htm. https://www.bls.gov/tus/charts/household.htm.

will always be the child-bearers. Even in situations of single-parent homes where the father raises the children, there are some things only a mother can give or teach. That part of the female experience will never go away unless human beings evolve to where men can have babies.

However, looked at from another angle, it is a perfectly valid argument because by the 1980s, in addition to the traditional duties of homemaking and motherhood, women had careers that demanded a disproportionate share of their time. Why shouldn't Guinevere experience the same tug-of-war on her time? Hence, we see writers like Bradshaw, Woolley, and Miles placing additional emphasis on the administrative nature of Guinevere's role as queen.

During the 1980s, Guinevere is finally given a fully-fleshed backstory, making her for the first time a truly three-dimensional character. As Barbara and Allan Lupack note, "A spate of recent novels by women have retold the story of Camelot from the queen's perspective…offer[ing] Guinevere's own views on her youth, her difficulties adjusting to the sweeping and radical social changes inherent in Arthur's reign, and her attempts to maintain her own independence, particularly in the face of patriarchal attitudes toward women."[463] This is a woman who doesn't simply magically show up on the scene when she's needed by a man—be he Arthur or Lancelot—but a real person who was shaped by her past, with dreams and ambitions of her own. Cooley writes of the

---

463   Lupack and Lupack. "The Forgotten Tradition," in *Arthurian Literature by Women: An Anthology*. New York: (New York: Routledge, 2013), 24.

Guinevere created by Sharan Newman, Marion Zimmer Bradley, and Persia Woolley: "Guinevere, High Queen of Camelot, is written with more variety than any other female character across feminist Arthuriana. Working within a literary tradition of a beautiful, educated Guinevere whose skills as a queen are of little importance when compared with her betrayal with Lancelot and her part in the fall of Camelot, these authors all reinterpret her character differently."[464] It is definite sign of growth for the character, giving her increased depth and realism, and also a subtle recognition that women are individuals who need not be tethered to their male relatives in order to have identity or purpose.

Sharan Newman

> "*Guinevere was not overly concerned, for in her whole life she had never had a difficulty that someone hasn't quickly helped her out of...someone would soon come to find her.*"[465]
> — *Guinevere* by Sharan Newman

One of the first authors to explore Guinevere's early life was Sharan Newman. Her 1981-1985 Guinevere trilogy is still one of the best-known, most studied, works of Guinevereian fiction, even more than thirty years after the final book was published. She was the first to explore Guinevere's youth, but also to give her

---

464   Cooley, "Re-vision from the Mists," 20.
465   Newman, Sharan, *Guinevere*, 1981 (New York: Tor, 1981, 1996), 10.

a clear character arc that spanned the entire trilogy and helped the reader grow attached to her even as she matured. Bonner summarizes her character arc:

> In the first novel of the trilogy, *Guinevere*, Newman follows Guinevere's life from her childhood to her marriage with Arthur....Newman continues Guinevere's development in *The Chessboard Queen* (1983), presenting Guinevere as a much more capable and active figure than she was in Malory and other writers...without portraying the queen as a shrew with no life of her own. Finally, Newman extends the narrative much further than most authors in the final novel *Guinevere Evermore* (1985). In the final book of the trilogy, Guinevere comes to terms with her own desires and needs and even leads her life without Arthur and Camelot.[466]

When we meet Guinevere, she is living a very sheltered life, and because of this she is rather self-centered and over-protected, even "emotionally stunted" as Harold J. Herman calls her.[467] She is being raised to be a typical nobly-born/aristocratic girl, with her education centered on domestic training, which she escapes as often as possible to be outside, where she is far more comfortable. The world Guinevere is raised in seems to be a fantasy in itself since it is highly-Romanized even though the rest

---

466 Bonner, "Guinevere as Heroine," 84.
467 Herman, Harold J., "Sharan Newman's Guinevere Trilogy," in *Lancelot and Guinevere: A Casebook*, ed. Lori Walters (New York: Routledge, 2002), 291.

of the country has moved beyond the Roman occupation. She lives in a villa with mosaic floors, murals on the walls, heated rooms, and even a Roman bath,[468] harkening back to the glory days of an occupying empire that long ago abandoned Britain. Given this willful delusion on a mass scale by her entire household, it is perhaps not surprising that Guinevere herself resides in a world at least partially of her own making.

A strong supernatural element pervades the plot of *Guinevere*. Guinevere befriends a unicorn and can see/hear faerie folk. Some critics, like Walters, argue that this isn't merely a nod to the fantasy genre, but represents Guinevere's desire to live in her own world and her inability to form relationships. Raymond Thompson cites "use of the faery world to indicate alienation within a character."[469] Others, like Gordon-Wise, take a more traditional symbolic approach, claiming the unicorn represents Guinevere's virginity and maidenhood, especially as it disappears upon her marriage to Arthur. She argues that this Guinevere experiences the supernatural as part of daily life because she is "a medial figure between the new Christian religion and the old goddess worship. Guinevere, herself a Christian like the rest of her family, accepts the numinous but remains poised between these two worlds."[470]

The in-between is a strong theme, coming up again and

---

468 Ibid., 292.
469 Thompson, Raymond M., *The Return from Avalon: A Study of the Arthurian Legend in Modern Fiction* (Westport: Greenwood Press, 1985).
470 Gordon-Wise, *The Reclamation of a Queen*, 130.

again in various pairings: the fantasy/real worlds, Roman/Britain, girl/woman, Christian/pagan. We see many of these dichotomies played out through Guinevere's relationship with others, especially her parents and household servants; Gaia and Timon, the two hermits she is sent to live with; and with those she encounters during her years in Cador's kingdom, where she is finally forced out of her childish bubble and compelled to participate in the real world. Herman argues, "Because Newman is principally concerned with the development of Guinevere from a teenager to an emotionally mature, self-reliant, altruistic woman, most of the first novel is devoted to a delineation of the character traits of Guinevere as a teenager and especially the effects of her parents and other members of the household upon her."[471]

This first book is Guinevere's journey from spoiled, self-absorbed child, to responsible, caring new wife. Bonner believes it is the first of many steps for the character. "Newman uses the first of her novels as an initiation or education for her heroine. Moreover, she clearly shows that Guinevere had, and will have, an existence with or without Arthur or any other man."[472] And that is perhaps the most important point. For the first time, Guinevere has had experiences that don't involve her famous husband and that can affect her independently of him, which means she develops her own opinions and viewpoints.

When *The Chessboard Queen* opens, Guinevere is married to Arthur, a proposal she was given the choice whether or not to

---

471 Herman, "Sharan Newman's Guinevere," 292.
472 Bonner, "Guinevere as Heroine," 89.

accept, unlike in many previous versions. Though it is her choice, her marriage to Arthur is not ideal. She and Arthur love one another, but he does not give her sexual satisfaction. She is also barren, which is seen as divine punishment. She is shunned by the other women of the court because she is childless, which only increases her sense of isolation.

Thus, the situation is ripe for Lancelot to enter the picture. Interestingly, even though he sees Guinevere as a goddess to adore, she does not immediately like him, feeling he is too perfect and too pious. But over time, she comes to realize they are a perfect fit, not only because she is terribly lonely, but both are outsiders, raised in an Otherworld of sorts—she in her Roman villa with a unicorn and faerie folk and he in the underwater palace of the Lady of the Lake.[473] Her attraction to Lancelot occurs in a flash, and every aspect of their relationship is equally intense. Finally, she has found a man who can sexually satisfy her.

By *Guinevere Evermore*, the third book in the series, Guinevere has grown from a selfish child into a warm, caring woman, sensitive to the concerns and emotions of others, but she is still in many ways weak and immature. She is unwilling to accept adult responsibility, and she often pretends to understand the running of the household, while allowing the servants to bear the true burden.[474]

In one of the strangest twists in modern Arthurian legend, Guinevere claims Galahad as her own child, even though he

---

473   Herman, "Sharan Newman's Guinevere," 43-45.
474   Bonner, "Guinevere as Heroine," 94.

belongs to Elaine and Lancelot, and raises him as her own. She says to him, "You are my child, Lancelot's and mine. It was his love for me that conceived you. You have my hair, my skin, and I claim you as my own... You must come to love me, for I am truly your mother."[475] This odd declaration not only shows the depth of Guinevere's need for a child but also that the delusions of her youth have not fully left her. Cooley suggests that this—and other incidents in modern Arthurian legend where Guinevere acts as a mother to either Galahad or Mordred—is a reflection of society having working mothers for the first time who "often run themselves ragged trying to juggle competing demands on their time."[476] Other critics, however, see it as simply an odd, perhaps a bit crazy, method of fulfilling a longing Guinevere can in no other way appease.

Unlike in previous versions of the legend, in Newman, it is not Guinevere's affair with Lancelot that ends up being the source of her downfall. In fact, as Bonner writes, Newman's Guinevere "takes full responsibility for the scandal [of her affair with Lancelot], saying 'It was my stupidity, my own willfulness, that caused this.' Thus, Guinevere is reconciled to Arthur, in a scene of confession very different from those of any other authors."[477]

The trouble, and Camelot's undoing, comes from Mordred, who seeks to shame Arthur and his wife by accusing Guinevere of using witchcraft to stay young, attract Lancelot, and keep

---
475   Newman, Sharan, *The Chessboard Queen*, 1982 (New York:, Tor, 1982, 1997), 283.
476   Cooley, "Re-vision from the Mists," 45.
477   Bonner, "Guinevere as Heroine," 95.

Arthur from attacking his enemies. She is tried by the bishops, and Arthur feels he can do nothing to help her. Here again, the supernatural comes into play. Merlin gives Guinevere a choice to become immortal or live and die in the mortal world. She chooses the mortal world and the possibility of death. Herman sees this as "a courageous decision. It is also, according to Merlin, the first time in her life she has made up her own mind, and is the first time she is afraid."[478] This is a major step for a character who has always depended on others.

Later, after Lancelot is exiled and Arthur is in Armorica fighting a war, Guinevere finds herself alone with Mordred, who is regent. He is a sadistic ruler and she is afraid of him. Nevertheless, she tamps down her own feelings in favor of defending her people and marries Mordred in exchange for allowing the women and children he had imprisoned to go free. Over time, using her new-found inner strength, she stands up to his abuse and figures out a way to get herself and Mordred's remaining prisoners to freedom. She says to Lancelot, "All my life, I waited patiently for someone to come along and rescue me. But with Mordred, I knew no one could. And I stopped waiting. After all these years, I finally rescued myself."[479]

Guinevere's journey is one many women can relate to. This was especially true in the 1980s when women who were born in a more father/husband-centric time finally woke up to see themselves as individuals who didn't need to depend on the men

---
478 Herman, "Sharan Newman's Guinevere," 46.
479 Newman, Sharan, *The Chessboard Queen*, 248.

in their lives to survive, financially or in any other way. Gordon-Wise notes that Guinevere's gradual independence is consistent with the novel's larger motif: "Newman's queen throughout much of this trilogy is not the fiercely independent queen of Parke Godwin's *Beloved Exile*, but this is in keeping with the theme of Newman's trilogy which closely follows Guinevere's voyage from a woman always relying on male wishes, desires, and rescues, to a truly adult woman who makes her own choices and therefore lives independently."[480]

Guinevere's independence comes to the fore after the battle of Camlann and its disastrous consequences. Guinevere and Lancelot willingly part and she goes to the home of her father, where she lives as an adviser and healer. To Gordon-Wise this is a fitting end to her story. "Unlike earlier versions of the myth which assign Guinevere to a nunnery where she spends the remainder of her life attempting to atone for her sin, Newman allows her queen a choice: to remain as wise dowager queen at Camelot with her successor Constantine, or to retire to the family estate. Her decision to return to her ancestral home is indicative of her transformation from sheltered daughter, wife, and lover to independent lady of the manor."[481] This is a Guinevere given much more freedom than her predecessors, even down to how she will spend the final years of her life, and she chooses to have peace at long last.

---

480 Gordon-Wise, *The Reclamation of a Queen*, 128.
481 Ibid., 127.

CHAPTER SIXTEEN

PERSIA WOOLLEY

"It's no easy business being queen of any country, and I should imagine a High Queen has more demands made upon her than most. I know you'll handle them well girl...and be a good mate besides...You're too much like your mother not to."[482]
— *Child of the Northern Spring* by Persia Woolley

"Through the Eyes of a Real Woman"

As the 1980s came to an end and the 1990s began, Persia Woolley was penning a completely different take on Guinevere. In the preface of the final book in The Guinevere Trilogy, *Guinevere: The Legend in Autumn* (1991), Woolley explains why she tackled such a well-trod subject: "It seems clear that although women look at the same events as men, they see very different things.... I felt that it was time we took a new look at an old story through the eyes of a real woman, and who better to see, know and understand the characters of the Round Table than the much-loved Queen at the heart of it."[483]

---

482   Woolley, Persia, *Child of the Northern Spring*, 1987 (Naperville: Sourcebooks, 2010), 8.
483   Woolley, Persia, *Guinevere: The Legend in Autumn*, 1993 (Naperville: Sourcebooks,

The events of the books largely follow Malory, and as a result are, in Lacy's view, "closer to medieval romance in plot and incident, but the story is revalued by an imaginative use of new motivations and relationships, making it more realistic in terms of present day conceptions of human nature."[484]

Woolley's Guinevere is purposefully a total departure from previous depictions of the character. Raised a pagan Celtic queen, she is impatient with the traditional womanly pursuits of carding, spinning, weaving, and sewing. Rather, she is more boyish. "By giving her a rough, tomboy background, I made sure she'd be looking at her new husband's world with fresh eyes," the author said.[485] In keeping with that characterization, Woolley's Guinevere is naturally beautiful, but unconcerned with her appearance, leading the reader to share her unconcern and focus on her character. "By redirecting both the reader's and Guinevere's attention from her physical appearance, Woolley is able to portray Guinevere's character strengths, not just as distinct from her looks, but in *spite* of them,"[486] argues Cooley.

As a queen, Guinevere is very much Arthur's equal. When she learns that Arthur would like to marry her, she weighs the pros and cons of his proposal with her father, considering first what it would mean for her people, as she views herself as their mother. When she accepts, Arthur takes her as his co-ruler, granting her

---

2011), i.
484   Lacy, *The New Arthurian Encyclopedia: New Edition*, 526
485   Woolley, *The Legend in Autumn*, ii.
486   Cooley, "Re-vision from the Mists," 21.

power and listening to her innovative ideas. This is consistent with the mores of the time of the book's writing. Cooley notes that by the 1980s when Woolley was writing, "women were beginning to see themselves represented by mayors, governors, and congresswomen, and feminist Arthurian authors contributed to this reputation by writing their own female politicians... Woolley give[s] Guinevere an opportunity to rule in the king's stead while he is away, and Woolley's Arthur even acknowledges Guinevere's success."[487] During this time, the idea of the "man of the house" was gradually fading and men were ceding marital power in favor of establishing a more equal married relationship.

Guinevere is highly independent, even slapping Malegant when he makes sexual advances toward her. His rape of her, and the transmittal of a life-threatening sexually transmitted disease, is the cause of her barrenness. This is a strikingly modern twist on an age-old plot point. "That Woolley writes the cause of Guinevere's barrenness to be her rape and subsequent illness demonstrates, for anyone doubting the seriousness of psychological damage, the physical consequences of trauma,"[488] writes Cooley. Woolley was also writing during the height of the AIDS epidemic, when cultural consciousness and fear of sexually transmitted diseases were at an all-time high, so consciously or not, this could have influenced her decision to take a non-traditional approach to Guinevere's barrenness.

Woolley's Guinevere is also a highly sexual character, and

---

487   Ibid., 28.
488   Ibid., 75.

being raised as a Celtic queen, she was not ashamed to admit it. "Woolley's [interpretation of] Celtic law offers a glimpse of what women's sexual liberation could look like in a society where sexual autonomy is legally and culturally sanctioned,"[489] writes Cooley. For Guinevere, the right to bed any man she chose was ingrained and expected. She says to Lancelot that to her, their lovemaking was a foregone conclusion, simply because she desired it.[490] Cooley does a masterful job contrasting Woolley's Guinevere with that of Marion Zimmer Bradley in regard to their attitudes toward sex:

> Woolley's Guinevere, a "Celtic queen" who worships a feminine aspect of the Divine, views sexuality as a woman's right, whereas Bradley's, a pious Christian, has been raised in the Church and views sexuality outside of marital duty as sinful, despite her affair with Lancelot. Their oppositional portrayals have the same effect, however. Woolley seems fully supportive of Guinevere's sexuality, and in fact, it is the Church who overrules her right as a Celtic queen and condemns her to death for adultery. Bradley emphasizes Guinevere's double standard that serves to anger and alienate some of her ladies-in-waiting. Both imply that sexual autonomy and empowerment among women should be celebrated, and that women should not resort to shaming each other

---

[489] Ibid., 59.
[490] Ibid., 60.

while engaging with their own sexuality in secrecy.[491]

Here again, Woolley's storyline strongly reflects the key social issues of the time. As the second wave of feminism wound down in the late 1980s and the third began to pick up steam in the early 1990s, issues of sexuality were hot topics. Birth control, rape, and abortion brought the right of a woman to choose what happens to her own body before, during, and after sex to the forefront of public debate. A result of this discourse was the conflict of woman against woman—much like we see with Bradley and Woolley's Guineveres in the above quote—resulting in what many term the "feminist sex wars."

Unable to have children of her own, Guinevere raises Mordred, viewing him as a child of her heart and serving as his main teacher. Having known him for so long and so intimately, she is perplexed when, later in life, he steals Arthur's throne. Guinevere makes a bargain with Morgan that she will abdicate the throne and retire to a convent. After Camlann, she honors her promise and Lancelot returns to searching for the Grail, as he did before their affair. Later, when she does return, Guinevere takes comfort in the assurance that her subjects have remained as loyal to her as she has always been to them and that they had threatened to rise up against Arthur if he had delayed any longer in returning her to her rightful place on the throne.

Given this characterization of Guinevere, which Cooley describes as "arguably the most outspoken and independent of all

---

[491] Ibid., 60.

the Guineveres written by feminist Arthurian authors,"[492] at least to her time, it is not surprising that Woolley is seen as one of the last great feminist writers of Arthuriana during the second wave of feminism.[493]

---

[492] Ibid., 32.
[493] Ibid., 113. The second wave of feminism is said to have ended in the 1980s.

CHAPTER SEVENTEEN

NANCY MCKENZIE AND ROSALIND MILES

"You are to write it down, Gwen. The story of your life. Of Arthur's deeds. Of the times."

If he meant to shock me, he succeeded.

"Me? Write it down? A woman's words? Whatever for?"[494]
— *Queen of Camelot* by Nancy McKenzie

Guinevere and Elaine

As the twentieth century drew to a close, two more female novelists turned their attention to Guinevere, with very different results. Nancy McKenzie's two Guinevere novels, *The Child Queen* (1994) and *The High Queen* (1995), were originally conceived of as one book by the author, but the publisher decided to split them into two, only to re-release them as a single volume, *Queen of Camelot*, in 2002.[495] Though not as widely studied, and perhaps not as popular as many of the other modern female authors discussed

---

494 McKenzie, Nancy, *Queen of Camelot* (New York: Random House, 2002, 1994, 1995), 7.
495 Noble, James, "Guinevere, the Superwoman," 205. The unified version contains a new prologue that takes place while Guinevere is in the convent.

in this book, McKenzie still makes noteworthy, though not altogether affirming, contributions to the character of Guinevere.

The Child Queen opens with the prophecies of a witch regarding Guinevere's fate, a role usually assigned to Merlin. Guinevere spends her childhood riding across the hills of Northern Wales and spending time with her cousin, Elaine, a relationship that will sour and spoil once Arthur enters the picture because he distracts Guinevere from giving her full attention to Elaine. Arthur and Guinevere have a strong marriage and he relies on her as a trusted advisor and she comforts him in times of stress.[496] Jealous of Guinevere and Arthur's relationship, Elaine later helps Malegant kidnap Guinevere and tricks Lancelot into marriage.

Publisher's Weekly blames Guinevere's equanimity at these events for the ultimate failure of the book to satisfy and for the negative light in which Guinevere is regarded. "Guinevere is unaccountably blind to Elaine's malevolence, and her characterization as a singular, strong and intuitive woman suffers accordingly. The book ends weakly, for the conflict between Elaine and Guinevere unfortunately comes to a head in a series of scenes where Guinevere behaves like nothing so much as a spoiled brat." Raymond Thompson writes along similar lines, comparing this relatively weakened—or perhaps we should call her traditional—Guinevere to Cinderella, who like the woman of fairy tales "must survive the machinations of her aunt and jealous cousin (Elaine), who try to prevent, then break up, her marriage to Arthur."[497]

---

[496] Lacy, 599.
[497] Thompson, *Women in Celtic Law*, 467.

It is true that Elaine seems almost more the main character than Guinevere, for in much of the book the action is based in Guinevere's *reaction* to Elaine's thoughts, words, and deeds, rather than on Guinevere's own agency. Guinevere seems to be constantly following the will of others—especially Elaine and the men in her life—rather than exerting her own, a characterization that lessens her in the eyes of the reader.

Perhaps this is an intentional evocation of the earlier, fragile Guineveres of Malory and his predecessors, but it does not sit well with the modern reader. Even at the very end of the book, Guinevere seems to feel as though her life will end with Arthur's death. She reflects: "Britain would miss him, certainly. But Britain would have other kings. It was I, Guinevere, who would not survive his passing."[498] This line of thinking may be meant to reflect her great love for Arthur, but it does not show Guinevere as having any confidence in her own ability to carry on, to continue alone the legacy she and Arthur began. Rather than reflecting the strong, modern woman, this Guinevere appears to be a throwback to the damsel in distress of previous legend.

In all, McKenzie does little to advance the character of Guinevere; rather, she pulled the character back to her pre-feminism roots, where she has little desire to be more than a puppet manipulated by those around her, a bubble tossed about by the sea. There is certainly nothing wrong with being true to the literary origins of a character, but when writing in the 1990s

---

[498] McKenzie, *Queen of Camelot*, 622.

for an audience raised to demand strength from their heroines, making this type of choice is risky, and in this case results in a step back for a character seemingly on an unstoppable march toward finally claiming greatness.

Rosalind Miles

> *"Deceiving Arthur was a daily ache. Loving Lancelot wounded her mortally as it kept her alive. All that was beautiful in their love was cruel and ugly, too. All this she saw every moment of every day...*
>
> *From minute to minute she twisted and turned like flotsam on the waves. She loved Lancelot now more than her own soul. But how could she love him when she still loved Arthur?*
>
> *If she still loved her husband, what was she doing with a lover?*
>
> *And if she did not love Arthur, what did that make her?"*[499]
> — Rosalind Miles, *Queen of the Summer Country*

On the heels of McKenzie's lackluster Guinevere, Rosalind Miles created a feministic Guinevere with the publication of *Guenevere: Queen of the Summer Country* in 1998. Her character was more in

---

[499] Miles, Rosalind, *Guenevere, Queen of the Summer Country* (New York: Three Rivers Press, 1998), 452-453.

keeping with her time, echoing Lacy's assertion that, "Arthurian female characters...mirror fantasies about and fears of women within the ages that produced them. In keeping with women's emergence in the twentieth century, many contemporary Arthurian fictions are more female-centered than ever before. Written by women authors, they are directed primarily at female audiences, and they depict the lives of their otherworld heroines in the intimate detail of realistic fiction."[500]

Miles' Guinevere is raised and trained for her future by her mother, a powerful woman who worships the Goddess, rules her own warriors, and engages in the ancient Celtic practice of changing her consort every seven years. Like her modern counterparts in the workplace, this Guinevere is trained never to show fear and, like so many of her readers, would prefer to remain single. In an interesting twist, Guinevere's mother rules Camelot, so it is established early as belonging to women—to Guinevere upon her mother's death—not to Arthur, as tradition dictates.

Johnson praises this Guinevere's steadfast nature and iron will. "Miles' Guinevere in *Guenevere: Queen of the Summer Country* has no problem with making decisions. She was raised by her mother and learned from an early age that she must be responsible for her own self as well of that of her kingdom. After her marriage to Arthur, she sees no reason to step down from her responsibility. Raised to be a strong leader, she has the confidence to make critical decisions which include overriding the King's

---

500   Lacy, *The New Arthurian Encyclopedia: New Edition*, 526.

command by ordering soldiers on the battlefield."[501]

Guinevere holds the cards in this Arthurian tale. As a headstrong woman, she is the one to propose marriage to Arthur—which serves Guinevere's interest because it saves her from marrying her kinsman, Malegant—and it is she who envisions their union as a first step in the effort to build a nation as high king and high queen. Upon being wedded, she makes Arthur both her husband and champion. And it is Guinevere who gifts Arthur with the Round Table and begins the order of knighthood.

Even after they've wed, Arthur treats Guinevere much like an equal. When Arthur is physically wounded or mentally exhausted, he defers to Guinevere to make decisions for the realm, a responsibility she gladly accepts. However, later on, as Arthur becomes more influenced by Christianity, he makes more decisions without her and she grows resentful.[502]

Even with her progressive role and attitude, bearing a child is still a prime responsibility for the queen. But instead of being barren and wracked with guilt as tradition dictates, Guinevere gives birth to a son, which Johnson sees as having a positive effect on the queen. "Giving birth to the future king and having a child to love enables this Queen Guinevere to enjoy a serenity that [other versions of the character] rarely experience."[503] However, this doesn't mean total happiness for Guinevere. She is disappointed that the babe isn't a daughter. While this is a shocking reaction to

---

501 Johnson, "Guenevere's Conflict," 28.
502 Ibid., 37.
503 Ibid., 34.

readers used to traditional Arthurian legend, it is in keeping with the matriarchal beliefs by which she was raised.

Her maternal happiness is short-lived, however. When her son is killed at age seven in a battle with the Saxons (one she begged Arthur not to involve him in), Guinevere retreats to Avalon, telling Arthur she will never forgive him and denying her role as queen. One would think this would be a perfect time for her affair with Lancelot to begin, but it does not.

It is only after Guinevere returns because the people need her, and only after her marriage to Arthur is essentially over, that Guinevere's love for Lancelot begins. The death blow to their wedded bliss takes place after Arthur's half-sister Morgan gives birth to a son, when, as in Malory, Arthur orders all male newborns killed in attempt to kill his incestuously conceived son, Mordred. This is too much for Guinevere, who withdraws her love and affection from the monster her husband has become.

In a twist on traditional legend, several times Arthur gives Guinevere the chance to put him away, to take a new lover as her mother did when one was needed. Though she loves Lancelot, she is wracked with guilt over her affair, and refuses, acknowledging they were both to blame for the problems in their marriage. Johnson explains, "[Rosalind] Miles present[s] the emotional roller coaster ride on an extremely conflicted Guinevere who struggles to reconcile her feelings for her lover and those for her husband whom she alternately loves, despises and respects."[504]

---

504 Johnson, "Guenevere's Conflict," 39.

Given his understanding of his own culpability in the situation, Arthur is hesitant to punish the affair. It is the public exposure that forces Arthur to act. [505]

After Lancelot leaves, Guinevere discovers she is pregnant and gives birth to her long-wished-for daughter. After that, they see each other once a year on Beltane, which as Johnson points out gives Guinevere the freedom to focus on her kingdom, rather than on her husband. "Miles' pagan Guinevere turns away from Lancelot because she believes her first responsibility is to her land and kingdom. The Queen convinces her people that Arthur is merely sleeping in Avalon, and living openly with Lancelot would contradict the notion that she believes her husband will return."[506] Johnson goes to emphasize Guinevere's continued activity after Arthur's death. "She continues the dream of Camelot among all her people who heartily accept her as their sole ruler."[507]

Every Woman a Goddess

For only the second time in Arthurian legend we have a non-Christian Guinevere, [508] this one from the Summer Country, "the last of the British lands not to become Christian."[509] Johnson shows Miles to be part of an emerging tradition among female

---

505 Ibid., 64.
506 Ibid., 65.
507 Ibid., 68.
508 The first time being the Guinevere created by Persia Woolley, who was the subject of Chapter Sixteen.
509 Ibid., 9.

Arthurian authors: "Like Bradley, Rosalind Miles also sets her Arthurian legend trilogy in a Great Britain that is leaving behind the Goddess and moving toward the patriarchal belief systems of the Christian church."[510]

This religious shift is not surprising when one looks at the culture of the time period the book was written. "Successful literature often reflects the times in which it is created and frequently mirrors changing societal belief systems and behaviors," writes Johnson. "During the second half of the twentieth century, an unprecedented upheaval in gender roles occurred as well as a youthful yearning to return to a simpler time which focused on community and the land. A result of this popular back-to-the-land movement was the rise of neo-paganism which, with its affirmation of women, enhanced the strengthening female persona."[511]

The rise of paganism was reflected in popular culture as well. Thanks in part to the success of films like *The Craft* and TV shows like *Charmed* in the mid-to-late 1990s, all things Wicca and witchcraft were in demand, especially among those in their teens and twenties. Large bookstores such as Borders and Barnes and Noble had entire sections dedicated to neo-paganism; journalists declared that embracing paganism was the newest form of adolescent rebellion. It was inevitable that these social changes would be reflected in contemporary reimaginings of Camelot as well. Johnson agrees. "As the world was evolving, so too did the Arthurian legend evolve as feminist writers set

---
510   Ibid., 8.
511   Johnson, "Guenevere's Conflict," 5.

the legend in a changing pagan world that would now be told through a female voice."⁵¹²

As goddess worship and "girl power" went hand-in-hand in pop culture, so too were they intertwined in the period's Arthurian legend. Johnson elaborates: "Traditionally, Arthurian legend was set in a Christian land inhabited by knights and kings whose good intentions were often thwarted by the evil doings of female characters. To circumvent this negative bias toward the legend's women, both Bradley and Miles initially provide a pre-Christian backdrop to the legend which automatically establishes the Goddess worship as an accepted way of life that is being negatively impacted by the arriving patriarchal Christians who seek to undermine the power of women."⁵¹³

Strong, not Feminist

In a 1999 interview with *The Independent*, Miles was asked about her motivation behind re-thinking Guinevere. "I wanted to recapture the active, regal women of this period," she said. "The only one we all know is Boadicea and we remember her because of her failure."⁵¹⁴ But in the same interview, she shies away from calling her retelling "feminist:"

I think feminism's time has passed. It's not passé, just

---

512   Ibid.
513   Ibid., 14.
514   Stanford, Peter, "The Books Interview: Rosalind Miles - A Feminist in Camelot," *The Independent* (1999).

passed. Thirty years ago we were fighting for equal pay, equal opportunities, free contraception, and we still haven't got them all. But, because of feminism, those issues have been addressed, progress has been made, prejudices shifted, the struggle diffused. And in the sense that society now accepts that what we used to call women's rights are human rights—equal pay and equal access to work, for example—then we are all feminists now.[515]

Miles' dismissal of feminism as a movement whose time had come and gone was also consistent with the time period in which she wrote. In the late 1990s and early years of the 2000s, feminism was waning. In a 2001 article, Barbara Epstein reported, "Feminist theory, once provocative and freewheeling, has lost concern with the conditions of women's lives and has become pretentious and tired,"[516] echoing many of her contemporaries' thoughts.

Fewer women reported being feminists. Many still supported the causes it stood for, but they no longer wanted to be associated with the word or the movement. Some saw the word as "limiting and exclusionary,"[517] while others didn't like the association it had taken on with so-called "feminazis," the radical faction of feminists. According to Martha Rampton, "Feminism's perceived silence in the 1990s was a response to

---

515   Ibid.
516   Epstein, Barbara, "What Happened to the Women's Movement?" *Monthly Review: An Independent Socialist Magazine* 53, Issue 01 (May 2001).
517   Rampton, Martha, "Four Waves of Feminism," *Pacific Magazine* (Fall 2008).

the successful backlash campaign by the conservative press and media, especially against the word feminism and its purported association with male-bashing and extremism."[518]

Feminist or not, for all of her revisionist efforts, was Miles successful in reshaping readers' conception of the character of Guinevere? It depends on whom you ask. Bonner writes about Miles and others of her mid-1980s to late 1990s generation, "At the hands of these contemporary [female] authors, Guinevere becomes a heroine, a figure that girls and women can read about and admire, not just for her well-documented external beauty, but for her integral strength and dynamics."[519] Miles' Guinevere is certainly a radical departure from previous versions, one who shows the potential of a female ruler in a non-Christian world, going against all the conventions that cast a bad light on Guinevere to begin with.

But Howey cautions heaping too much praise on Miles and the advancements she may have made. "While Miles' book presents itself as a feminist version of the legend, Guinevere does very little to earn the reader's respect and many other major female characters in the novel (such as Morgan) are demonized."[520] If Howey is correct, perhaps there are shades of Marion Zimmer Bradley's quandary in Miles' work. Maybe she wrestled with creating a strong Guinevere without diminishing her other female characters, just as Bradley seems to have done when

---

518 Ibid.
519 Bonner, "Guinevere as Heroine," 100.
520 Howey, "Once and Future Women," 277.

redeeming Morgaine. In an article in the journal *Arthuriana*, Roberta Davidson describes just this pattern of female portrayal in modern Arthurian literature:

> The equation works with predictable regularity: when Guinevere is good, Morgan (et al.) is bad. When Guinevere is bad, Morgan (et al.) is good. Even the nature of "goodness" or "badness" in the characters is remarkably uniform. When Guinevere is bad, she presented as over-sexed and selfish, sometimes scheming, and always clearly unworthy of Arthur, who is more "truly" in love with the protagonist. She is usually blond. When the "Morgan" figure is bad, she is over-sexed, selfish, inevitably scheming, and out to use or destroy Arthur. However, creative license is not entirely dead—in Morgan's case her hair is neither uniformly blond nor black, but "of what color it shall please God." Conversely, the favored protagonist is seldom depicted in a hyper-sexualized way. Indeed, she is more often described as "boyish" and, in fact sometimes appears disguised as a boy. She is unconcerned with her own appearance, despite her beauty;...she is independent, unconventional, and uncertain if she wants to be a wife.... She is the mirror image, in other words, of the "bad" woman, a pattern which may not be entirely accidental.[521]

---

[521] Davidson, Roberta, "When King Arthur Is OG 13," in *Arthuriana* 22, no.3 (2012): 13.

As we've seen, this is a pattern that held true throughout the 1980s and 1990s. Luckily, after the turn of the century, authors would reject this "either/or" way of thinking and allow multiple Arthurian women to be strong at the same time.

CHAPTER EIGHTEEN

GUINEVERE POST-2000 AND LAVINIA COLLINS

The Arthurian Market Slows

With the dawning of the twenty-first century—a full thousand years after Guinevere first graced Arthurian legend with her written presence—one would think Guinevere's time might have finally come. Perhaps, but it wasn't through new work championed by the traditional publishing industry. In her thesis, Sara Cooley cites a study showing "no fewer than forty books on Arthurian themes were published in the United States in the year 2000 alone,' [but] only a handful of these have been written through the perspectives of female characters."[522]

Why? She blames the post-feminist movement, which caused "the freshest story, the most creative spin [to] no longer include the feminist politics that have been declared outdated and irrelevant to women today."[523] And that is a real possibility. As mentioned in the last chapter, during the early 2000s, the feminist movement suffered from a severe slowdown, that

---

522 Cooley, "Re-vision from the Mists," 112.
523 Ibid.

continues to this day[524] in parts of the world. Many women from all walks of life, in the United States, Britain, and other countries, have argued that the fight is no longer relevant, with some even claiming feminism has harmed gender relations or made men's hatred of women worse.[525] "Many though believe this kind of thinking [feminism] belongs in the past. Today, western women have achieved much, though not all, of what they set out to. They now often stand above men in terms of personal achievement," cites a 1999 BBC article questioning whether or not feminism was still relevant at the turn of the millennium.[526]

While there was a post-feminist movement[527] and it could have influenced interest (or lack thereof) in Guinevere, the lack of recent novels about her has more to do with the publishing industry than it does with culture. As an author who had a Guinevere book on submission to all the major publishers in the late 2000s, I can attest to a perplexity regarding that type of book. While I had several editors very keen to work on my book and we went to acquisitions twice at a Big Five publishing house (and once at a top ten house), the publishing houses expressed reticence. Some had been burned by previous underperforming Arthurian books, others were already reissuing older works and

---

524 Although the United States seems to have had a resurgence since the 2016 presidential election.
525 Gallagher, Michael, "Is feminism relevant in 2000?" *BBC News Online*, 28 December 1999.
526 Ibid.
527 It divided the country at least up until the 2016 election gained steam. The first female president on a major party ticket and her opposition being a documented misogynist reignited the feminist movement into what is now clearly a fourth wave.

didn't want the competition, and there were a few that simply didn't know how to market that type of book.

While traditional publishing houses were busy ignoring the potential in Guinevere, independent (a.k.a. self-published) authors looked at the market, realized it had been more than a decade since a Guinevere book was published, and took up the call to arms. Looking at the top twenty fictional books for adults[528] about Guinevere published since 2000 that are available on Amazon as of this writing, the most visible—based on number of reviews, star rating level, search placement, and awards won—are those by Lavinia Collins and myself.[529] Therefore, the Guinevere books by those two authors will be the last two discussed in this book.

Lavinia Collins

"Tell me you want me," he murmured, kissing me once more, gently pulling on my lip with his teeth, leaning away as I leaned towards him, trying to kiss him deeper. So, this is what he wanted. After my resistance last night, he wanted to feel that he had won me round. I was not sure that he had not, but I was not going to yield a position of even the slightest

---

528   Cheryl Campanello and Nancy McKenzie both have highly successful Guinevere series intended for the teen or young adult market.

529   As of this writing, my novel *Daughter of Destiny* has won nine awards and been short-listed in two others. My novel *Camelot's Queen* has won seven and been long- or short-listed in four others. Both books have been named Books of the Year, *Daughter of Destiny* by Chanticleer Reviews in 2015 and *Camelot's Queen* by Author's Circle in 2016. For a full list of awards, please visit https://nicoleevelina.com/awards/.

power if I did not have to." [530]
— *Guinevere: A Medieval Romance* by Lavinia Collins

Lavinia Collins is a feminist scholar who has a degree in medieval literature from Oxford and has written three fictional series on famous Arthurian women, including Guinevere, Morgan, and Morgause. Her Guinevere trilogy was published in mid-2014 as *Warrior Queen* (Book 1), *A Champion's Duty* (Book 2), and *Day of Destiny* (Book 3), and then later the same year as a boxed set titled *Guinevere: A Medieval Romance*.

According to a 2014 interview,[531] Collins' Guinevere trilogy is based off her reading of Malory. Her Guinevere is a Breton[532] sent from her home to marry the younger Arthur after he conquered her homeland, resulting in the deaths of her mother, brothers, and the man she was supposed to marry. Arthur wants her, sight unseen, because she is descended from Maeve, the warrior queen of the Breton, who, it is claimed, has Otherworldly blood. He believes Guinevere may be able to save him from the destiny Merlin tells him awaits him. Guinevere unwillingly leaves her kingdom and elderly father behind and goes to Camelot to marry Arthur, whom she has never met but hates with obvious reason.

---

530 Collins, Lavinia, *Guinevere: A Medieval Romance* (London: The Book Folks, December 2, 2014), no page number given in the ebook.
531 Medieval Bex, "Interview with Lavinia Collins, author of *The Warrior Queen*," interviewed by Rebecca E. Lyons, June 5, 2014.
532 I believe she may be the first to give Guinevere this heritage.

At first, being a Queen is a whole new experience for Guinevere because although she was a princess in her kingdom, she never had to act like one. Eventually, she learns to enjoy her new role and even falls in love with Arthur. He initially welcomes her in his war council and as a warrior, allowing her to fight alongside him against an enemy threatening to take his lands in France. But when Guinevere is wounded in battle and a mysterious French knight saves her life, Arthur is so upset by her injury that he decides he can't bear to worry about her anymore. He bans her from war and sends her home to Britain.

As one might expect, the knight is Lancelot. When Lancelot comes to court at Camelot, Guinevere tries to snub him, but finds herself attracted to him. She initiates the affair, pressuring Lancelot when he resists.[533] Their affair is based in mutual passion, but also in Guinevere's need to exert control of her life, which she lost when Arthur banned her from war.

Some suspect what is going on between Lancelot and Guinevere so the castle is fraught with gossip. Arthur doesn't believe a word of it, but enemies are watching the two closely. Lancelot is forced to leave in search of the Holy Grail in an attempt to refute the rumors and keep Guinevere safe. With her champion and lover gone, Guinevere seeks solace in Arthur's arms, but as time passes, she finds Lancelot's absence growing heavier upon her heart and her enemies growing in numbers.

---

533 Here Collins seems to be playing with the idea of consent in a sexual relationship, flipping the traditional gender roles to make a statement perfectly timed to public consciousness which was on high alert with "rape culture" being in the news.

The Sexual Side of Guinevere

One of the things Collins's Guinevere is well-known for is her sexual agency, which makes her a direct contradiction to Malory and other early portrayals of the character. The trilogy is more overtly sexual than previous versions – "bordering on erotica,"[534] according to Leonide Martin, a retired California State University professor. But given the contemporary success of series like *Fifty Shades of Gray*, is that really very surprising? Collins is reacting directly to what her audience wants. As Brewer reminds us, "Modern Gueneveres...show how our images of the heroine and our expectations as to how she will behave have changed in the course of time. The authors are now much more explicit about, and make much more of sexual matters, and in this respect we can see a new race of liberated young Gueneveres has sprung up in the last few decades."[535]

Some readers criticize Collins for including a *Mists of Avalon*-like ménage à trois between Guinevere, Arthur, and Kay (rather than with Guinevere, Arthur, and Lancelot as in *The Mists of Avalon*). A Goodreads[536] user named Terric853 writes, "So why did I only give this three stars? See how the title says it's 'A Medieval Romance?' I'm no prude, but 50% of the book

---

534 Martin, Leonide, review of *Guinevere: A Medieval Romance*, by Lavinia Collins, Goodreads, January 25, 2017.
535 Brewer, "The Figure of Guenevere," 286.
536 As Collins' books are so new that there is no critical literature available, at least that I can find, I am using reviews from readers on Goodreads and Amazon to get a sample of reader opinions. Plus, just as characters evolve over time, so do methods of reviewing books, and today scholarly critical analysis is not the only method.

was graphic sex—between Guinevere and Arthur; between Guinevere and Lancelot; and a three-way between Guinevere, Lancelot and someone else (not named due to spoiler issues)."[537] An Amazon reader named Jillian wrote, "[I]t reads like the sex scenes were written first, then they decided to add an Arthurian theme to make it sell and filled it in around the sex. I don't mind sex scenes, but in this book many of the sex scenes don't make sense, felt disingenuous, and they are used to carry the whole book. Which is probably why the world-building attempts failed for me entirely, like they were an afterthought, which made the story completely lack charm."[538] Readers such as this seem to yearn for the romance of the old tales, rather than graphic sex that can be readily obtained in non-Arthurian literature.

Others aren't as bothered by it. Tricia Preston writes, "It was interesting to view the action through the perspective of one of the strong female characters of the legend. There *is* an incredible quantity of romance and racy sex, verging on the salacious at times...but the author does give us a splendid insight into the chivalry and camaraderie of the time."[539] Bex Lyons, late medievalist and research associate at the University College of London, doesn't even give the sex a thought. "Lavinia Collins is a medievalist, and it shows. This trilogy of books is a lovely homage to the medieval Arthurian tradition—with Malory

---

537 Terric853, review of *Guinevere: A Medieval Romance*, by Lavinia Collins, Goodreads, June 2, 2016.
538 Jillian, review of *The Warrior Queen*, by Lavinia Collins, Goodreads, December 1, 2014.
539 Preston, Tricia, review of *Guinevere: A Medieval Romance*, by Lavinia Collins, Amazon, June 21, 2016.

referenced and evoked throughout—as well as post-medieval feminist Arthuriana, as epitomized by Marion Zimmer Bradley's *The Mists of Avalon*. Collins gives the leading lady of Arthurian literature a new voice, and some new and interesting motivations and associations, whilst sticking to the essentials of Malory's plot structure."[540]

Sex is definitely an area where this Guinevere is different from her previous incarnations, who were exhorted to be chaste and then castigated when they failed. "Whereas romance is an Arthurian fascination that has persisted from medieval writings, sex and sexuality, especially women's, has been given little positive attention in Arthurian literature...to describe even the most sexually active Arthurian woman as 'sexually liberated' would be shallow...[because] it [must] include the freedom to reject or enter into sexual relationships fearing neither exploitation nor punishment,"[541] writes Cooley.

This comment highlights the very idea Collins sought to change. Her Guinevere certainly is given a reason for being as sex-positive as she is. In the Breton society of Collins' creation, women are warriors and they have a strong voice in the family and society. This is what Guinevere is used to; she is the one with the power. Then all of sudden, she is forced into the British world in which women are treated like brood-mares and slaves, quite a shock to her independent system. Luckily, in Arthur, she finds a

---

540 Lyons, Bex, review of *The Day of Destiny*, by Lavinia Collins, Goodreads, August 21, 2014.
541 Cooley, "Re-vision from the Mists," 58.

man who loves her for her strength, and in Lancelot, she finds someone who can handle her passion.

A Mixed Reaction

In regard to Collins' portrayal of Guinevere as a character, readers give mixed reviews. On the positive end, Cynthia T. Cannon sees her as "not just a pale and timid woman, but more of a daring and independent person."[542] Elma Grove enthuses, "[A]t last, we have a Guinevere for our time, yet one who is also firmly rooted in the medieval world of the narrative. Without anachronism, Collins gives us brilliant access to the queen's thoughts and emotions, her keen intelligence, strength, and compelling human responses to those surrounding her and to circumstances both within and beyond her control."[543] And Goodreads user Joy writes, "Guinevere isn't just a gentile [sic] prize, victim of manipulation or a vindictive adulteress. She's a woman of strength, character, desires, willfulness, and intelligence. She's a heroine and powerful force in Arthurian Britain."[544]

But others aren't buying it. The "contradictions and waffling"[545] in her character Jillian points out make this Guinevere much like earlier versions, which might be intentional given

---

[542] Cannon, Cynthia T., review of *Guinevere: A Medieval Romance*, by Lavinia Collins, Goodreads, May 22, 2016.
[543] Grove, Elma, review of *The Warrior Queen*, by Lavinia Collins, Goodreads, April 17, 2014.
[544] Joy, review of *The Day of Destiny*, by Lavinia Collins, Goodreads, November 12, 2014.
[545] Jillian, review of *The Warrior Queen*. by Lavinia Collins, Goodreads, December 1, 2014.

that Collins based her story on Malory. As we saw in Chapter Seven, his Guinevere varies wildly throughout, going from noble to treacherous at warp speed, and swooning over Lancelot one minute, while berating him the next. Perhaps Collins' is simply following this lead.

However, it doesn't sound like knowing the answer would matter much; readers who don't like this Guinevere don't seem to care about the reasons for her unattractive qualities. Sheila writes on Goodreads, "I would have enjoyed this book more if Guinevere had been even remotely likable. She was a selfish petulant child through the entire book. Her actions ruined lives and destroyed everything good in the story. However, she did not care. Almost everything bad that happens in the book is her fault. She's actually surprised when someone (usually Kay) calls her on it."[546] Book blogger Geek Girl in Love writes, "What bugged me is that she's so freaking self-centered. She can't seem to grasp that there is an entire kingdom which will be totally ruined if she can't control her libido... She can't see or doesn't care that all these acts of personal rebellion don't get her any further towards self-determination but they do hurt a ton of people."[547] Others called her "a pretty messed up person,"[548] "shallow,"[549] "selfish,"[550]

---

[546] Sheila, review of *Guinevere: A Medieval Romance*, Lavinia Collins, Goodreads, May 19, 2016.
[547] Geek Girl in Love, "Book Review: The Guinevere Trilogy, by Lavinia Collins," September 22, 2014.
[548] Ibid.
[549] Martin, review of *A Medieval Romance*, Goodreads.
[550] Daneesha, review of *Guinevere: A Medieval Romance*, by Lavinia Collins, Goodreads, March 25, 2016.

and "dumb."[551]

With only a few years having elapsed since the books' publication, the jury is out on Collins' overall contribution to Guinevere's evolution. She clearly updated the character by allowing her to claim her sexuality and by making her "a strong accomplished warrior"[552] who is worthy of respect in her own right. But as for advancing her role, some readers say there wasn't enough gravitas to the material to call this much of an evolution. Erica writes on Goodreads, "It was a light read, with an interesting perspective—but cotton-candy, light, fluffy and not much substance, but enjoyable regardless."[553] Obviously, only time will tell what Collins' overall impact on the history of Guinevere will be.

---

551 Geek Girl in Love, review of *The Guinevere Trilogy*, Goodreads, September 22, 2014.
552 Ankiel, Janet, review of *Guinevere: A Medieval Romance*, by Lavinia Collins, Goodreads, May 12, 2016.
553 Erica, review of *Guinevere: A Medieval Romance*, by Lavinia Collins, Goodreads, May 27. 2016.

CHAPTER NINETEEN

NICOLE EVELINA

"I was once a queen, a lover, a wife, a mother, a priestess, and a friend. But all those roles are lost to me now; to history, I am simply a seductress, a misbegotten woman set astray by the evils of lust.

This is the image painted of me by subsequent generations, a story retold thousands of times. Yet, not one of those stories is correct. They were not there; they did not see through my eyes or feel my pain. My laughter was lost to them in the pages of history..."

It ends now. I will take back my voice and speak the truth of what happened... All I ask is that mankind listen to my words, and then judge me on their merit. [554]
— *Daughter of Destiny* by Nicole Evelina

Guinevere and Me: Personal Reflections

Including my own novels in this book may seem a bit self-serving and strange, but I wrote my Guinevere's Tale trilogy with the

---

[554] Evelina, Nicole, *Daughter of Destiny* (Maryland Heights, Missouri: Lawson Gartner Publishing, 2016), 1, 2.

intention of changing the paradigm for her character so I am as much a part of her evolution as the others examined within this volume. Like Lavinia Collins, my books are too new for there to be much critical analysis, so instead I am going to relay my intent.[555] What others may decide about me and my books in the future is up to them.

I wrote my books under the strong influence of Marion Zimmer Bradley and somewhat under the influence of Parke Godwin and Nancy McKenzie, all of whom I read before attempting my own novels. I loved *The Mists of Avalon*, especially Bradley's vision of Avalon, but I disliked the way the author seemed to feel that both Morgan and Guinevere couldn't be strong, capable women at the same time, which is how I pictured them. Because of this, I have done my best to uphold the dignity and strength of both characters in my work, making them women who stand in opposition to one another like magnets of reverse polarity, while bowing down to no one, not even one another. Godwin influenced my portrayal by getting me to think about Guinevere's life after Arthur's death, which in turn led me to thinking about her life before she married him. McKenzie was a strong subconscious influence on my portrayal of Elaine and her close, familial relationship with Guinevere. Because these other author's portrayals could color how I wrote my own version of the

---

[555] I will not, however, subject you to reviews of my own books because I am certainly not an objective third party and attempting to use them as though I am strikes me as wrong. Those who are interested can read them on Amazon, Goodreads or any number of blogs.

tale, I decided to take the advice of William Morris, who "once remarked that the best way to deal with old stories was to close the book and retell them as new stories for yourself."[556]

Why I chose to write about Guinevere isn't a simple question to answer. As we have seen, literature tells us painfully few things about Guinevere, other than she married Arthur, was barren, had an affair with Lancelot, etc. But no one's identity should be reduced to a handful of incidents. Guinevere had a childhood, a family, and dreams for her future. She was a queen and may or may not have been a mother. As for her infamous affair, every situation has a context that is important to understanding it, even when it's the climax that is remembered. Guinevere had reasons for acting as she did, and she didn't do it in a vacuum. The circumstances surrounding her affair are just as important as the act itself. The medieval tale of her ending her days in a convent is convenient and moral, but we all know life is messy and usually doesn't end tied up in a nice bow. Chances are good there was far more to Guinevere's story than we've ever heard.

The Guinevere's Tale trilogy (*Daughter of Destiny, Camelot's Queen* – both published in 2016 – and *Mistress of Legend*, forthcoming in 2018) is my attempt to give context to the bits of Guinevere's life that tradition gives us. In it, Guinevere tells her own story—from the age of eleven to well into her

---

556 Brewer, "The Figure of Guenevere," 279. I purposefully didn't read any other Arthurian fiction while I was writing my trilogy. I didn't read many of the authors mentioned in this book until after my novels were published and I began the research that would lead to this book.

fifties—seeking to right the wrongs history has thrust upon her, to clear away the mists of time, and to give the reader a clear picture of who she really was, virtues, sins, and all. As she says in the prologue: "I deserve to be able to bear witness before being condemned by men who never saw my face. Grieve with me, grieve for me, but do not believe the lies which time would sell. All I ask is that mankind listen to my words, and then judge me on their merit."[557]

The world needs strong female characters now more than ever. Guinevere, despite her sullied reputation, is an archetype that women of every age can look up to. A few years ago, Merida in *Brave* showed us that a Disney princess can be strong and accomplish a mission without a man at the end to bring about her happily ever after. Legendary ones can do the same. If King Arthur existed, Guinevere would have lived in a similar culture to Merida, in a time and place when women had more rights than in the rest of the world. Even 1,500 years later, Guinevere shows us that as women, while we naturally love and nurture, we can also lead ourselves and others, taking our destinies into our own hands and shaping our own future while positively influencing others.

To me, Guinevere is a perfect example of how strong is more than just physical strength. Yes, my Guinevere can wield a sword and leads troops into battle, but that's not the only way in which she shows strength. Over the course of the trilogy, my Guinevere is a woman who is tapped for roles she never expected—much

---

557 Evelina, *Daughter of Destiny*, 2.

less desired—and deals with repeated heartache, the loss of loved ones, jealousy, abuse, and expectations that would bow lesser women. She shows us that being a strong woman means carrying on even in your darkest hours and emerging on the other side stronger than you were before.

Breaking with Tradition by Inventing Guinevere's Early Years

Barbara Gordon-Wise writes:

> [T]he traditional treatment of Guinevere begins with her marriage to Arthur and ends with enclosure in a nunnery after his death. Details of her existence before marriage are extremely scanty and generally they allude only to her father. After the fall of Camelot and Arthur, Guinevere is without exception depicted safely ensconced in the arms of the patriarchal Christian church. Obviously an independent Guinevere would have presented many difficulties…it has been left to modern fantasy to flesh out the maiden aspect of the queen.[558]

She continues this thought a few pages later, noting that even the versions that have Guinevere fall in love with another before marrying Arthur, usually Lancelot—as in Heber's 1830 poem "Morte D'Arthur," Richard Hovey's late nineteenth century play

---

558 Gordon-Wise, *The Reclamation of a Queen*, 58.

Lancelot and Guenevere, and Tennyson—"focus on Guinevere's life before marriage only to create sympathy for her ultimate betrayal of Arthur. There is no true depiction Guinevere as maiden/virgin since her existence is totally dependent on men."[559]

I approached the book that would become *Daughter of Destiny* wanting to give Guinevere context. After all, we have an entire tradition built around Arthur's birth narrative at Tintagel castle, so why do we not know anything about the young Guinevere? That she was raised by a strong woman was a given for me. I couldn't fathom how she could be reared otherwise and go on to be the powerful, intelligent queen I envisioned. When I read about the Votadini tribe of what is today southern Scotland and their historical connection to Wales, the very place I wanted to set Guinevere's childhood, I knew I had her maternal linage. For her paternal ancestors, I kept with the traditions dating back to Geoffrey of Monmouth by making them Roman.

Much of Guinevere's personality is shaped by her family and her upbringing. She is a very selfish girl who gets somewhat better with age, maturity, and experience. Narcissism is a common trait among children, especially those without siblings, and is in keeping with the way Guinevere has been portrayed throughout the course of Arthurian tradition. It also makes sense because as the only surviving child of the thirteen her parents sired, she was coddled and protected because she was their only direct heir. Unfortunately, this also made her very self-centered.

---

[559] Ibid., 61.

Her time in Avalon teaches Guinevere a modicum of humility, but not as much as some people display naturally. Later, after Guinevere marries Arthur, she is the most powerful woman in the land, so her worldview remains centered on herself, as it did for many historical rulers.

I would like to believe my Guinevere doesn't show much of the rashness that characterized early versions of her character, but she is still jealous. Between Elaine being besotted with Arthur and then Lancelot (in books 1 and 2) and Morgan vying for Arthur's attention (in book 2), I don't personally see how that trait can be eradicated from Guinevere's personality without turning her into a "featherhead" like Bradley's Guinevere or making her blind to Elaine's involvement as she seems to be in McKenzie.

Pagan vs. Christian

Making Guinevere a priestess of Avalon is probably my most controversial move, at least according to readers. While some people like the change, others resent what they see as me taking away Morgan's traditional power or customary role and giving it to Guinevere. Gordon-Wise explains Guinevere's tangential traditional relationship with magic:

> Guinevere, though never as blatantly associated with magic and sorcery as Morgan la Fee, [sic] still becomes tainted with the elements traditionally characteristic with witches or the practice of witchcraft. Once the figure of

the queen became linked with adultery and then lechery, the association with witchcraft became more marked. It has been left to modern fantasy writers either to erase this negative image or to posit more strongly the beneficial aspect of the witch archetype—the Wise Woman.[560]

I wasn't about to erase the tradition, so I followed Marion Zimmer Bradley's lead and made Guinevere as well as Morgan priestesses, the more acceptable version of a witch. Though it is not common, I've never come across anything in tradition that says both women can't be priestesses with varying gifts of the Sight.

I needed Guinevere to grow up somewhere she'd have strong women other than her mother as role models, so I chose Avalon, which reminded me of the all-girls high school that was so important to my own formation. When Cooley wrote, "[I]t is important for these authors to write a Guinevere who takes inspiration from the women before and around her because essential to women's understanding of their status in society is the recognition of all the successes and failures of the women who came first that contributed to the present place,"[561] she was referring to Persia Woolley and Sharan Newman, but she could just as well have been talking about me and the way I viewed the importance of Avalon in Guinevere's life.

Guinevere lives in Avalon for a formative period of her life,

---

560 Gordon-Wise, *The Reclamation of a Queen*, 79.
561 Cooley, "Re-vision from the Mists," 29.

from the age of eleven through fifteen.[562] Having her experience that interval in an isolated location with a bunch of other women meant she wasn't subject to the prevailing thoughts and influences of the time that said men were dominant, Christianity was the only way, etc. In this little cocoon, Guinevere was free to nurture the outspokenness and intelligence that her mother instilled in her[563] and it made her a much stronger woman than she might have been had she stayed in Northgallis. I thought of it kind of like going off to an all-girls boarding school, one where she would make lifelong friends and rivals—such as Morgan—just as girls do today.

As for Guinevere's paganism, at the time I wasn't aware that Woolley and Miles had already created a pagan Guinevere, but it made sense to me given that she likely would have lived right in the time of greatest conflict during the decline of the old Celtic pagan beliefs and the rise of the new Christian faith. Scholars suggest that goddess worship may have lasted through around 500 A.D., and we know that even after that, many common people remained pagan. Johnson writes, "By recognizing the existence of a Goddess worshipping society being overcome by Christianity during the time when the legendary King Arthur may have reigned, the authors [Bradley and Miles, but the statement is also true of me] are able to bring a new perspective to the traditional

---

562 Fourteen was legal marrying age for a girl under Brehon law.
563 Guinevere's mother raised her with beliefs rare to post-Roman Britain but more common to her native Votadini tribe in what is now southern Scotland.

telling of the Arthurian legend."[564] This conflict also powers the political struggles in my trilogy, as seen in the relationships between Arthur and Father Marius, as well as Guinevere and Morgan's interactions with the Lady of the Lake.

Like Lavinia Collins, I chose to make my Guinevere a warrior, which is in keeping with the traditions of pre-Roman Celtic Britain, and also with the practices of the historical tribes of southern Scotland, such as the Votadini, from whom Guinevere's maternal line descends. It also sets her up well to be Arthur's equal in ruling the kingdom and fighting in war.

In order to give Guinevere a complete early life and show her as a full person independent of Arthur, she had to be in love with someone before him. Most authors who have given Guinevere a first love have chosen to make it Lancelot, but I wanted to go in a different direction. The more I explored the legend, I realized that in some versions, Mordred isn't alone in confronting and exposing Lancelot and Guinevere. Sometimes Aggrivane is with him. I started wondering why, which eventually led me to fuse Guinevere's early love of Aggrivane with his later betrayal. Also, because Lot is Aggrivane's father and Lot's kingdom of Lothian is in the Votadini lands, it was helpful for Guinevere to already have a connection to their family through Aggrivane.

---

564 Johnson, "Guenevere's Conflict," 15-16.

The Dark Side of History

One of the more distasteful parts of the Arthurian legend (as it relates to Guinevere) occurs in my second book, *Camelot's Queen*. It is an incident that was glossed over for a long time, but that more writers are beginning to resurrect. "Recent authors also tend to be less reticent on the subject of Meliagaunt's carrying off of Guenevere when she went a-Maying, and to turn the episode into a case of rape with rather more graphic detail than is to be found in earlier retellings. Our modern anxieties about rape, perhaps, find indirect expression through these recent fictions."[565]

I knew when I approached this series that I would not shy away from Malegant's rape of Guinevere. To me, it was integral to the legend. Like other female authors, I was not willing to let such a personal female experience be treated lightly, or gleefully. I wanted to be sure I approached it with respect. Cooley notes that men and women treat rape differently in the legends:

> The theme of ravishment is common in Arthurian legends—usually as a plot device to show the courage and chivalry of knights who rescue damsels from this fate… many of the medieval stories of ravishment that come to contemporary readers show ambiguous portrayals of assault in which the effect of the incident on the woman is passed over in favor of rhetorical fawning over the savior knight. It is only when the stories are told from

---

565 Brewer, "The Figure of Guenevere," 286.

the perspectives of female characters that we can see the reality of those assaults—not just the details of the incident itself, but the events leading up to the assault, the nature of the assault itself, and the severe physical, emotional and psychological impact of the assault on the woman and those close to her, even long after the incident has taken place.[566]

I did my best to ensure the kidnapping and rape were integral to the plot and to show how they affected Guinevere's life. Therefore, my version of Guinevere suffers both mentally and physically for a lengthy period of time after Malegant's abuse, nearly losing her mind when it is coupled with Arthur's betrayal. It is only after time and Avalon's version of therapy that she can learn to move past her experiences. Plus, rape is an ancient weapon of war, so including this in an incident that also has political ramifications is historically accurate.

A Woman in a Man's World

Usually, the Grail Quest is the purview of the men of Camelot. As Carlos Sanz Mingo writes about books that pre-date Bernard Cornwell's Warlord Chronicles (2004-2016), "It has to be said that, to the best of our knowledge, no former account included women in the actual search of the cauldron (or Grail) except as

---

566   Cooley, "Re-vision from the Mists," 64.

a means to achieve it."⁵⁶⁷ While I have not read Mr. Cornwell's books, women play a key role in the search of the Grail in my version of events. As in many other tales, they are its guardians, but in my story, Guinevere at first plans to go with Arthur on the quest. Even when Morgan interferes with those plans, Guinevere, Morgan, and Grainne (another priestess of Avalon) must work together using their different gifts of The Sight to give Arthur and his knights direction as to where to begin looking.

Rejecting the Convent

As noted throughout this book, the traditional ending for Guinevere is to live out her remaining life in a convent, usually in reparation for her sins. "Guinevere's story, like Arthur's, ends tragically. Perhaps it is this fact that prompts so many women to set all or part of their retellings in Avalon, a place of refuge and escape," argue Alan and Barbara Lupack.⁵⁶⁸

That may have been the case traditionally, but in recent years, more and more authors are choosing another ending for Guinevere, one that keeps her actively in the world. Newman, Woolley, and Miles each show her as a healer and wise woman in her golden years, but I have chosen a different tack, one in keeping with the woman I have created. In my third Guinevere book, *Mistress of Legend*, Guinevere not only outlives Arthur,

---

567 Mingo, Carlos Sanz, "In This Tale of Arthur the Women Do Shine," *Acta Universitattis Danubius*. Vol. 6, no 2, 79.
568 Lupak and Lupak, "The Forgotten Tradition," 24.

but she moves on with her life, seeking refuge in her mother's homeland and becoming crucial to the Votadini's survival when they are threatened not only by the civil war that erupts after the battle of Camlann, but also by the Saxons and Angles seeking to expand their foothold in Britain. By keeping Guinevere in an active role, I wanted to emphasize her agency even well into old age, showing that she did not wither and cower once the men in her life were gone, but found strength within to continue influencing the future of her country in a new way.

Without realizing it, I think I may have been influenced in this regard by seeing so many active older women around me. The average life expectancy of women today is 81.1 years[569] and women are routinely holding on to their jobs well beyond retirement age. I didn't set out to write Guinevere as a role model for aging women, but a busy Guinevere who exercises her mind and body is certainly much better than one like White's who bemoans her lost youth and mourns the wrinkling of her girlish beauty.

It was indeed possible for a woman of Guinevere's time to live to old age. It's difficult to find age records from the year 530 A.D., but we can reasonably assume it would have been close to what it was in 1000 A.D.—fifty-one years.[570] As historian Deborah Harkness notes, if a person lived through 1) childhood, when many deaths occurred, 2) childbirth for women, 3) teen

---

[569] Welch, Ashley. "Life Expectancy for White Women Falls Slightly in U.S.," CBS News, April 20, 2016.
[570] Woodbury, Sarah, "Life Expectancy in the Middle Ages," *Romance and Fantasy in Medieval Wales*, March 27, 2012.

years and work accidents for men and boys, and 4) war for men (and my Guinevere), it wasn't uncommon for them to live into their sixties or seventies.[571]

Hopefully, through my novels I can provide a fully-fleshed out character for women young and old alike to look up to in the generations after me. It's my hope that as women continue to claim their power in modern society, they will learn from Guinevere's mistakes, emulate her strengths, and claim her as the heroine and role model she should be. After all, if Arthur gets to be "the once and future king," who is constantly being resurrected and reinvented by authors and filmmakers, why shouldn't his wife have the same privilege?

---

571 Harkness, Deborah "Worldview." Master Class lecture, Past Tense: History as Resource and Inspiration from Hedgebrook, Whidbey Island, WA, March 7, 2014.

CONCLUSION

Having explored over one thousand years of history and traced Guinevere's rise from literary sinner to feminist icon, the natural question we are left with is "What next?"

The obvious answers are: 1) we have no way of knowing, and 2) the sky is the limit. As we've seen Guineveres who represent everything from models of rigid morality for women to those who seem to have few sexual inhibitions at all, I think it safe to say anything goes as we look to the future. As Brewer points out, "We no longer censure Guinevere—all is understood, all forgiven. She is set free to become a private person, the image of young loveliness or professional competence, and we do not demand that she should maintain the dignity of England's Queen."[572]

Given this new open mindset in regard to the character and how we've seen her embody social ideology in the past, I can imagine that future literature will hold Guineveres who are gay,[573] persons of color,[574] and even single mothers—perhaps Guinevere was left to raise her children alone after the Battle of Camlann

---

572 Brewer, "The Figure of Guenevere," 288.
573 These likely already exist, but have not yet hit the literary mainstream.
574 This wouldn't be out of the realm of historical possibility, as there have been ethnically diverse people in England since at least Roman times. Fans of the television show *Merlin* will note its Guinevere was a person of color, but that doesn't count for the purposes of my argument because it is television, not literature.

made her a widow. Some authors may move the Arthurian legend into modern times and depict Arthur and Guinevere equally sharing household duties and child-rearing. I also have no doubt we will soon see transgender Arthurian legend given how much the issue of gender pervades the consciousness of America as of this writing.

I, for one, would love to see Guinevere continue to take on a feministic role, fighting for issues important to women in the twenty-first century. I bet many others will follow in the footsteps of Lavinia Collins to provide a counterpoint to the "slut shaming" of Guinevere prevalent in traditional Arthurian legend. Perhaps someone will use Guinevere to tackle body image—she doesn't have to be the skinny, traditionally beautiful blonde-haired, blue-eyed woman; if changing her appearance worked for T. H. White, it can work for anyone else—or reproductive rights, equal pay, equal representation in government, or something else that's not even on the radar of the average woman yet. Given the recent controversy surrounding "rape culture," the backlash against victim-shaming, and emphasis on a woman's right to say no, I would expect that Guinevere's kidnapping and subsequent abuse by Malegant will remain fertile ground for authors for years to come as well.

That is the beautiful thing about the Arthurian legend. Its themes are universal and timeless so it can be adapted to any time period or place. The most important thing is that those of us who contribute to the Arthurian legend continue to show Guinevere as an empowered woman, regardless of the other details of our stories. We owe that to ourselves, to the generations of women who will come after us, and to Guinevere herself. Never again should she be the silent, passive woman of Geoffrey of Monmouth or the guilt-ridden harpy of Tennyson or White. Just as women fought for hundreds of years (and in some parts of the world are still fighting) to be recognized as equal to men and there is no going back, neither will Guinevere step back into Arthur's shadow.

What Guinevere needs now is widespread popular exposure. Despite one thousand years of literary history, her story is still relatively unknown in comparison to the men of Camelot. As I was preparing to write this conclusion, I stumbled across a blog post in which the female writer admits to not knowing Guinevere existed until she watched the television show, *Merlin*. "What? He [Arthur] had a queen? He was married? Who knew!"[575] ("Everyone, you ninny," I wanted to say. Apparently, I was wrong.)

While I hope this is an extreme case, it makes clear that writers of the Arthurian legend, particularly females, have a lot of work to do toward placing Guinevere firmly in the minds of the general public. Hopefully, someone—whether it is an author mentioned in this book or a new contributor to Arthuriana—will hit it big with a runaway bestseller about a strong Guinevere

---

[575] Legendary Women, "A Woman of Legend: The Once and Future Queen Guinevere," Medium.com, accessed August 15, 2017 (December 18, 2014), https://medium.com/legendary-women/a-woman-of-legend-the-once-and-future-queen-guinevere-e9783938d134

that makes her as popular and irresistible to Hollywood and big business as Harry Potter. I dream of the days when Guinevere's name is on everyone's lips, books and movies about her abound, and little girls are begging to dress up as her for Halloween.

Until then, we have a wide variety of literature to choose from as we pick books for ourselves and our children, as well as lessons to learn from each retelling. Just as every time period tells us about its people, every version of Guinevere's story teaches us about where our societies have been and where they have the potential to go in the future. Plus, with the advent of self-publishing, for the first time in history, any person who can write has the ability to be the next Malory, Tennyson, or T. H. White, shaping the next incarnation of Guinevere. In the words of Roberta Davidson, "Reflecting upon our literary 'foremothers' in a time when women have found their voices as a party of the literary mainstream and have the power to tell old stories in new way is our latest contribution to the Matter of Arthur. Where we will take it next, only time can tell."[576] I personally can't wait to find out.

---

576 Davidson, "When King Arthur is PG 13," 15.

SOURCES

Ahern, Stephen. "Listening to Guinevere: Female Agency and the Politics of Chivalry in Tennyson's 'Idylls.'" *Studies in Philology*, vol. 101, no. 1 (2014): 88–112. http://www.jstor.org/stable/4174780.

"American Time Use Survey," Bureau of Labor Statistics, United States Department of Labor. December 20, 2016. Accessed August 15, 2017. https://www.bls.gov/tus/charts/household.htm.

Ankiel, Janet. Review of *Guinevere: A Medieval Romance* by Lavinia Collins. Goodreads, May 12, 2016. https://www.goodreads.com/review/show/1636474143.

Beal, Rebecca S. "Guenevere's Tears in the Alliterative *Morte Arthure*: Doubly Wife, Doubly Mother, Doubly Damned," in *On Arthurian Women*, ed. Bonnie Wheeler and Fiona Tolhurst. 1-9. Dallas: Scriptorium Press, 2001.

Benson, C. David. "The Ending of the Morte Darthur" in *A Companion to Malory*, edited by Elizabeth Archibald. 221-238. Woodbridge: D.S. Brewer, 2000.

Bethlehem, Ulrike. "Guinevere, a Medieval Puzzle: Images of Arthur's Queen in the Medieval Literature of England and France." Doctoral Universität, Bochum, 2001.

Bonner, Katherine Alice. "Guinevere as Heroine: Her Development, Dynamics and Demise in the Works of the Middle Ages Through the Present," M.A., Georgia College & State University, 2000.

Bovey, Alice. "Women in Medieval Society." The British Library. April 30, 2015. https://www.bl.uk/the-middle-ages/articles/women-in-medieval-society.

Brewer, Elizabeth. *T. H. White's The Once and Future King*. Cambridge: D.S. Brewer, 1993.

—— "The Figure of Guenevere in Modern Drama and Fiction." In *Lancelot and Guinevere: A Casebook*, edited by Lori Walters, 279-290. New York: Routledge, January 4, 2002.

Bromwich, Rachel. "Celtic Elements in Arthurian Romance: A General Survey." In *The Legend of Arthur in the Middle Ages: Studies presented to A.H. Diverres by Colleagues, Pupils, and Friends*, edited by P. B. Grout et al. 41-55. Cambridge: D.S. Brewer; Torowa N.J., U.S.A.: Biblio Distribution Services, 1983.

—— *Trioedd Ynys Prydein*. Cardiff: University of Wales Press, 2014.

Bruce, Christopher W. "Guinevere the False." *The Arthurian Name Dictionary*. New York: Garland, 1999.

Bumke, Joachim. *Courtly Culture: Literature and Society in the Middle Ages*. London: Duckworth, 2004.

Burns, Jane E. "Which Queen?: Guinevere's Transvestism in the French Prose Lancelot." In *Lancelot and Guinevere: A Casebook*, edited by Lori Walters, 247-266. New York: Routledge, January 4, 2002.

Cannon, Cynthia T. Review of *Guinevere: A Medieval Romance* by Lavinia Collins. Goodreads. May 22, 2016. https://www.goodreads.com/review/show/1646232764.

Capellanus, Andreas. "De Arte Honeste Amandi [The Art of Courtly Love], Book Two: On the Rules of Love." Medieval Sourcebook, accessed July 17, 2017. http://sourcebooks.fordham.edu/source/capellanus.asp.

Chamberlain, David. "Marie de France's Arthurian Lai: Subtle and Political." In *Culture and the King: The Social Implications of Arthurian Legend*. 15-34. Albany: State University of New York Press, 1994.

Comer, Stephanie. "Behold Thy Doom is Mine: The Evolution of Guinevere in the Works of Chrétien de Troyes, Sir Thomas Malory, and Alfred, Lord Tennyson." Master's thesis, Eastern Michigan University, 2008. http://commons.emich.edu/cgi/viewcontent.cgi?article=1163&c

ontext=theses.

Cooley, Sara Diane. "Re-vision from the Mists: The Development of a Literary Genre of Feminist Arthuriana as an Allegorical Response to Second Wave Feminist Politics." Senior capstone project, Paper 520, Vassar College, 2015. http://digitalwindow.vassar.edu/cgi/viewcontent.cgi?article=1517&context=senior_capstone.

Davidson, Roberta. "When King Arthur Is PG 13." *Arthuriana* 22, no. 3 (2012): 5–20. http://www.jstor.org/stable/43485970.

Day, David. *The Quest for King Arthur*. London: Michael O'Mara, 1999.

Daneesha. Review of *Guinevere: A Medieval Romance* by Lavinia Collins. Goodreads. March 25, 2016. https://www.goodreads.com/review/show/1590172142.

Duggan, Joseph J. *The Romances of Chrétien de Troyes*. New Haven: Yale University Press, 2014.

Edwards, Elizabeth. "The Place of Women in the Morte Darthur." In *A Companion to Malory*, edited by Elizabeth Archibald, 37-54. Woodbridge: D.S. Brewer, 2000.

Ellis, Kimberly. "Lancelot and Guinevere: The Love Affair through the Ages." Hanover College, December 12, 2000. http://vault.hanover.edu/~battles/arthur/affair.htm.

Ellis, Peter. *Celtic Women: Women in Celtic Society and Literature*. Grand Rapids: William B. Eerdmans Publishing Company, 1995.

Epstein, Barbara. "What Happened to the Women's Movement?" *Monthly Review: An Independent Socialist Magazine* 53, issue 01 (May 2001). https://monthlyreview.org/2001/05/01/what-happened-to-the-womens-movement/.

Erica. Review of *Guinevere: A Medieval Romance* by Lavinia Collins. Goodreads. May 27, 2016. https://www.goodreads.com/review/show/1650434353.

Evans, Michael R. *Inventing Eleanor: The Medieval and Post-Medieval Image of Eleanor of Aquitaine.* London: Bloomsbury, 2016.

Falsani, Teresa Boyle. "Parke Godwin's Guenevere: An Archetypal Transformation." *Quondam Et Futurus* 3, no. 3 (1993): 55–65. http://www.jstor.org/stable/27870245.

Fletcher, Robert Huntington. "The Arthurian Material in the Chronicles Especially Those of Great Britain and France." In *Studies and Notes in Philology and Literature*, Vol. X. Boston: Ginn and Company, 1906.

Fries, Maureen. "Female Heroes, Heroines, and Counter Heroes." In *Popular Arthurian Traditions,* edited by Sally K. Slocum. 5-17. Bowling Green: B.G.S.U.P.P., 1992.

——— "The Poem in the Tradition of Arthurian Literature." In *The Alliterative Morte Arthure: A Reassessment of the Poem*, edited by Karl Heinz Goller. 30-43. Cambridge: D.S. Brewer, 1981.

Fulton, Helen. "Arthur and Merlin in Early Welsh Literature: Fantasy and Magic Naturalism." In *A Companion to Arthurian Literature,* edited by Helen Fulton. Chichester, England: Wiley-Blackwell, 2009.

Gallagher, Michael. "Is feminism Relevant in 2000?" *BBC News Online,* December 28, 1999, http://news.bbc.co.uk/2/hi/americas/575161.stm.

Geek Girl in Love. "Book Review: The Guinevere Trilogy, by Lavinia Collins." September 22, 2014. https://geekgirlinlove.com/2014/09/22/book-review-the-guinevere-trilogy-by-lavinia-collins/.

Ginnel, Laurence. "Marriage." In *The Brehon Laws*, 1894, chapter 8, section 1. http://www.libraryireland.com/Brehon-Laws/Marriage.php.

Goldsmith, Barbara. *Other Powers: The Age of Suffrage, Spiritualism and the Scandalous Victoria Woodhull.* New York: Alfred A. Knopf, 1998.

Gordon-Wise, Barbara. *The Reclamation of a Queen: Guinevere in Modern Fantasy.* New York: Greenwood Press, 1991.

Gossedge, Rob and Stephen Knight. "The Arthur of the Sixteenth to Nineteenth Centuries." In *The Cambridge Companion to the Arthurian Legend*, edited by Elizabeth Archibald and Ad Putte, 103-119. Cambridge: Cambridge University Press, 2009.

Grove, Elma. Review of *The Warrior Queen* by Lavinia Collins. Goodreads. April 17, 2014. https://www.goodreads.com/review/show/912691576.

Harkness, Deborah "Worldview." Master Class lecture, Past Tense: History as Resource and Inspiration from Hedgebrook, Whidbey Island, WA, March 7, 2014.

Herman, Harold J. "Sharan Newman's Guinevere Trilogy." In *Lancelot and Guinevere: A Casebook*, edited by Lori Walters. 291-309. New York: Routledge, January 4, 2002.

Higham, N.J. *King Arthur: Myth-Making and History*. London: Routledge, 2009.

Hoberg, Tom. "In Her Own Right: The Guenevere of Parke Goodwin." In *Popular Arthurian Traditions*, edited by Sally K. Slocum. 68-79. Bowling Green: Bowling Green State University Popular Press, 1992.

Hodges, Kenneth. "Guinevere's Politics in Malory's 'Morte Darthur.'" *The Journal of English and Germanic Philology* 104, no. 1 (2005): 54–79. http://www.jstor.org/stable/27712477.

Hopkins, Andrea. *The Book of Guinevere*. Salford: Saraband, 2004.

Hopkins, Annette Brown. "The Influence of Wace on the Arthurian Romances of Crestian de Troies." PhD thesis, University of Chicago, 1912. Menasha: George Banta., 1913.

Howey, Ann. "Once and Future Women: Popular Fiction, Feminism and Four Arthurian Rewritings." PhD thesis, University of Alberta, Spring 1997. http://www.collectionscanada.gc.ca/obj/s4/f2/dsk3/ftp04/nq21579.pdf.

Howey, Ann and Stephen R. Reimer. *A Bibliography of Modern Arthuriana* (1500-2000), Cambridge: D.S. Brewer, 2006.

Jillian. Review of *The Warrior Queen* by Lavinia Collins. Goodreads. December 1, 2014. https://www.goodreads.com/review/show/1120444295.

Jillings, L. G. "The Ideal of Queenship in Hartman's Erec." In *The Legend of Arthur in the Middle Ages: Studies presented to A.H. Diverres by Colleagues, Pupils, and Friends*, edited by P. B. Grout et al. Cambridge: D.S. Brewer; Torowa N.J., U.S.A.: Biblio Distribution Services, 1983113-128.

Johnson, Jacquelyn Sweeney. "Guenevere's Conflict: Pagan Love or Christian Ethics." Master's thesis, Longwood University, 2003. http://digitalcommons.longwood.edu/etd/121.

Joy. Review of *The Day of Destiny* by Lavinia Collins. Goodreads. November 12, 2014. https://www.goodreads.com/review/show/1104270293.

Ju, Anne. "Women's Studies at Cornell Evolves over 40-year History to include Sexual Minorities." *Cornell Chronicle*. November 4, 2009.

Kennedy, Edward Donald. "Introduction." In *King Arthur: A Casebook*. New York: Routledge, 2013.

Knight, Stephen. "Queen Guinevere." *The Politics of Myth*. 63-86. Strawberry Hills, NSW: ReadHowYouWant, 2015.

Korrel, Peter. *An Arthurian Triangle: A Study of the Development and Characterization of Arthur, Guinevere and Mordred*. Leiden: E.J. Brill, 1984.

Krueger, Roberta L. "Desire, Meaning and the Female Reader." In *Lancelot and Guinevere: A Casebook*, edited by Lori Walters. 229-246. New York: Routledge, January 4, 2002.

Lacy, Norris J. *The New Arthurian Encyclopedia: New Edition*. New York: Taylor and Francis, 2013.

Le Saux, Françoise Hazel Marie. *A Companion to Wace*. Woodbridge:

Boydell & Brewer, 2010.

Legendary Women. "A Woman of Legend: The Once and Future Queen Guinevere." Medium.com. December 18, 2014. Accessed August 15, 2017. https://medium.com/legendary-women/a-woman-of-legend-the-once-and-future-queen-guinevere-e9783938d134.

Leyser, Henrietta. *Medieval Women: A Social History of England 450—1500*. London: Phoenix Press, 2003.

Lupack, Allan and Barbara Lupack. "The Forgotten Tradition." In *Arthurian Literature by Women: An Anthology*. 3-30. New York: Routledge, 2013.

Lyons, Bex. Review of *The Day of Destiny* by Lavinia Collins. Goodreads. August 21, 2014. https://www.goodreads.com/review/show/1032760743.

Macleod, Sharon Paice. *Celtic Myth and Religion: A Study of Traditional Belief.* Jefferson: McFarland & Co., Inc., 2012.

Mancoff, Debra N. "To Take Excalibur: King Arthur and the Construction of Victorian Manhood." In *King Arthur: A Casebook*, edited by Edward Donald Kennedy. 257-280. New York: Routledge, December 1, 1995.

Markale, Jean. *Women of the Celts*. Rochester, Vt: Inner Traditions International, 1986, 1972.

Martin, Leonide. review of *Guinevere: A Medieval Romance* by Lavinia Collins. Goodreads. January 25, 2017. https://www.goodreads.com/review/show/1883086029.

Mason, Eugene. "Introduction." In *French Medieval Romances: From the Lays of Marie de France*. Auckland, New Zealand: The Floating Press, 2013.

—— "Introduction." In *Arthurian Chronicles: Roman de Brut*. Auckland: The Floating Press, 2013.

Matthews, John. *King Arthur: Dark Age Warrior and Mythic Hero*. New York: NY Rosen Publishing, 2008.

Matthews, John and Caitlin. *The Complete King Arthur: Many Faces, One Hero*. Rochester, Vt: Inner Traditions, 2017.

Medeiros, Jessica. "Why Marie De France Was A Medieval Bad Ass." *The Odyssey*. August 22, 2016. https://www.theodysseyonline.com/why-marie-de-france-was-medieval-bad-ass.

Medieval Bex. "Interview with Lavinia Collins, author of The Warrior Queen." Interview by Rebecca E. Lyons, June 5, 2014. https://medievalbex.com/2014/05/06/interview-with-lavinia-collins-author-of-the-warrior-queen/.

Merriman, James Douglas. *The Flower of Kings: a Study of the Arthurian Legend in England Between 1485 and 1835*. Lawrence: The University Press of Kansas, 1973.

Mingo, Carlos Sanz. "In This Tale of Arthur the Women do Shine." *Acta Universitattis Danubius*, Vol. 6, no. 2, 74-94. http://journals.univ-danubius.ro/index.php/communicatio/article/view/1585.

MorgauseofOrkney. "'The Poisoned Apple'- Thoughts," *In My Defens*, August 29, 2014. http://morgauseoforkney.tumblr.com/post/96110372023/the-poisoned-apple-thoughts.

Noble, James. "Guinevere, the Superwoman of Contemporary Arthurian Fiction." *Florilegium*, vol. 23.2 (2006): 197-210. https://journals.lib.unb.ca/index.php/flor/article/viewFile/12554/20003.

Noble, Peter. "The Character of Guinevere in the Arthurian Romances of Chrétien De Troyes." *The Modern Language Review* 67, no. 3 (1972): 524–535. http://www.jstor.org/stable/3726121.

Perkin, Harold. *The Rise of Professional Society: England Since 1880*. New York: Routledge, 2016.

Preston, Tricia. Review of *Guinevere: A Medieval Romance* by Lavinia

Collins. Amazon. June 21, 2016. https://www.amazon.co.uk/Guinevere-medieval-romance-Lavinia-Collins/dp/1505488729

Quilligan, Maureen. "Arthur's Sister's Story." *The New York Times*. January 30, 1983. http://www.nytimes.com/1983/01/30/books/arthur-s-sister-s-story.html.

Raluca Radulescu. "Why the Legend of King Arthur Still Resounds Today." *Newsweek*. February 3, 2017. http://www.newsweek.com/king-arthur-round-table-myth-literature-552155.

Rampton, Martha. "Four Waves of Feminism." *Pacific Magazine*. Fall 2008. https://www.pacificu.edu/about-us/news-events/four-waves-feminism.

Rhys, John. *Studies in Arthurian Legend*. Oxford: Clarendon Press, 1891.

Ross, Meredith. "The Sublime to the Ridiculous: The Restructuring of Arthurian Materials in Selected Modern Novels." PhD diss., University of Wisconsin–Madison, 1985.

Roth, Mark. "The Historic Roots of the Middle Class." *Pittsburgh Gazette*. November 20, 2011. http://www.post-gazette.com/local/region/2011/11/20/The-historic-roots-of-the-middle-class/stories/201111200308.

Samples, Susann. "Guinevere: A Re-Appraisal." In *Lancelot and Guinevere: A Casebook,* edited by Lori Walters. 219-228. New York: Routledge, January 4, 2002.

Sheila. Review of *Guinevere: A Medieval Romance* Lavinia Collins. Goodreads. May 19, 2016. https://www.goodreads.com/review/show/1643196189.

Silver, Carole G. "'The Defence of Guenevere': A Further Interpretation." *Studies in English Literature, 1500-1900*, 9.4 (1969): 695–702. http://www.jstor.org/stable/450041.

Simpson, David L. "Chivalry and Courtly Love." The School for New Learning, DePaul University. Accessed July 14, 2017. http://condor.depaul.edu/dsimpson/tlove/courtlylove.html.

Slocum, Sally K., ed. "Popular Arthurian Traditions." In *Popular Arthurian Traditions*, edited by Sally K. Slocum, Bowling Green: B.G.S.U.P.P., 1992.

Stanford, Peter. "The Books Interview: Rosalind Miles - A Feminist in Camelot." *The Independent*. 1999. http://www.independent.co.uk/arts-entertainment/the-books-interview-rosalind-miles-a-feminist-in-camelot-1090684.html.

Struve, Laura. "The Public Life and Private Desires of Women in William Morris's 'The Defence of Guenevere.'" *Arthuriana* 6.3 (October 3, 1996): 15-29. http://morrisedition.lib.uiowa.edu/StruveDG.pdf.

Swabey, Fiona. *Eleanor of Aquitaine, Courtly Love, and the Troubadours*. Westport: Greenwood Press, 2014.

Swanson, Kelsey. "Guinevere: Victorian Gender, Sexuality and Nature." Literature 330: Romancing Arthur, Harlaxton College, April 8, 2010. https://www.harlaxton.ac.uk/academics/downloads/honors/SwansonKelsey.pdf.

Terric853. Review of *Guinevere: A Medieval Romance* by Lavinia Collins. Goodreads. June 2, 2016. https://www.goodreads.com/review/show/1656965950.

Thomas, Alfred. *Reading Women in Late Medieval Europe: Anne of Bohemia and Chaucer's Female Audience*. New York: Palgrave Macmillan, 2015.

Thompson, Jack George. *Women in Celtic Law and Culture*. Lewiston: Edwin Mellen, 1996.

Thompson, Raymond M. *The Return from Avalon: A Study of the Arthurian Legend in Modern Fiction*. Westport: Greenwood Press, 1985.

Tichelaar, Tyler. "While King Arthur was Away, Did Guinevere with Mordred Play?" Children of Arthur. Accessed June 12, 2017. https://childrenofarthur.wordpress.com/2011/06/19/while-king-arthur-was-away-did-guinevere-with-mordred-play/.

—— *King Arthur's Children*. Ann Arbor: Modern History Press, 2010.

Tolhurst, Fiona. "What Ever Happened to Eleanor? Reflections of Eleanor of Aquitaine in Wace's *Roman de Brut* and Lawman's *Brut*." In *Eleanor of Aquitaine: Lord and Lady*, edited by Bonnie Wheeler and John Carmi Parsons, 319-336. New York: Palgrave Macmillan, 2008.

Umland, Rebecca. "The Snake in the Woodpile: Tennyson's Vivien as Victorian Prostitute." In *Culture and the King: The Social Implications of the Arthurian Legend*, edited by James P Carley, Valerie M Lagorio, and Martin B Shichtman, 274-287. Albany: New York State University of New York Press, 1994.

Vallas, Estelle. "Feminist Icon or Ruthless Warrior? Guinevere in Bernard Cornwell's The Warlord Chronicles." In *Theorising the Popular*, edited by Michael Brennen, 136-149. Newcastle upon Tyne, UK: Cambridge Scholars Publishing, 2017.

Walters, Lori. "Introduction." In *Lancelot and Guinevere: A Casebook*, edited by Lori Walters, xiii-lxv. New York: Routledge, January 4, 2002.

Welch, Ashley. "Life Expectancy for White Women Falls Slightly in U.S." *CBS News*. April 20, 2016. http://www.cbsnews.com/news/life-expectancy-for-white-women-falls-slightly-in-u-s/.

Whalen, Logan. *A Companion to Marie de France*. Boston: Brill, 2011.

Whitaker, Muriel. "Unifying Makers: Lancelot and Guinevere in Modern Literature and Art." In *Lancelot and Guinevere: A Casebook*, edited by Lori Walters, 159-180. New York: Routledge, January 4, 2002.

Wikipedia. "Guinevere." Accessed January 23, 2017. https://en.wikipedia.org/wiki/Guinevere.

Woodbury, Sarah. "Guinevere (in Welsh Gwenhwyfar)." Romance and Fantasy in Medieval Wales. March 27, 2012. http://www.sarahwoodbury.com/guinevere-in-welsh-gwenhwyfar/.

—— "Life Expectancy in the Middle Ages." Romance and Fantasy in

Medieval Wales. March 11, 2014. http://www.sarahwoodbury.com/life-expectancy-in-the-middle-ages/.

Wyatt, Siobhan. *Women of Words in Le Morte Darthur: The Autonomy of Speech in Malory's Female Characters*. London: Springer International Publishing, Palgrave Macmillan, 2016.

PRIMARY SOURCES:

Benson, Larry D., ed. and Edward E. Foster, rev. *King Arthur's Death: The Middle English Stanzaic Morte Arthur and Alliterative Morte Arthure*. Medieval Institute Publications Kalamazoo, Michigan, 1994. http://d.lib.rochester.edu/teams/text/benson-and-foster-king-arthurs-death-alliterative-morte-arthur-part-iii.

Bradley, Marion Zimmer. *The Mists of Avalon*. New York: Random House Publishing Group, 2001.

Bradshaw, Gillian. *In Winter's Shadow*. 1981. Naperville: Sourcebooks Landmark, 2011.

Caradoc of Llancarfan. *The Life of Gildas*. Celtic Literature Collective. http://www.maryjones.us/ctexts/gildas06.html.

Collins, Lavinia. *A Champion's Duty*. London: The Book Folks, 2014.

—— *Guinevere: A Medieval Romance*. London: The Book Folks, 2014.

—— *The Day of Destiny*. London: The Book Folks, 2014.

—— *The Warrior Queen*. London: The Book Folks, 2014.

De France, Marie. *Marie de France: Poetry*. International Student Edition. New York: W. W. Norton & Company, 2015.

De Troyes, Chrétien. *Lancelot, or The Knight of the Cart*. Herklion Press, 2013.

Evelina, Nicole. *Camelot's Queen*. Maryland Heights, MO: Lawson Gartner Publishing, 2016.

—— *Daughter of Destiny*. Maryland Heights, MO: Lawson Gartner Publishing, 2016.

—— *Mistress of Legend*. Maryland Heights, MO: Lawson Gartner Publishing, forthcoming.

Godwin, Park. *Beloved Exile*. Reprint edition. New York: Avon Books, 1994.

Krishna, Valerie. *The Alliterative Morte Arthure: A New Verse Translation*. Washington, D.C.: University Press of America, 1983.

Lacy, Norris, J. *The Lancelot-Grail Reader: Selections from the Medieval French Arthurian Cycle*. New York: Garland Pub., 2000.

Layamon. *Roman de Brut*. Auckland: The Floating Press, 2013.

McKenzie, Nancy. *Queen of Camelot*. New York: Random House, 1994, 1995.

Malory, Thomas. "Le Morte d'Arthur." In *The King Arthur Collection*. Rochester: Maplewood Books, 2014.

Malory, Thomas. *The Morte Darthur, Parts Seven and Eight*. Edited by Derek Brewer. Evanston, Illinois: Northwestern University Press, 1987, 1968.

Miles, Rosalind. *Guenevere, Queen of the Summer Country*. New York: Three Rivers Press, 1998.

—— *The Child of the Holy Grail*. New York: Crown, 2001.

—— *The Knight of the Sacred Lake*. New York: Crown, 2000.

Monmouth, Geoffrey. *The History of the Kings of Britain*. Peterborough, Ontario: Broadview Press, January 1, 2008.

Morris, William. *The Defence of Guenevere and Other Poems*. New York: Longmans, Green and Co., 1908.

Nennius, Bill Gunn and Mark the Hermit, ed. *The Historia Brittonum*. London: John and Arthur Arch, 1819.

Newman, Sharan. *Guinevere*. New York: Tor, 1981, 1996.

—— *Guinevere Evermore* New York: Tor, 1981, 1996.

—— *The Chessboard Queen*. New York: Tor, 1985.

Stewart, Mary. *The Merlin Trilogy*. New York: Eos, 2004.

Stone, Brian, trans. "Alliterative Morte Arthure" In *King Arthur's Death*. London: Penguin Books, 1988, 7-168.

Tennyson, Alfred Lord. "Guinevere" *Idylls of a King*. Public domain book, 2012. https://www.amazon.com/Idylls-King-Baron-Alfred-Tennyson-ebook/dp/B0082Z5JBA.

Wace. *Arthurian Chronicles: Roman de Brut*, translated by Eugene Mason. Auckland: The Floating Press, 2013.

White, T. H., *The Once and Future King*. London: HarperCollins, 1994.

Woolley, Persia. *Child of the Northern Spring*. Naperville: Sourcebooks, 2010.

—— *Guinevere: The Legend in Autumn*. Naperville: Sourcebooks, 2011.

—— *Queen of the Summer Stars*. Naperville: Sourcebooks, 2011.

Index

A

A Champion's Duty, 10, 208
adultery, 7, 13-15, 20-21, 24, 33,
  37, 46-47, 50-50, 57, 59, 61,
  62n134, 64, 68-70, 72-75,
  77-78, 85-87, 97-102, 106,
  111, 120-121, 131, 147, 163,
  168-169, 182, 188, 197, 209,
  218, 223
Agravain, 87, 95-96, 100, 225
Aggrivane. *See* Agravain
Ahern, Stephen, 114-116, 122-123
Alliterative Morte Arthure, 8, 12,
  90-94, 106
Amazon, 11, 207, 210n536, 211
Amesbury, 98, 100-112
Amhar. *See* Amr
Amr, 19, 33
Anir, *See* Amr
Arthur, King, 11-12, 14-15, 21,
  25, 31, 33, 38-41, 46-47, 50,
  53, 59, 61-62, 68, 70, 74, 76,
  83-88, 94, 99-100, 107, 108,
  112, 114-118, 120-121, 134-
  135, 138-139, 146-149, 154,
  156-158, 162-163, 168-169,
  179, 182-183, 186-187, 196-
  198, 204, 208-211, 220
Avalon, 22, 49, 158, 160, 197-
  198, 217, 222-223, 227-228

B

Badon, 14
Beal, Rebecca S., 92-94
Bedivere, 13, 21, 148, 166, 168-169
Bedwyr. *See* Bedivere
Beloved Exile, 19, 161-166, 216
Benson, C. David, 91, 97-98,
  102-103
Bertholai, 84
Bethlehem, Ulrike, 17
Bible, 8, 44, 78, 99
Boece, Hector, 24,
Bonner, Katherine Alice, 27, 41-
  42, 49-50, 52, 55, 61-63, 68,
  72-73, 76, 101, 104, 112-113,
  118, 120-122, 126, 128-129,
  131, 139, 140, 144-145, 154,
  157, 159, 173, 178, 180-182,
  192, 202
Book of Guinevere, The, 6, 24, 29,
  47, 65, 77
Bors, 96, 141
Boy and the Mantle, The, 78
Bradley, Marion Zimmer, 9,
  27-28, 151-160, 177, 188-
  189, 199, 200, 202, 212, 217,
  222-224
Bradshaw, Gillian, 10, 23, 166-
  171, 176
Breton (language), 5, 12

Breton (from Brittany), *See* Brittany
Brewer, Elizabeth, 119, 129, 136, 138-140, 142-143, 168, 174, 210, 218, 226, 231
Britain, 18, 30, 36-38, 48-49, 51, 94, 119, 145-146, 152, 154, 162, 164, 167, 179-180, 193, 198, 206, 209, 213, 224n563, 225, 228, *See also* England
Brittany, 47n84, 77, 207, 212
Bromwich, Rachel, 11-12, 16, 35-38, 38-39
Bruce, Christopher W., 84, 111
Bumke, Joachim, 69n159, 74
Burns, Jane E., 84-86

C

Cador, 15, 180
Caerleon, 52-53, 93, 157
Cai. See Kay
Camelot, 2, 7, 13, 14, 17, 21, 23-24, 26, 48, 51, 62, 69, 88, 97, 100, 105, 111-112, 114, 117, 134, 146, 158, 163, 169-171, 173, 176-178, 182-184, 195, 198-199, 208-209, 220
Camelot (movie), 1, 137
Camelot (musical), 22, 95
Camelot's Queen, 207n529, 218, 226
Camille, 86
Camlann, Battle of, 14-15, 19, 24, 38, 171, 184, 189, 229, 231
Cannon, Cynthia T., 213
Capellanus, Andreas, 68-70
Caradoc of Llancarven, 46
Catholic Church, 2, 42-44, 155, 158, 166, 188, 198, 220, *See also* Catholic religion; Christianity
Catholic religion, 8, 108, *See also* Catholic Church; Christianity
Celtic law, 23, 31-32, 38-39, 43, 48, 188, 224n562
Celtic myth, 7, 13-14, 33-34, 36, 40, 47
Celtic women, 32-33, 36, 38, 146, 188, 195
Chamberlain, David, 78
Champion's Duty, A, 208
chastity, 44, 52, 53, 76, 78, 86, 88, 99, 100, 106, 117, 119, 212
Chessboard Queen, The, 178, 180, 182-183
Child Queen, The, 191-194
Child of the Northern Spring, 185-190
chivalry, 60, 101-102, 116, 211, 226
Chrétien de Troyes. *See* de Troyes, Chrétien
Christianity, 42, 54, 94, 104, 152, 153, 155, 158-159, 165, 179, 188, 196, 198, 200, 220, 224, *See also* Catholic Church; Catholic religion
Cistercian, monks 7, 17, 82, 89, 143
Clarent, 90, 94

Claris et Laris, 21
Cleodalis, 83
Collins, Lavinia, 205, 207-215, 225, 232
Comer, Stephanie, 4-5, 44, 66-67, 71, 74-75, 101, 105, 111, 112-114, 117-119, 122-124
convent, 22-23, 44-45, 52-53, 59-60, 63, 82, 93, 100, 104, 105, 110-112, 118, 141, 155, 159, 164-170, 184, 189, 191n495, 218, 220, 228
   as refuge for women, 22, 100,
   as source of female power, 23, 44-45, 169, 170
   Guinevere in, 22-23, 52-53, 59-60, 63, 93, 100, 105, 110-112, 119, 141, 159, 164-70, 184, 189, 191n495, 218, 220, 228
Cooley, Sara, 3, 146, 149, 153-154, 173, 175-177, 182, 186-189, 205, 212, 223, 226
courtly love, 7, 20, 46, 55-56, 59, 67-76, 80, 116, 128, 166
"Culhwch and Olwen," 31, 33
Cywyrd Gwent, 16, 35

D

Davidson, Roberta, 147, 203, 234
Day, David, 56, 97-98
Day of Destiny, 208, 212-213
Daughter of Destiny, 207n529, 216-230
De Excidio Britanniae, 14
de Champagne, Marie, 45, 66, 68, 71, 73-75,
de France, Marie, 7, 20, 21, 57, 76-80, 81
de Troyes, Chrétien, 7, 20-21, 27, 64-81, 87, 91-92, 100-101, 106, 113, 126, 131
Defence of Guenevere, 8, 27, 125-131
devil/demon, 89, 110, 203
Dialogue of Melwas and Gwenhwyfar, The, 30-31
Diu Crone, 18-19
Du Cor, 78
Duggan, Joseph J., 37

E

Eden, Garden of, 26
Edwards, Elizabeth, 105-106
Eleanor of Aquitaine, 45, 55-57
Elaine, 10, 86-87, 99, 102, 111, 113, 117, 141, 143, 146, 182, 191-193, 217, 222
Ellis, Kimberly, 117, 121
Ellis, Peter, 32-33, 48n88,
England, 51, 55, 57, 99, 108, 135n342, 152, 231n574, *See also* Britain
Epstein, Barbara, 201
Erec and Enid, 65
Etain, 36

Evans, Michael R. 57
Evelina, Nicole 11, 216-230
Eve, 2, 8, 16, 17, 21, 26, 42, 43, 51, 88, 94, 97
evil 2-3, 7, 60-63, 66n148, 77, 88, 95, 106, 123, 129, 200, 216

F

Faerie Queen, The, 107
Fairy of the Lake, The, 18
Fairy Queen, 79
fallen woman, 8, 110n262, 112, 123-124
Falsani, Teresa Boyle, 124, 129-130, 164-165
female authors, 3, 10, 133, 145-146, 149, 154, 191, 195, 198-199, 202, 225, 232
female characters, 9, 17, 28-29, 85, 88, 92, 114, 130, 138, 143, 145, 147-148, 152, 154, 165, 172-173, 177, 94-195, 199-200, 202-204, 210, 218, 225, 233
feminism, 1-3, 9-10,17, 28, 49, 79, 144, 148-151, 153-154, 159-160, 171-174, 177, 187, 189-190, 193-194, 199-202, 205-206, 208, 212, 232
  feminist Arthuriana, 79, 144, 149, 154, 159-160, 171, 177, 187, 190, 194-195, 199-202, 204, 208, 212, 216,230, 232, 234
  Fourth Wave, 206n524, 206n527
  Second Wave, 3, 10, 17, 19, 25, 28, 133, 138, 144, 153, 169, 171-172, 175-176, 183, 185, 187, 189-190, 202-203
  suffrage and, 119-120
  Third Wave, 3, 6, 10, 17, 25, 29, 152, 154, 185, 189, 193, 199-204
  unpopularity of, 199-201, 205-206
Firelord, 19, 161-163
Flower Bride, 7, 33-34, 36, 40, 47
France, 56, 100, 208
French Arthurian Legend, 5, 7, 19, 21, 24, 58, 64-81, 84, 88, 91, 101
Fries, Maureen, 26-27, 34, 53, 73, 76, 92-93, 104, 133
Fulton, Helen, 37

G

Galahad, 20, 181-182
Gallagher, Michael, 206
Garden of Eden, 26
Garlin of Gore, King, 18
Gawain, 21, 87, 95, 101,
Gaynore, 12, *See also* Guinevere
Geek Girl in Love (blogger), 214-215

gender, 28, 80, 85, 115, 122, 145-146, 148, 152, 158, 160, 175, 199, 206, 209n533, 232
Genesis, 26, 43
"Gereint and Enid," 33
German, 5, 12, 18-19
Geoffrey of Monmouth, 7, 11, 15, 18, 27, 37, 41-42, 46, 48-56, 58-59, 61-63, 89, 91, 104, 106-107, 221, 233
Ginevra, 12, *See also* Guinevere
Ginnel, Laurence, 48
Ginover, 12, *See also* Guinevere
Givevara, 12, *See* also Guinevere
Glastonbury, 25, 46, 101
God, 44, 97, 100n235, 155, 156, 157, 158
goddess worship, 17, 152-153, 158, 179, 195, 198-200, 224
goddesses, 16-17, 36, 152, 181, 195, 199
Godwin, Park, 10, 19, 161-166, 171, 184, 217
Gogrvan/Gogfran/Ocvran the Giant, 16, 18, 35
Goldsmith, Barbara, 120n295
Goodreads, 11, 210-215
Gordon-Wise, Barbara, 5, 16-17, 22-23, 26, 28, 35, 38, 49, 51, 62, 75, 78, 83-85, 89, 112, 117, 120, 122, 147-148, 155, 158, 160, 163-168, 171, 174, 179, 184, 220, 222-223
Gossedge, Rob, 108, 128

Great Campaigns, The, 137
Green Man, The, 137
Grove, Elma, 213
Guanhumara, 11, 65, *See also* Guinevere
Guenever, 12, *See also* Guinevere
Guenevere: Queen of the Summer Country, 194-195
Guenevere, 27, 77, 82, 92-93, 95, 125-130, 138, 163, 174, 194-195, 210, 226, *See also* Guinevere
Guenhumara 11, 147, *See* also Guinevere
Guiamor, 21, *See also* Guinevere
Guinevere
  agency of, 10, 26, 73, 149, 161, 166, 172, 193, 201, 210, 228, 232
  appearance of, 7, 15, 50, 58, 63, 76, 86, 115, 137, 139, 166, 186, 203, 229, 233
  as child, 3, 176-179, 180, 182, 192, 216, 220-224, 229
  as downfall of Camelot, 22-24, 51, 88, 100, 112, 158, 169, 177, 220
  as healer, 25, 184, 228
  as minor character, 2, 6, 26, 41, 49, 53, 63, 65, 92, 106-107, 118, 136
  as model of courtly love, 67-76, 116, 128
  as mother to her people, 4, 29,

183, 186, 197
as object of affection, 67-68, 88, 139
as pagan, 10, 165, 186, 198, 222-225
as possession, 31
as role model, 4, 20, 44, 65, 103, 106, 130, 160, 172, 219, 223, 298-230, 231
as strong woman, 11, 29, 72, 76, 126, 147, 167, 172, 192-193, 195, 200-203, 211, 215, 217, 219-221, 223-224, 233
as symbol of:
   Eve, 2, 8, 16, 17, 21, 26, 42, 43, 51, 88, 94, 97
   Goddess, 16-17, 36, 116, 152, 181
   Grief, 92-94
   ideal woman, 45, 65-67, 71, 76, 103, 123, 136
   Lancelot's fatal flaw, 88, 97, 100, 121
   Mary Magdalene, 8, 16, 17, 51, 104, 123
   morality for Arthur's court, 8, 79, 105, 120
   sovereignty, 17, 36, 47
as warrior, 169, 195, 208-209, 212, 215, 225
barren, 2, 19, 51, 56, 61, 116, 142, 156, 173-174, 181, 187, 189, 196, 218
children of, 19-20, 92, 182, 189, 196, 198
dependent on men, 76, 139, 146, 149, 151-160, 193, 221
death of, 15, 24-25, 62
duty to correct men/knights, 67, 71, 105, 115-116
equality with Arthur, 10, 29, 72, 161-163, 174, 186-187, 195, 196, 209, 224-225, 233
family of, 17-19, 83, 92, 155-156, 167, 195, 197, 208, 220-221, 224
fear of Arthur and/or Mordred, 53, 59, 62, 87, 93, 111
grief of, 52, 57, 92-94, 106, 219
guilt of, 7, 20, 51, 57, 59-60, 84, 87-89, 91, 106, 112-113, 117, 155, 157, 170, 196-197, 233
historical authenticity, 14-15, 41, 136, 154
inconsistent characterization of, 8, 40, 65-66, 74, 80, 101, 103, 104, 105, 115, 197, 208, 213
in convent, 22-23, 52-53, 59-60, 63, 93, 100, 105, 106, 110-112, 118, 141, 159, 164-70, 184, 189, 191n 495, 218, 220, 228
independence of, 8, 44, 72-83, 85, 126, 128-130, 157-158, 164-168, 176, 180, 183,

184, 195, 200, 209, 212-213, 217, 220, 232
kidnapping of, 7, 13, 33, 46-48, 66, 94, 99, 164, 192, 227, 232
lineage, 18, 50, 58, 221
lovers of, 20-21
name, 1, 11-12
personality of:
  cold, 65, 95
  evil/unlikeable, 30, 40, 61, 63, 66, 72-73, 77, 86, 95, 111, 115-116, 12-131, 136, 138, 140-143, 147, 156
  good person 40, 58, 65, 74, 40, 148, 161, 167, 178, 181
  immature, 180-182, 192
  intelligent, 31, 134, 148, 161, 162, 211-214, 221, 224
  jealous, 68, 74, 77, 87, 113, 116, 139-143, 162-163, 199, 222
  lonely, 147, 181
  manipulative, 65-66, 75, 77-78, 96, 126-131, 137, 141-142, 148-149, 204
  no personality, 27, 75, 88, 148
  passive, 49, 148, 155, 193, 233
  prideful/self-centered, 66, 69, 93, 113, 128, 137, 104-142, 178, 180, 192, 200-221

seductress 77, 79, 121, 137, 142, 164, 204
weak, 9, 22, 50, 105, 115, 139, 140, 141, 144, 146, 149, 151-160, 167, 181, 192-193
power over Lancelot, 67-71, 76, 83, 120, 126
rescue of, 13-14, 31, 46-47, 66, 87, 99-100, 128, 157, 164, 168, 177, 183, 195, 207, 210-213
rumors about, 95-96, 99-100, 111, 209
sexuality of, 1, 11, 80, 121, 188-189, 212
treason of, 14, 46, 51-52, 92, 94, 106, 126
True and the False, the, 8, 17, 38-39, 82-85, 110n262
unfeminist portrayals of, 9, 146-147, 151-159
See also Gaynore, Ginevra, Ginover, Givevara, Guanhumara, Guenever, Guenevere, Guiamor, Gwehywfar, Gwenhwyfach, Gwenhwyfawr, Gwenwhyfar, Gwynnever, Waynor, Wehaver, Wenneuereia, Winlogee
Guinevere (Sharan Newman), 178-180
Guinevere: A Medieval Romance, 208-215

Guinevere Evermore, 178, 181
Guinevere's Tale, 216, 218
Guinevere: The Legend in Autumn, 185
Gwehywfar, 11, 16, 30, 33, 35-36, 65, See also Guinevere
Gwenhwyfach, 17, See also Guinevere
Gwenhwyfawr, 17, See also Guinevere
Gwenwhyfar, 37-39, See also Guinevere
Gwinfreda, 12, See also Guinevere
Gwydre, 33
Gwyn ap Nudd, 33
Gwynnever, 12, See also Guinevere
Gwythyr ap Greidawl, 33, 36

H

Harkness, Deborah, 229
Heresy, 62n134
Herman, Harold J., 178, 180-181, 183
Higham, N.J., 136
High Queen, The, 191
History of the Kings of Britain, The, 15, 18, 48, 52, 58-59
Hoberg, Tom, 146-148, 162-163, 165
Hodges, Kenneth, 97, 102
homosexuality, 78
Hopkins, Andrea, 6, 24, 29, 47, 65, 77

Hopkins, Annette Brown, 50, 59-60
Howey, Ann, 98-99, 133, 148, 154, 156, 159, 162-163, 169, 172, 202
Hughes, Thomas, 107

I

Idylls of the King, 8, 110-125, 132
incest, 59, 83, 197
Industrial Revolution, 109, 135n342
In Winter's Shadow, 10, 23, 166-171

J

James I, 108
Jillings, L. G., 104
Johnson, Jacquelyn Sweeney, 42, 152, 155-158, 173. 195-200, 224
Ju, Anne, 145

K

Kay, 1, 20, 31, 66, 210, 214
Kennedy, Edward Donald, 88, 120
kidnapping, 7, 13, 33, 46-48, 66, 86, 94, 99, 164, 192, 227, 232
King Arthur. See Arthur, King
King Garlin of Gore. See Garlin of Gore, King

King Leodgrance of Cameliard. *See*
   Leodgrance of Cameliard, King
Knight of the Cart, The, 64-81
Knight, Stephen, 108, 168
Korrel, Peter, 19, 40, 46, 51, 59,
   62, 78, 107
Krueger, Roberta L., 67
Kulwch, 31

L

Lacy, Norris J., 26, 45, 56, 82,
   103, 175, 186, 192, 195
Lancelot, 13-14, 30, 33, 47, 64-
   74, 76, 84, 86-89, 95-97, 99-
   106, 111-115, 117, 121, 126,
   130-131, 138-141, 157, 159,
   181-184, 188-189, 197-198,
   209-211, 225
   as model of courtly love 68-72
   enthralled by Guinevere 67-
      71, 76, 83, 126
   superhuman strength of
      69n131, 70-71, 100
Lancelot, 24, 65-68, 86-89, 92
Lancelot: A Novel, 137
Lancelot-Grail Cycle, 82-90
Lanval, 21, 76, 77-78
Lanval, 21, 77-78
Lanzelet, 19, 21
Layamon, 7, 12, 25, 27, 40, 42,
   55-56, 60-63, 89, 91
Le Saux, Françoise Hazel Marie,
   56, 58-59

Leodagan, 85
Leodgrance of Cameliard, King, 18
Leyser, Henrietta, 43-45
Life of Gildas, The, 7, 46-48
Llacheu, 19, 33
Loholt, 19, 24
Love triangle
   Guinevere/Arthur/Lancelot,
      33, 64-65, 139, 141, 156-
      157, 210-211
   Guinevere/Arthur/Mordred, 61
   Isolde/Tristan/Mark, 33-34
Lust, 2, 7, 26, 68, 77, 137, 216
Lupack, Allan, 176, 227
Lyons, Bex, 207, 211-212

M

McKenzie, Nancy, 10, 191-193,
   207n528, 216, 222
Mabinogion, The, 31, 33
Macleod, Sharon Paice, 32, 38
Magdalene, Mary, 8, 16, 17, 51,
   104, 123
magic, 12, 152-154, 222
Malegant, 13, 46, 66, 94, 187,
   192, 196, 226-227, 232, *See
   also* Medraut, Medrawd,
   Melegraunce, Meliagaunt,
   Melwas
Malory, Thomas, 1, 8, 19, 27, 83,
   89-110, 113-114, 130, 132,
   138-141, 143, 152, 178, 186,
   193, 197, 208, 210, 212, 214,

Mancoff, Debra, 120, 135
Marie de Champagne. *See* de Champagne, Marie
Marie de France. *See* de France, Marie
Markale, Jean, 32
Martin, Leonide, 210, 214
Mason, Eugene, 56-58, 61, 77, 79
Matthews, Caitlin, 12, 14-16, 31, 33, 36, 38-40, 65, 78, 110
Matthews, John, 12, 14-16, 17, 30-31, 33, 38-40, 47, 65, 78
Matthews, John and Caitlin, 12, 14-16, 31, 33, 38-40, 65, 78, 100
Medeiros, Jessica, 80
Medieval Bex, 208
Medraut, 33, *See also* Malegant
Medrawd, 38-40, *See also* Malegant
Meigle, 24
Melegraunce, 99, *See also* Malegant
Meliagaunt, 226, See also Malegant
Melwas, 7, 13, 30-31, 34, 46, *See also* Malegant
Merlin, 12, 13, 49, 83, 183, 192, 208
Merriman, James Douglas, 53-54, 108
Middle Ages, 2, 5, 6, 7, 8, 18, 22-24, 26, 27, 41-44, 49, 51, 55, 62n134, 67, 78-79, 85, 89, 94, 105-106, 109, 116, 119,132, 136, 143, 152, 156, 165-167, 170
Miles, Rosalind, 10, 25, 28, 176, 191, 194-198, 200-202, 224, 228
Mingo, Carlos Sanz, 227
Misfortunes of Arthur, The, 107
Mistress of Legend, 218, 228

Mists of Avalon, The, 9, 28, 151-161, 210, 212, 217
monk, 7, 14, 17, 21, 25, 45-46, 48, 50, 82, 87-89, 106, 118, 143, 170-171
Monmouth, Geoffrey, 7, 11, 15, 18, 37, 41, 48-54, 58, 89, 91, 104, 106, 107, 221, 233
Mordred, 13-14, 19-21, 24, 37, 39, 48, 50-53, 57, 59-62, 83, 87, 91-96, 99-100, 107, 112, 163, 168, 175, 182-183, 189, 197, 225
Morgan, 12, 17, 21, 49, 83, 87, 94, 96, 99, 146, 154, 159-160, 162-163, 175, 189, 197, 202, 203, 208, 217, 222-225, 227-228, *See also* Morgaine; Morgana
Morgaine, 9, 152, 157, 159-160, 203, *See also* Morgan; Morgana
Morgana, 162-163, *See also* Morgan; Morgaine
Morgause of Orkney (blogger), 96-97
Morte d'Arthur, 8, 18, 19, 83, 90, 94-96, 98-99, 103, 107, 109, 220
Morte le Roi Artu, 86
Morris, William, 8, 27-28, 109, 125-131, 163, 218
murder, 25, 39, 84, 87, 96, 99, 197

N

Nennius, 14
New Age movement, 18
Newman, Sharan, 10, 25, 28, 172-

184, 223, 228
neo-paganism, 152-133, 199, *See also* paganism; Wicca
Noble, James, 25, 138, 156, 158, 191
Noble, Peter, 65, 70-71
Normans, 30

O

Ocvran/Gogrvan, 18
Ogfran the Giant, 16, 30, 35
Once and Future King, The, 9, 137-144
original sin, 3, 43, 97
Otherworld, 12-13, 47, 61, 79, 181, 195, 208

P

paganism, 10, 47, 53, 152-153, 165, 180, 186, 198-199, 222-224, *See also* neo-paganism
Paris, Gaston, 69
patriarchy, 9, 22-23, 29, 122-123, 144-150, 153, 155, 158-160, 172-174, 176, 198, 201, 219-220
Peredur, 19
"Peredur, Owein and Lunet," 33
Perlesvaus, 19, 24
penance/repentance, 17, 22, 23, 50-54, 88, 93, 100, 101, 104, 112, 118, 130, 158
Perkin, Harold, 135
Picts, 24, 162
Poisoned Apple, The, 8, 95-98
Preston, Tricia, 211

priestess, 216, 222, 223, 228
primogeniture, 51
prostitute, 7, 78, 79, 85, 120, 137
Protestant, 8, 108, 132

Q

Queen of Camelot, 191, 193
Quilligan, Maureen, 152

R

Radulescu, Raluca, 134
Rampton, Martha, 201
rape, 7, 13, 33, 39, 47, 157, 158, 187, 189, 208, 209n533, 226-227, 232
rape of the Flower Bride, 7, 47
Reimer, Stephen R., 133
religion, 2, 8, 54, 108, 117, 132, 152, 153, 156, 158, 179, 199
"Rhonabwy's Dream," 33
Rhys, John, 20, 36
Romance of Yder, The, 21
Roman de Brut, 19, 55-60, 62-63
Ross, Meredith, 87-88, 101, 103, 108-109, 130, 138, 142-143, 152
Roth, Mark, 135n342
Round Table, 58, 96-97, 103, 185, 196
Ruin of Britain, The, 14

S

Samples, Susann, 50, 72
Saxons, 14, 30, 33, 60, 164, 197, 229
Scotland, 24, 108, 221, 224n563, 225

Scotorum Historiae, 24
self-publishing, 207, 234
sexuality, 1, 11, 80, 121, 168, 180, 188-189, 208-215
Shahar, Shulamith, 16
Silver, Carole G., 127, 129
Simpson, David L., 69
sin, 1, 3, 8, 22-24, 43, 50-51, 53, 54, 57, 59, 66, 68, 85, 97-98, 100, 101, 104-106, 109, 117, 118, 121, 123, 130, 156, 169, 184, 188, 219, 228, 231
Slocum, Sally K., 27, 53, 147
Spenser, Edmund, 107
Stanford, Peter, 200
Stewart, Mary, 9, 21, 147-149
Struve, Laura, 128, 130
suffrage, 29, 119-120
Summer Country, 34, 198
Sutcliff, Rosemary, 9, 21, 147
Swabey, Fiona, 55
Swanson, Kelsey 112, 115, 121-122
Sword at Sunset, 147

T

Tennyson, Alfred Lord, 6, 8, 27, 102, 109, 110-124, 126, 127, 130, 132, 141, 146, 233, 234
Thelwall, John, 18
Thomas, Alfred, 79
Thompson, Jack George, 48, 192
Thompson, Raymond M., 137, 179, 192
Tichelaar, Tyler, 15, 52-53, 61, 91, 92, 93-94
Tintagel, 49, 221
Tolhurst, Fiona, 56-57, 92
Treece, Henry, 137
triplets, 35
True and False Guineveres, 8, 17, 38-39, 82-85, 110n262
twins, 17, 35

U

Umland, Rebecca, 120, 127-128
United States, 5, 28, 94, 134n342, 145, 175n462, 191, 205, 206, 232

V

Vallas, Estelle, 31
Vansittart, Peter, 137
Victorian Era, 6, 8, 9, 109, 110-124, 129-130, 132, 136, 143
Vikings, 30
Virgin Mary, 16, 44-45
virgin/whore polarity, 79, 85, 203
virginity, 42, 179, 221
Vortigern, 18
Vulgate Cycle, 7, 17, 38, 82-89, 90, 148

W

Wace, 7, 19, 27, 40, 42, 55-63, 68, 91, 106
Wales, 20, 30-38, 192, 221
Walters, Lori, 14, 33, 40, 47, 58, 67,

72, 75-76, 86, 102, 105, 107-109, 115, 132, 147, 149, 172, 179
warrior, 32, 38, 50, 61, 163, 169, 195, 208, 209, 212, 215, 219, 225
Warrior Queen, 208, 211, 213
Waynor, 12, 90, *See also* Guinevere
Wehaver, 112, *See also* Guinevere
Welch, Ashley, 229
Welsh literature, 30-38
Welsh Triads, 34-38
Wenhaver, 12, 61, *See also* Guinevere
Wenneuereia, 12, *See also* Guinevere
Whalen, Logan, 79
Whitaker, Murie, 132, 136, 142
White, T.H., 1, 9, 12, 27-28, 94, 126, 132-144, 229, 232, 233, 234
Wicca, 153, 199
Winlogee, 12, *See also* Guinevere
witch/witchcraft, 14, 62, 78, 83, 182, 192, 199, 222-223
Women
   as Arthurian authors, 3, 10, 133, 145-146, 149, 154, 190, 191, 195, 198-199, 202, 205, 216-230, 233, 234
   Celtic, 32-33, 36, 38, 146, 188, 195
   Greek, 33, 56
   Middle Ages, 18, 21, 22, 23, 41-45, 49, 51, 67, 78, 85, 89, 105, 136, 156, 170
   Victorian Era, 6, 8, 9, 109, 110-124, 129-130, 132, 136, 143
   1950s, 136, 142
   1960s, 142, 145-149
   1970s, 2, 3, 17, 133, 136, 138, 145n372, 148-149
   1980s, 3, 10, 17, 19, 25, 28, 133, 138, 144, 153, 169, 171-172, 174-176, 183, 185, 187, 189, 190n493, 202, 203
   1990s, 10, 17, 25, 152, 154, 185, 189, 193, 199-203
   post-2000, 3, 6, 29, 204, 232
   in the workplace, 2, 28, 120, 162, 165, 172-173, 174, 176, 182, 187, 195, 229
   marriage and, 5, 43, 47, 48, 70, 72, 122, 148, 174
   rights of, 3, 9, 32, 38, 122, 145, 165, 173, 201, 219, 232
   suffrage of, 29, 119-120
women's rights, 3, 9, 32, 38, 122, 145, 165, 173, 201, 219, 232
women's studies, 4, 145
Woodbury, Sarah, 36n53, 229n570
Woolley, Persia, 10, 25, 28, 176, 177, 185-190, 198n508, 223, 224, 228
World War I, 2, 134, 135n342
World War II, 134, 135n342
Wyatt, Siobhan, 102, 105

Y

Yder, 21
Ymddiddan Melwasa Gwenhwyfar, 30
York, 52, 57
young adult fiction 5, 207n528

Before You Go

Thank you for reading this book. If you enjoyed it, please leave a review on Amazon and/or Goodreads. Word of mouth is crucial for authors to succeed, so even if your review is only a line or two, it would be a huge help.

To be the first to find out about future books and insider information, please sign up for my newsletter. You will only be contacted when there is news, and your address will never be shared.

Also by Nicole Evelina:
- *Daughter of Destiny* (Guinevere's Tale Book 1) (Arthurian historical fantasy)
- *Camelot's Queen* (Guinevere's Tale Book 2) (Arthurian historical fantasy)
- *Been Searching for You* (contemporary romantic comedy)
- *Madame Presidentess* (historical fiction)

Future releases include:
- *Mistress of Legend* (Guinevere's Tale Book 3) – Early 2018

Please visit me at http://nicoleevelina.com/ to learn more.

I love interacting with my readers! Feel free to contact me on Twitter, Facebook, Goodreads, Pinterest, or by email. You can also send snail mail to: PO Box 2021, Maryland Heights, MO 63043.

About The Author

Nicole Evelina is an award-winning historical fiction and romantic comedy writer whose four novels have won nearly 20 awards. The first two books in her Guinevere trilogy, *Daughter of Destiny* and *Camelot's Queen* were named Books of the Year by Chanticleer Reviews and Author's Circle, respectively. Her most recent novel, *Madame Presidentess*, a historical novel about Victoria Woodhull, America's first female presidential candidate, was the first place winner in the Women's US History category of the Chaucer Awards for Historical Fiction.

Her mission as a writer is to rescue little-known women from being lost in the pages of history. While others may choose to write about the famous, she tells the stories of those who are in danger of being forgotten so that their memories may live on for at least another generation. She also writes from the female point of view since the male perspective has historically been given more attention.

Nicole is one of only six authors who completed the first week-long writing intensive taught by #1 *New York Times* bestselling author Deborah Harkness in 2014. She is a member of and book reviewer for the Historical Novel Society as well as a member of the International Arthurian Society - North American Branch, Historical Fiction Writers of America, Novelists, Inc., Romance Writers of America, Romantic Novelists Association, Missouri Writers Guild, St. Louis Writer's Guild, Alliance of Independent

Authors, Independent Book Publishers Association, and Midwest Independent Publishers Association.

When she's not writing, she can be found reading, playing with her spoiled twin Burmese cats, cooking, researching, and dreaming of living in Chicago or the English countryside.

Acknowledgements

Thank you to the St. Louis County library Oak Bend Branch for asking me to give a presentation on Guinevere during National Women's History Month. It was in my research for that lecture that this book was born. I never thought I would write non-fiction, especially about Guinevere. But given the amount of information I couldn't fit into a 60-minute talk, it seemed only natural.

Thank you as well to the gentleman at my November 2016 lecture at the Oak Bend Branch on Victoria Woodhull who suggested I write non-fiction. I wish I knew your name because I had never considered it until you mentioned it. This book is a direct result of your presence at that talk.

Publishing a book takes a tribe and I've got a great one. Thanks to my editor, Kelly Gamble for her thoughtful consideration of every aspect of this book, as well as the fine tooth comb she took to my footnotes and sources. You are an angel! Thanks to Jenny Quinlan for her help with the beautiful cover and to Nada Qamber for the layout. You make me look so professional!

My thanks to the St. Louis County library and all of the libraries across the country who provided dissertations and theses for me to read, but especially to Georgia College and State University, for the extra effort they put into ensuring I had the opportunity to read Ms. Bonner's research.

A special shout out to my beta readers: Tyler Tichelaar, Jim Palmer, Courtney Marquez, and my mom. Your input, thoughts, objections (Jim!), and opinions made this book so much stronger. I really appreciate your time and effort. Special thanks to Tyler for his in-depth comments and editing. Seriously, man, I couldn't have done this so well without you!

I would be remiss if I didn't thank Dr. Benjamin Moore, my undergraduate thesis advisor, who taught me how to research so many years ago. I never thought that writing about the similarities between Beatrice in *Much Ado About Nothing* and Queen Elizabeth I would lead to this! You'll appreciate that although the final version of this book is in Chicago Style, all my notes are written in MLA style – it is still what I'm most comfortable with!

Thanks to my parents for their support and to my editorial assistants (fur babies), Connor and Caitlyn, for their love and comfort. You have my heart and all my love.

And finally, thanks to everyone who reads this book. An author is nothing without readers. I really appreciate your willingness to read about such a niche subject. I hope you are enlightened and come away knowing something new about this great mythological and literary queen; I know I did.

www.ingramcontent.com/pod-product-compliance
Lightning Source LLC
Chambersburg PA
CBHW021121300426
44113CB00006B/233